The Tourist's Gaze
Travellers to Ireland 1800-2000

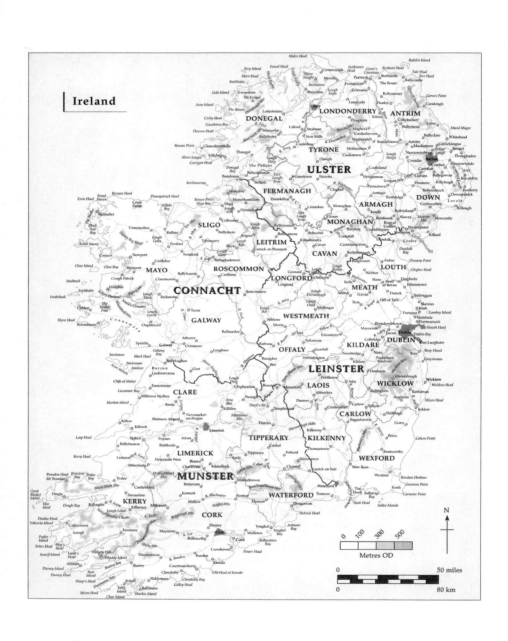

Ireland

The Tourist's Gaze

TRAVELLERS TO IRELAND
1800–2000

Edited by
Glenn Hooper

CORK UNIVERSITY PRESS

First published in 2001 by
Cork University Press
University College
Cork
Ireland

British Library Cataloguing in Publication Data
A CIP catalogue record for this book is available from the British Library

Library of Congress Cataloguing-in-Publication Data
The tourist's gaze : travellers to Ireland, 1800-2000 / edited by Glenn
Hooper.
    p. cm.
    Includes bibliographical references and index.
    ISBN 1-85918-277-1 (alk. paper) -- ISBN 1-85918-323-9 (pbk. : alk.
paper)
    1. Ireland--Description and travel.   2.
Travelers--Ireland--History--19th century.   3.
Travelers--Ireland--History--20th century.   I. Hooper, Glenn,
1959-   .
  DA969.T68 2001

  914.15'04'8--dc21

                                        2001017289

ISBN 1 85918 277 1 hardcover
ISBN 1 85918 323 9 paperback

Typeset by Tower Books, Ballincollig, Co. Cork
Printed by ColourBooks Ltd, Baldoyle, Dublin

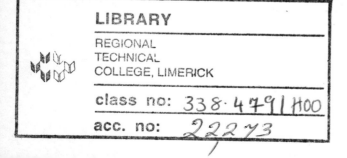

Contents

PART II 1852–1921

PART III 1921–2000

For Oonagh & Dearbhla

Acknowledgements

In the course of putting this anthology together I have become indebted to several institutions. My thanks to the Linenhall Library, Belfast, the libraries of University College and Trinity College Dublin, the Royal Irish Academy, the National Library of Ireland, the National Library of Scotland, the British Library, and the library of the University of Aberdeen, especially the Interlibrary Loan and Special Collections Departments.

I also wish to thank a number of friends and colleagues for their help with queries about Ireland, travel and anthologies. On a more specific note, I wish to thank Michael Cronin for reading an earlier draft, and for the Ovid reference, Betty Hagglund for help with Quaker queries, and Margaret Kelleher and Alasdair Pettinger for their very full and generous commentaries. Graham Huggan, Peter Hulme, C.J. Woods and Tim Youngs all read earlier drafts, and saved me from several mistakes, for which I am extremely grateful. I wish to thank Fintan Cullen for sharing his anthology experiences, and Declan Kiberd, Seamus Deane, and Kevin Whelan for their guidance, encouragement and generosity throughout. I would also like to express my gratitude to Morton Gauld for his Latin glosses, and to Bill Naphy for additional Latin references. My thanks, finally, to Catherine Cox and Pauric Dempsey, who graciously supported the project, and to my extremely patient commissioning editor, Sara Wilbourne. Oonagh Walsh read the thing through almost as many times as I, and I am especially thankful for her efforts, although all mistakes remain mine.

The Publishers wish to thank Matthew Stout for permission to reproduce the map of Ireland on p. ii.

Preface

In Bruce Chatwin's *In Patagonia* detours and digressions spin effortlessly from the central narrative, although one memorable moment – a consideration of Samuel Coleridge's passion for travel – prompts this reflection: 'Coleridge himself was a "night-wandering man", a stranger at his own birthplace, a drifter round rooming-houses, unable to sink roots anywhere. He had a bad case of what Baudelaire called "The Great Malady: Horror of One's Home".'[1] Chatwin, perhaps more than many other modern travel writers, was all too aware of the restrictions of home, even if the limitations imposed upon gay and bisexual men by the late 1970s had begun to ease, and a reformulation of sexual politics was well underway. But the horror of one's home to which Chatwin alludes, the reason why some travellers leave to do what they do, poses an obvious question: why travel? To visit other countries, to become, if only partially and provisionally, of another culture, is a still-tempting experience. We may be pampered by the ease of long-haul flights, unimpressed by the range of destinations now on offer, but the rush of excitement borne by being temporarily displaced remains strong. Nevertheless, one wonders whether the appetite for travel has been at all compromised. Some of the political presumptions about exotic cultures no longer exist, the hardships and difficulties that were once the mainstay of the traveller's lot have changed beyond recognition; so has the desire for travel altered significantly?

The answer, in a word, is no; or certainly not much. There are undoubtedly many motives behind the desire to travel, but one of its central tenets still appears to remain; that if travel allows for anything it allows for the possible reinvention of the self.[2] To leave home behind, to venture abroad, to encounter the exotic or different in uncompromising ways, suggests a transformation of the self, often despite ourselves. If travel does anything, it might be argued, it removes us from that which is familiar, slackening our ties to home, family, even national identity. Indeed this shedding of the old self constitutes for many the very essence of travel, with the traveller removed from the domestic and the routine, presented with all that is defamiliarizing and, at least potentially, strange.

The sense of possibility, the opportunity to reinvent, or to simply imagine oneself as an amalgam of shifting identities, exists in many cases. And for the travel writer especially, such experiences can be remarkably liberating, with choices enlarged, and opportunities for invention apparently endless.

Over the last decade or so critical interest in the travel-narrative form has accelerated at an astonishing rate. Anthologies and readers, monographs and essay collections, have all sought to explain our continuing, and growing, interest in the travel narrative.[3] However, while recent criticism has done a great deal to promote the genre, and to explain much of what underlies the ideology of travel literature, a number of earlier (mid-twentieth century) works set the trend. One book in particular, compiled just after the Second World War, revealed an interest in several of these questions. The 1950s may seem a less than auspicious era for a theoretical discussion of travel (think of the young Philip Larkin in his bicycle clips, determinedly avoiding continental Europe), but when the travel critic M.A. Michael and his contributors presented their work, the time could not have been more appropriate. Indeed, a book which discussed escape, freedom and solitude after the destruction and limitations of warfare must have seemed glorious indeed. Michael's *Traveller's Quest: Original Contributions towards a Philosophy of Travel* includes essays from Henri Bordeaux, Freya Stark, Ella Maillart, Walter Starkie, Rupert Croft-Cooke, Alec Waugh and others, yet for all the variations of style and content, one thing keeps the essays together: a sense that travel can be a precious, almost spiritual experience if properly conducted. *Traveller's Quest* represents a significant effort to think through the implications of travel, the environmental impact of mass tourism, and the sorts of technological advances that have changed travel, sometimes for the better. The collection begins by contemplating the reason for travel itself, even if, like much on the subject, it struggles with problems of definition:

> Travel, indeed, is one of those things of which it is easier to say what it is not, than to define. In the first place, it is necessary to distinguish true travel from going abroad for a holiday, which may be travel, but is usually just a turning-down of the leaf to mark our place in the book of life which we then lay aside for a few weeks and with it our cares and responsibilities. Then there are the journeyings of those whose profession or job takes them abroad. These people may travel, as well as journey, but such travel is subsidiary and so cannot count as true travel. What then is travel? It would be easier, perhaps to say who is a traveller. At any rate, it should be possible to construct an ideal type.[4]

Despite Michael's honest appreciation of the difficulties inherent in such a subject, his collection stresses time and again how travel is tied to a developing or transient sense of self. 'The modern traveller travels for himself alone', he argues, 'his reasons for going are purely personal, as are the gains of his travels'.[5] But *Traveller's Quest* is also a product of its time, with the increasing pressures of modern life acting as an additional stimulus to leave home:

> We tolerate, rather than like our fellows. Those who suffer the daily degradation of riding in the underground railways of London often find themselves even loathing their fellows. The majority of urban dwellers have had their natures warped by modern civilization …What fools we are to live as most of us do, in huge cities under artificial conditions that sour our souls and sap our fundamental virtues![6]

Pitting the soul against the sour experience of city life, Michael conjures up a scene more reminiscent of an Escher lithograph than daily commuting, an image of blind automatons on a conveyor of dull and empty repetition. Nevertheless, this view of the purpose of travel animates many of Michael's essayists, with several of them stressing the need for independence and freedom, focusing almost exclusively on the restorative, revitalizing benefits of travel. Even the essay titles equate travel with seclusion, and with an almost total disavowal of modernity: 'Remote Places', 'The Lure of Solitude', 'The Quest for a better Life and a better Self', 'To Get Away from it all': these give some sense of the direction of their writings.

Although the reasons for travel given by Michael's contributors are convincing enough, one wonders how circumscribed and historically determined they are. An emphasis on the self is developed by several writers, but how far this is a predominantly twentieth-century view, and to what extent it was actually shared by travel writers throughout the century, is another thing. Travel literature, no less than other genres, has felt the pressures of history, especially as the experience of travel has modified itself noticeably over the last two centuries. Improved roads, the advent of the railway, better hostelries: these changing circumstances made for significantly greater numbers of travellers in the nineteenth century, and were reflected in the books which were subsequently written, largely in terms of bringing to the attention of travellers previously inaccessible places. But how did earlier travellers from, say, the early modern period respond? What enticed them to travel, what sorts of preoccupations did they share, and how did their writings reflect their physical experiences? More importantly, what pressures were experienced by travellers who journeyed to Ireland? Was Ireland different from what they expected, or less threatening, or exotic in ways they were not prepared for?

TO IRELAND

'Wonder', suggests Stephen Greenblatt, 'was the central figure in the initial European response to the New World, the decisive emotional and intellectual experience in the presence of radical difference'.[7] The New World captivated and at times bewitched its visitors, and prompted feelings of incomprehension and fascination. Although the sense of difference experienced in North America was more extreme than that encountered in Ireland, a level of awe was nevertheless experienced by many travellers, an incredulity at how a country so geographically proximate to other European cultures and civilizing influences could remain so alien. The majority of those who wrote on Ireland in this period were English, and their accounts were often penned not as travel narratives in the obvious sense, but as commentary and analysis of the country and its inhabitants for political purposes. Barnaby Rich, in *A New Description of Ireland* (1610), wrote of how the Irish have 'lived like barbarians in woods, in bogs, and in desolate places, without politic law or civil government, neither embracing religion, law, nor mutual love',[8] and although Sir John Davies, in *A Discovery of the True Causes why Ireland was never entirely Subdued* (1612) enthused about the 'good temperature of the ayre, the fruitfulnesse of the soyle, the pleasant and commodious seats for habitation', he also remarked on how untamed the country remained, and what needed to be done to make it manageable: 'For the husbandman must first breake the land before it bee made capeable of good seede; and when it is thoroughly broken and manured, if he do not forthwith cast good seede into it, it will grow wilde againe and beare nothing but weeds.'[9] Barnaby Rich was a soldier who first served in Ireland in 1573, and who wrote a number of texts dealing with Irish issues, such as *The Survey of Ireland* (1609), and *The Irish Hubbub* (1617), while Sir John Davies was Ireland's solicitor-general and attorney-general from 1603 to 1619. In neither case, therefore, should we be surprised to find discussion of Ireland as a place of political instability. Although Fynes Moryson is known as one of the great travellers of his day, his *Itinerary* (1617) expresses concerns similar to Davies', with the practicalities of security appearing paramount: 'First, to establish the maintenance of some necessary forts planted within land remote from seas and rivers ... [which] might not only keep the Irish in awe, but be to the state as it were spies to advertise all mutinous and seditious inclinations.'[10] Of the earlier travellers to Ireland whose accounts survive, then, a common trope is not just the threatening nature of Irish life, but the practical matters of fortifications and the physical preservation of the colony. The emphasis is therefore rather different from that in later accounts, and instead of some of the pleasurable elements we commonly associate with travel, many writers reveal an explicitly political agenda. Indeed, it would appear that early modern travellers to Ireland were concerned less with self-discovery than with self-preservation, and their accounts are frequently affiliated to, and spring from, the discourses of imperialism, commerce, even of soldiery and warfare.

In early modern Ireland, when parts of the country were associated with intractability and sedition, travellers (broadly speaking) reflected a common set of concerns. The sense of obligation to record detail relating to security, and to comment on the primitive state of the Irish, is clear from the majority of surviving accounts. There is a similarly shared perspective amongst later writers, although the specific circumstances in the country have changed, leading to a new set of preoccupations. For example, in the late seventeenth century, when politics are just as volatile, but where a confidence born of long residence in the country exists, a different emphasis by British travellers emerges. If we take just three examples from this period – William Brereton's, *Travels* (1635), William Petty's, *The Political Anatomy of Ireland* (1672), and John Stevens's, *A Journal of my Travels* (1689) – Ireland appears less as an ungovernable site than as a spectacle, a country that may be travelled in with greater confidence. In Brereton's *Travels* a consideration of the Irish themselves, but especially what marks them out as different to an English gaze, is evident: 'Some gentlewomen of good quality here I observed clothed in good handsome gowns, petticoats and hats, who wore Irish rugs, which have handsome, comely, large fringes, which go about their necks.'[11] For William Petty food and the simple pleasures of the Irish are worth detailing: 'The diet of these people is milk, sweet and sour, thick and thin, which also is their drink in summer-time, in winter small-beer or water. But tobacco taken in short pipes seldom burnt, seems the pleasure of their lives',[12] while even John Stevens, caught up with the distractions of war, can take time to describe Irish apparel: 'Very little clothing serves them, and as for shoes and stockings much less. They wear brogues being quite plain without so much as one lift of a heel, and are all sewed with thongs, and the leather not curried'.[13] For each of these writers Ireland is interpreted less as a terrifying wilderness, or as a place of tribal warfare and strife, than as domestic spectacle. It might be argued that a political intention lies behind these domestic appraisals, and that what is important about their construction is less the detail of Irish domestic life provided than the image of a domesticated and pacified Irishry which reassuringly emerges. Nevertheless, although these narrators concentrate on Irish difference, they do not ascribe to it the element of fear discernible in many of the earlier seventeenth-century accounts.

The following century saw a considerable growth in both the numbers of accounts published, and in the appetite for descriptions of travellers' trials and tribulations, but it also saw an interesting development within travel more generally. In 1769, just four years before Samuel Johnson and James Boswell embarked on their tour of the Scottish Highlands, John Bush published his tour of Ireland, entitled *Hibernia Curiosa*. Bush's journey, like that of Johnson and Boswell, saw a reorientation of the notion of centre and periphery, as parts of Scotland and Ireland were transformed from inaccessible and aesthetically unattractive regions, with little to recommend them, to rediscovered venues of primitive delight. Indeed, the timing of these two journeys is noteworthy, for just as these travellers were heading off to the pleasures of Irish bogs and Scottish moors, many of their contemporaries were still packing for continental Europe, determined to see and experience as much 'real' culture as they could. The Grand Tour, in other words, was still in its heyday, with many educated and wealthy young men regarding it as the most effective way of consolidating their education.[14] There was, of course, a downside to this type of tourism. As Turner and Ash suggest, the Grand Tour followed:

> a shift in the focus of culture and of economic and political power. The wealthy and educated, of states whose position of dominance in the world is comparatively new, visit countries that have passed their peak of prestige and creativity but are still venerated for historic and cultural reasons. Thus Romans visited Greece and the eastern Mediterranean; the English, from the sixteenth century onwards, visited Italy; and in this century Americans 'do' Europe. The new world pays its respects to the old.[15]

Nevertheless, continental Europe was seen not just as a place to visit, but as a useful, sometimes necessary finishing stage in many young men's lives. The Grand Tour, suggests Roger Hudson, 'in its purest form was the culmination of the rich young eighteenth-century Englishman's education', an opportunity to see for himself 'the landscapes of antiquity, and to view the ruins and statuary that survived'.[16]

How did an interest in Ireland emerge throughout the eighteenth century when the Grand Tour was the travelling experience many wealthy young Britons expected to make? For one thing, eighteenth-century Ireland was a rather different country from its earlier incarnations and, most important of all, was a relatively pacific country. The military campaigns of the sixteenth and seventeenth centuries were at an end, and although a simmering discontent remained, travel accounts reflected this new-found ease, noting to a much greater extent the natural beauties of the landscape, rather than the volatile nature of the Irish inhabitants which was such a leitmotif of earlier writers. For example, John Bush wrote of Irish poverty, of the hardship endured in the cities as well as in the countryside, but also of the improved cultural conditions perceived by at least some Irish residents: 'if the gentility of Dublin is spoken of, with any view to a comparison with that of London, it is with an air and manner that plainly bespeaks a presumed superiority on the side of Dublin'.[17] And such comments helped to encourage visitors to Ireland at a time of increasing interest in Britain's Celtic fringe. Moreover, as traditional Grand Tour destinations in continental Europe became somewhat less accessible, impeded as they were by war (especially throughout the 1740s and early 1750s), travellers increasingly turned to the remoter parts of the British Isles, especially to parts of Ireland and Scotland. As Gold and Gold suggest, 'Preoccupation with the "Grand Tour" as a framework for travel had led to a neglect of Britain. The search for domestic locations for travel reinforced a new interest in exploring Britain as a suitable pastime for the upper classes.'[18]

'After 1763', suggests Roger Hudson, 'the Grand Tour was at its height'.[19] Nevertheless, the publication of Edmund Burke's *A Philosophical Enquiry into the Origin of Our Ideas of the Sublime and Beautiful* in 1757 caused many to re-evaluate the natural world, and humanity's relationship to it, even in the apparently prosaic surroundings of rural Ireland. While the impact on specific writers is not that easy to determine – one of the best-known travellers to Ireland for this period was Arthur Young, whose *Tour in Ireland* (1776–79) is especially renowned for its agricultural statistics – this change in aesthetics created an environment in which areas previously regarded as remote and uncultivated became more acceptable. A further reason for the renewed interest in the Celtic fringe, especially Scotland, concerns the emergence of a more vibrant British identity. Although Linda Colley writes of 'Runaway Scottophobia' in England after 1760,[20] and notes that distrust between the Scots and English manifested itself in a variety of ways, she remarks on how after the rebellion of 1745 Scotland rapidly ceased to be seen as the 'old enemy', and more as a 'useful, loyal and *British*' partner.[21] This reorientation of the notion of centre and periphery, in which unknown and indifferently imagined areas became more attractive, is one of the catalysts in the increase of travellers to both Scotland and Ireland in the late eighteenth century. Thomas Pennant's *Tour in Scotland 1769* (1771), Samuel Johnson's *A Journey to the Western Islands of Scotland* (1775), and James Boswell's *The Journal of a Tour to the Hebrides* (1786), all helped to focus interest on relatively unexplored areas, even if one of the principal reasons for doing so was an unacknowledged reappreciation of the political structure of Britain.

Although it is unwise to overemphasize links between Ireland and Scotland as far as eighteenth-century travel writing is concerned, the fact that a changing set of political circumstances led to an increased interest in Scotland has some bearing on nineteenth-century perceptions of Ireland, when the Act of Union created a similarly reinvigorated interest. In Scotland, many post-1745 writers, especially English writers, travelled northwards in order to assess a once seditious, though clearly integral, part of Britain. After 1800 many English travellers approached Ireland with something of the same eagerness, determined to read Ireland as a natural offshore extension of the British state, as yet uneasily yoked in Union, but possessing great potential nevertheless. Indeed, some writers arrived with an open curiosity about Ireland and the Irish, seeking to explore this largely 'unknown' neighbouring territory, and burying the notion of political discord at the root of the Union in favour of harmony with the 'Sister Isle'. Sir Richard Hoare, in his *Journal of a Tour in Ireland* (1807), described Ireland as 'unvisited and unknown', the English as 'a rambling nation', and the main objective of travel being to extract 'research and information'.[22] Like many of his compatriots Hoare attempted to disavow an earlier historical relation to Ireland in the hope of creating afresh the Anglo-Irish relationship. Similarly, J.C. Curwen, in his *Observations on the State of Ireland* (1818), explained his interest in 'visiting a country, which, although almost within our view, and daily in our contemplation, is as little known to me, comparatively speaking, as if it were an island in the remotest part of the globe',[23] while John Alexander Staples, in *A Tour in Ireland, in 1813 and 1814* (1817), described Ireland as 'a country that Englishmen in general know less about, that they do of Russia, Siberia or the Country of the Hottentots'.[24] Not surprisingly, a level of double-think underlay these initiatives as narrators struggled with the concept of Union with a country still associated with insurrection (the 1798 rebellion witnessed terrible cruelties, and resulted in approximately 30,000 deaths). As ever, Ireland was the Janus-faced 'Sister', the place where old certainties were continually under pressure of erasure or modification, and where Britain apparently had to play catch-up to Irish twists and turns.

Although it can be useful to cite the interest generated among travellers in Ireland after the Act of Union as comparable to the motivation seen in Scotland in the 1760s and 1770s, Ireland differed significantly from Scotland in one more major respect. A catastrophic event was to draw travellers to Ireland at mid-century and afterwards in numbers which greatly exceeded those to Scotland, and which provoked intense discussion and speculation regarding Ireland and its future. The Great Famine, from 1845 to 1850, with severe after-effects until 1852, caused untold suffering and horrific loss of life through starvation, disease and emigration, and resulted in a decline in population of almost two million individuals by 1852. The height of the famine drew numerous commentators to Ireland, and resulted in harrowing descriptions of misery, as well as the often remarkable efforts made to alleviate it. But the years after the 'great calamity' are the most interesting as far as developments in travel writing are concerned, for the 1850s saw the publication of a number of accounts which sought to disseminate information regarding the newly depopulated state of the country, and the economic opportunities which this presented to enterprising investors and settlers. Indeed, the publication of the 1851 census confirmed the fact of massive population decline, and encouraged travellers such as Harriet Martineau and John Ashworth to stress the limitless potential for expansion, economic as well as social, which Ireland now held.[25] It is a remarkable moment, but one which encapsulates the often contradictory responses which Ireland provoked in her visitors.

The nature of travel undertaken in Ireland, as well as the type of traveller, altered a good deal throughout the nineteenth century. One of the most obvious changes is the gradual rise in the numbers of women travellers, such as Anne Plumptre, Henrietta Chatterton, Harriet Martineau, Theresa Cornwallis West, and several others, who all made forays throughout the country. Their increasing presence reflects the changing circumstances governing travel in Ireland, as in Britain, which was considerably eased as a result of improvements to the country's roads, and the development of the railway. That said, when Mary Ann Grant and Anne Plumptre travelled, in the first decades of the nineteenth century, conditions remained difficult and hazardous, as the extract from Plumptre in this anthology makes clear. Triggered to some extent by the publication of other women's travel accounts — such as Mary

Wollstonecraft's *Letters Written during a Short Residence in Sweden, Norway and Denmark* (1796) – figures like Plumptre began to establish women's travels as notable contributions in their own right. Indeed Plumptre's narrative is a surprisingly full account in which information on antiquities, history and architecture is interwoven with mineralogical queries and a desire to comprehend Ireland above all else:

> If we are anxious to be introduced to a knowledge of the face of their country, to understand its natural advantages and disadvantages, its customs and manners, its civil and political state, that we may be enabled to compare them with our own, and judge between them and ourselves, – a much deeper interest will surely be excited when these injuries, these comparisons, relate to an object so near to us as a SISTER.[26]

The play here on Ireland as kinsfolk as well as geo-political entity effectively communicates the sense of optimism shared by many post-Union travellers, although Plumptre remained throughout a cautious traveller who took pains to avoid giving offence, and who deflected attention away from herself at several points: 'No tourist could now venture to write down a memorandum in the presence of company: I carefully avoided it, and reserved till evening, when I had retired to my own apartment, the task of taking down my notes and observations.'[27]

Given the caution exercised by Plumptre one wonders how women's accounts differed from men's, and whether women travellers were more inclined to be generous, or to find in Irish social life greater reasons for explaining the high instances of poverty and dereliction. Shirley Foster suggests that 'the woman writer often represents foreigners sympathetically, as individuals with whom she tries to identify rather than as symbols of an alien "otherness"'.[28] Although a case may be made for regarding certain women writers as less blatantly antagonistic than their male counterparts it is difficult to sustain the notion of female empathy or sensitivity in relation to Ireland. There are some outspoken critics of government policy, such as Asenath Nicholson, whose feelings of wearied disgust are evoked all too clearly during her Famine journey. But male writers such as Osborne and Tuke were just as outraged and outspoken. An argument might indeed be made for Ireland as an exceptional case, a place that provoked greater independence on the part of women travellers, especially English women travellers who found less to fear in a country with which they felt some affinity.

Perhaps a more obvious explanation lies in the fact that an ever increasing number of travel accounts reflected the discourse of British imperialism of the early and middle nineteenth century, a discourse which was to flower supremely in the 1880s and 1890s. The nineteenth century was stamped by the rhetoric of empire, and many of its travellers mirrored, and in some cases passionately articulated, empire politics. In fact so interwoven is the theme of empire among nineteenth-century travel accounts that one finds many instances of journeys undertaken which are nothing less than political evaluations of foreign countries. Elleke Boehmer suggests that travellers' 'rough, rudimentary descriptions charted unknown lands in the same tentative and provisional way as did early maps'.[29] And many travellers did document the lands through which they passed, and amassed detail about cultural practice, language, religion and politics. Others made their agenda even more explicit, and assessed the strength of foreign armies, land or coastal defences, the positions of towns or cities – all practical information for territorially acquisitive nations. These writers combined travel with a genuine sense of patriotism and they journeyed, not just for the betterment of self, but, as Rana Kabbani suggests, 'for their *patria*'.[30]

This view of the traveller as imperial scout has been occasionally raised, although the publication of Edward Said's *Orientalism* in 1978 explicitly identified the relationship between empire and travel, especially in the nineteenth century. Said pointed to the travel narrative's role in the development of Orientalist discourse, and argued that such writing 'strengthened the divisions established by Orientalists between the various geographical, temporal, and racial departments of the Orient.'[31] Said's comments acted to bring the role of the travel writer into sharper focus, and his presentation of the travel narrative as political document fundamentally changed the way in which these texts were critically received. More importantly, subsequent interpretations of travellers' accounts, particularly those who wrote of non-Western societies, have been heavily influenced by Said's work.[32] This is evident even amongst those critics in fundamental disagreement with Said's central thesis, and it is interesting to note that the majority of critical interpretations published after *Orientalism* discuss the connection between travel and imperialism, even when their primary focus lies elsewhere. This is not to say that a general interpretation of travellers' accounts is possible. Indeed, many nineteenth-century travel accounts suggest rather complex negotiations, with many travellers displaying considerable tact, while many mid- and late-twentieth-century accounts convey great insensitivity. Nevertheless, even where the scales are delicately balanced, where the writing is carefully modulated to avoid giving offence, the power differential between the traveller and the native still tends to favour the former. Even the 'tourist', that most castigated of individuals, feels him/herself superior in another country.

Although many travellers to Ireland displayed an attitude that may be broadly defined as colonialist, and engaged in forms of representation that reflected Ireland as an economically backward place in need of paternal guidance, others had different concerns. A notable number, for example, saw the country in terms of simple pleasures and of its capacity to fulfill needs that could not be satisfied elsewhere. Many journeyed in search of a lost idyll, believing Ireland to be the keeper of a cultural purity. In the early nineteenth century this search was largely conducted throughout the Wicklow hills, or around Killarney, but as the nineteenth century progressed, the traditionally harsher, more austere West of Ireland received the greatest attention. Mayo, Connemara, the extreme and most destitute parts of Galway: these became the new sites of pilgrimage, as travellers went, firstly, in search of scenery on a grander scale, and then on increasingly anthropological forays. Indeed, throughout the two hundred years covered by this anthology, there is a remarkable consistency in terms of attitudes displayed by travellers towards the West. Even now, it remains a region associated with an Arcadian innocence, a place which offers the possibility of renewal and regeneration above all else. Ironically, towards the end of the nineteenth century, Irish revivalists viewed the West in much the same light, a view that ignored the realities of poverty, and conspired to imprison the region as a place of timeless, unchanging integrity. As Catherine Nash suggests, the West 'came to stand for Ireland in general, to be representative of true Irishness. It could be seen as a way of access into the Irish past through its language, folklore, antiquities, and way of life, yet also be conceived of as outside time, separated from normal temporal development'.[33] And certainly in the nineteenth century the West had the greatest number of Irish-speakers, was more remote than many other places from Britain, appeared topographically harsh, and yet beautiful at the same time. It was also, as we will see, the place most affected by famine.

Although the West still dominates when discussion turns to a consideration of the 'true' or 'authentic' Ireland, for many travellers Ireland's broad appeal as a place removed from contemporary concerns prevailed throughout the nineteenth century, and well into the twentieth. Several extracts in this anthology suggest that personal security issues, not surprisingly, emerged during the late teens and early 1920s, and that the image of Ireland as pastoral idyll was no longer entirely apt. Nevertheless, in the 1930s, and especially in the 1940s and 1950s, the picture of Ireland as a haven of bucolic ease, a place to abscond to when life got a little hectic, re-emerged. Indeed, the anti-modern strain so evident among many of Michael's essayists is typical of how travellers responded to Ireland in the 1940s and 1950s, especially those visiting after the war when, as Martin Ryle suggests, Ireland was looked upon as a 'refuge from modernity'.[34] In Ryle's opinion the numbers of travellers visiting Ireland in the 1950s 'was at its zenith', and he argues that the attractions of Ireland, with its cheap and abundant food rather than 'the strictly enforced rationing and high prices in England', was one of the principal reasons for the marked increase in the number of English travellers to Ireland.[35] If Ireland had been for a time eclipsed by more exotic locations, or seen as less appealing by a type of luxury tourist, then its notorious underdevelopment and distinct lack of industrial progress was now regarded as a boon. The image of Ireland in the 1950s, it is generally perceived, was of a society that valued a more traditional way of life, and which had successfully countered the excesses of modernity, despite many Irish people's association of that particular decade with desperately high levels of unemployment and emigration. Travellers' impressions in the 1960s and 1970s are a little harder to gauge, although the noticeable drop in travel narratives during that period is possibly best ascribed to the emergence of violence. Unlike previous Irish crises, the conflict in Northern Ireland succeeded in warding many travel writers off during these decades, and it is only from the 1980s onwards that we begin to see their numbers rise again.

THE ANTHOLOGY

Travel literature, even over the last two centuries, has had a chequered history. Quite apart from how politically suspect it has periodically been, it has confused many readers by allying itself to different genres. At a certain level the idea of a genre with a fluid set of rules, an evolving sense of itself, and a vaguely defined set of parameters might appear innocuous enough, but it does invite questions. What is especially noteworthy about M.A. Michael's collection, for example, is not just that he asks why people travel, what motivates them, what their experiences have been, and how they would advise others to do similar deeds, but the fact that he does not address how any of his contributors actually write up their experiences afterwards. Not surprisingly, Holland and Huggan remind us that travel writing, 'however entertaining, is hardly harmless, and that behind its apparent innocuousness and its charmingly anecdotal observations lies a series of powerfully distorting myths about other (often, "non-Western") cultures', but they also ask 'But what, exactly, *is* a travel book? By which criteria should it be judged?'[36] Clearly any attempt to establish disciplinary or critical parameters is nothing less than problematic, and if one defines the field on the basis of authorial profession the water becomes even more muddied, with inevitable connections arising between profession and alleged narrative form. As suggested above, in the early modern era many narratives were penned by military personnel, cartographers, and civilian settlers, and were medleys of historical rumination, imaginative writing and factual reportage. The nineteenth century undoubtedly saw the development of a greater sense of order, a move away from casual jottings and the sorts of historical and antiquarian narratives that frequently masqueraded as travel accounts, but even here the travel narrative was a notoriously slippery affair, a type of writing that flirted with a range of interests and styles (notice how many modern bookstores still categorize uneasily, frequently using the term 'travel biography' to describe the form). Holland and Huggan suggest that the best way to deal with the problem is to regard travel narratives as 'occupying a space of discursive conflict' and they cite Rob Nixon who writes of the 'semi-ethnographic, distanced, analytic mode' and the 'autobiographical, emotionally tangled mode' that characterize many travel accounts.[37] Although Nixon's description encapsulates the confusion that arises among many readers, it also reminds us of the woven nature of the form, its essentially volatile mode.

To what extent are these hybrid, complexly constructed narratives reflected in this anthology? It certainly includes travel narratives that embraced the notion of hybridity in many respects – drawing on ethnography, journalism, and so forth – but I have attempted as far as possible to differentiate between travel and related literatures. Accounts which at least describe themselves as travel narratives, tours, journeys, and suchlike, have been chosen, while texts whose primary purpose was quite different have been avoided. This is not to deny that many of the travellers included in this work visited Ireland on business, or with some objective in mind other than 'recreation', but it is to say that the extracts chosen are at least recognizable as travel narratives. By the beginning of the nineteenth century, travel literature, through the sheer number of texts then in print, had achieved an identifiable form, which alleviates the difficulty of differentiating between formally ambiguous narratives to a considerable degree. This is not to suggest that a uniformity binds these extracts together, but simply suggests that some sort of order or rationale has been attempted.

If the beginning of the nineteenth century may be regarded as a useful departure point for an anthology of travel (Mary Louise Pratt conveniently cites the 1799 publication of Mungo Park's *Travels in the Interior Districts of Africa* as ushering in a new way of writing),[38] it is especially appropriate for a selection of 'Irish' documents, since the period 1800–2000 constitutes such an important set of Irish historical dates: from the Union of Great Britain and Ireland, to the formation of a new Executive in Northern Ireland, and with some of the key moments of Irish history in between (Catholic Emancipation, the Famine, Fenian agitation, the Land League, the Gaelic Revival, the 1916 Rising, Partition, the War of Independence, the Civil War, Civil Rights, the Troubles). Do these political issues impact on the Irish travel narrative? While the physical and material detail of travel has obviously altered in significant ways in the last two hundred years, many of the motivations for visiting Ireland remain the same. What brought travellers to Ireland in 1800 was remarkably similar to what brought them in 1900 and in 2000: a desire to understand the country, to engage with the peculiarities of its culture, to speculate on its long-term political future. Of course the Irish countryside – the hallowed sites of the West, the literary spaces of Dublin, Galway and the Aran Islands – constitute any amount of additional reasons for visiting the island. But Ireland's religious antagonisms, its image as a place simultaneously of sordid deprivation and pastoral innocence, its almost gothic appetite for historical trauma, was what really stimulated interest. This is not to say that it is only in the last two hundred years that Ireland has had this appeal. From the early modern period, when travel was becoming a necessary element in the formation of empire, we know that travellers to Ireland voiced such, frequently political, concerns. To be sure, Ireland's sublime and romantic views, its pristine otherness, its scenic attributes were also duly noted. But even here, politics was never that far away. As these extracts will show, even where a place associated with natural beauty forms the basis for a traveller's tour of Ireland, political considerations frequently intrude.

No doubt readers of this anthology will have their own opinions on the suitability of the extracts I have selected, and may be surprised or disappointed if certain writers are absent. Nevertheless, I consider myself liberated from the usual charges of attempting to shape the curriculum, or canon-formation, since these texts really are, with one or two notable exceptions, the literary underclass. The majority of these texts have been marginalized and remain out of print, and despite the scholarly interest recently developed, are unlikely to see a widespread readership in the immediate future. Moreover, since this is the first anthology exclusively devoted to travellers' impressions of Ireland, there is nothing to compare it with. There is no canon against which to establish an anti-canon, no agreed list of authors against whom one might respond, and few rules. The only canon against which this anthology may be set is the 'literary' one, the one which still largely excludes what it regards as non-literary works, such as travel writing, print media, biography, critical writing, memoirs, letters, and so on. For these reasons I have selected extracts on the basis of what has interested me above all else, situating apparently playful accounts alongside those which tackle serious political and economic issues, which I believe is part of the appeal of travel writing anyway. John Urry suggests that there 'is no single tourist gaze as such. It varies by society, by social group and by historical period.'[39] These extracts, by authors not born or raised in Ireland reflect the diversity of experience over two hundred years of Irish history.

NOTES AND REFERENCES

1 B. Chatwin, *In Patagonia* (London: Pan, 1979), p. 87.
2 Of course a liberal, rather than exclusively existential, use of the term 'self' exists among many theorists of travel. See J. Urry, *The Tourist Gaze: Leisure and Travel in Contemporary Societies* (London: Sage, 1990), G. Robertson et al. (eds), *Traveller's Tales: Narratives of Home and Displacement* (London: Routledge, 1994), J. Duncan & D. Gregory (eds), *Writes of Passage: Reading Travel Writing* (London: Routledge, 1999), R. Kaur & J. Hutnyk (eds), *Travel Worlds: Journeys in Contemporary Cultural Politics* (London: Zed, 1999), and M. Cronin, *Across the Lines: Travel, Language, Translation* (Cork: Cork UP, 2000).
3 See, for example, D. Porter, *Haunted Journeys: Desire and Transgression in European Travel Writing* (New Jersey: Princeton UP, 1991), J. Buzard, *The Beaten Track: European Tourism, Literature, and the Ways to Culture, 1800–1918* (Oxford: Clarendon, 1993), T. Youngs, *Travellers in Africa: British Travelogues, 1850–1900* (Manchester: Manchester UP, 1994), N. Thomas, *Colonialism's Culture: Anthropology, Travel and Government* (Cambridge: Polity, 1994), D. Spurr, *The Rhetoric of Empire: Colonial Discourse in Journalism, Travel Writing, and Imperial Administration* (Durham: Duke UP, 1994), M. Frawley, *A Wider Range: Travel Writing by Women in Victorian England* (London: Associated UP, 1994), A. Blunt, *Travel, Gender, and Imperialism* (London: Guilford, 1994), E. Bohls, *Women Travel Writers and the Language of Aesthetics 1716–1818* (Cambridge: Cambridge UP, 1995), R. Jarvis, *Romantic Writing and Pedestrian Travel* (Basingstoke: Macmillan, 1997), A. Pettinger (ed.), *Always Elsewhere: Travels of the Black Atlantic* (London: Cassell, 1998).
4 M. Michael, *Traveller's Quest: Original Contributions towards a Philosophy of Travel* (London: Hodge, 1950) p. 5.
5 Ibid., p. 2.
6 Ibid., p. 13.
7 S. Greenblatt, *Marvelous Possessions: the Wonder of the New World* (Chicago: Chicago UP, 1991), p. 14.

8 Cited in J.P. Harrington, *The English Traveller in Ireland* (Dublin: Wolfhound, 1991), p. 85.

9 Sir John Davies, A Discoverie of the true Causes why Ireland was never entirely subdued, nor brought under obedience of the Crowne of England (London: Jaggard, 1612), pp. 4–5.

10 Cited in C. Litton Falkiner, *Illustrations of Irish History* (London: Longmans, 1904), p. 296.

11 Cited in Harrington, *The English Traveller* (note 8 above), p. 116.

12 Ibid., p. 123.

13 Ibid., p. 134.

14 Much has been written on the Grand Tour, including G. Trease, *The Grand Tour* (London: Heinemann, 1967), C. Hibbert, *The Grand Tour* (London: Methuen, 1987), R. Hudson (ed.), *The Grand Tour, 1592–1796* (London: Folio, 1993), and E. Chaney, *The Evolution of the Grand Tour* (London: Cass, 1998). See also, P.G. Adams, *Travelers and Travel Liars 1660–1800* (Berkeley: UCLA Press, 1962), and C.L. Batten, *Pleasurable Instruction: Form and Convention in 18th Century Travel Literature* (Berkeley: UCLA Press, 1978).

15 L. Turner & J. Ash (eds), *The Golden Hordes: International Tourism and the Pleasure Periphery* (London: Constable, 1975), p. 29.

16 Hudson, *The Grand Tour* (note 14 above), p. 13.

17 Cited in Harrington, *The English Traveller* (note 8 above), p. 161.

18 J.R. Gold & M.M. Gold (eds), *Imagining Scotland: Tradition, Representation and Promotion in Scottish Tourism since 1750* (Aldershot: Scolar, 1995), p. 41.

19 Hudson, *The Grand Tour* (note 14 above), p. 21.

20 L. Colley, *Britons: Forging the Nation 1707–1837* (New Haven: Yale UP, 1992), p. 117.

21 Ibid., p. 119.

22 R.C. Hoare, *Journal of a Tour in Ireland, 1806* (London: Miller, 1807), p. ii–iv.

23 J.C. Curwen, *Observations on the State of Ireland* (2 vols, London: Baldwin, 1818), vol. I, p. 7.

24 J.A. Staples, *A Tour in Ireland, in 1813 and 1814* (Dublin: Napper, 1817), p. 238.

25 The Comparative Table of the Census of Ireland was published on 13 October 1851.

26 A. Plumptre, *Narrative of a Residence in Ireland* (London: Colburn, 1817), preface.

27 Ibid., p. 90.

28 S. Foster, *Across New Worlds: Nineteenth-Century Women Travellers and their Writings* (Hemel Hemstead: Harvester, 1990), p. 24.

29 E. Boehmer, *Colonial and Postcolonial Literature* (Oxford: Oxford UP, 1995), p. 17.

30 R. Kabbani, *Europe's Myths of Orient: Devise and Rule* (London: Macmillan, 1986), p. 6.

31 E. Said, *Orientalism* (orig. pub. 1978, London: Penguin, 1987) p. 99.

32 See also S. Clark (ed.), *Travel Writing and Empire: Postcolonial Theory in Transit* (London: Zed, 1999).

33 C. Nash, 'Embodying the Nation – The West of Ireland Landscape and Irish

Identity', in B. O'Connor & M. Cronin (eds), *Tourism in Ireland: a Critical Analysis* (Cork: Cork UP, 1993), pp. 86–7.

34   M. Ryle, *Journeys in Ireland: Literary Travellers, Rural Landscapes, Cultural Relations* (Aldershot: Ashgate, 1999), p. 27.

35   Ibid., p. 39.

36   P. Holland & G. Huggan (eds), *Tourists with Typewriters: Critical Reflections on Contemporary Travel Writing* (Ann Arbor: Michigan UP, 1998), p. 8.

37   Ibid., pp. 10–11.

38   M.L. Pratt, *Imperial Eyes: Travel Writing and Transculturation* (London: Routledge, 1992), pp. 74–5.

39   Urry, *The Tourist Gaze* (note 2 above), p. 1.

Editorial Note

These extracts, from accounts of travels in Ireland, are taken largely from first editions, although wherever I have used later editions (and translations) I have included publication details where available. I have tried to disturb the original extracts as little as possible, although a very small number of adjustments were necessary, such as the anglicizing of a number of American spellings. In the case of an archaism – Swisserland for example – I have opted for the modern spelling, and in the case of one or two writers – Ashworth for instance – I have introduced new paragraphing. All of the extracts are continuous pieces, and all glosses are in square brackets immediately following the phrase or quotation. I have chosen to retain all capitalized and italicized emphases, and in the case of texts bearing lengthy titles I have occasionally abbreviated, although in all cases the details provided are ample.

Each extract is prefaced with a header, providing publication details and a short biography wherever possible. Although many of the biographical details come from a number of sources, in several cases I have adapted and combined references to present the most appropriate information. I wish to acknowledge my use of *The Dictionary of National Biography*, *Chambers Biographical Dictionary*, *Webster's New Biographical Dictionary*, *Who's Who?*, *The Dictionary of English Biography*, as well as the *English Biographical Index* and the *American Biographical Index*. Extracts have been arranged in order of when they were first published, rather than when the tour actually took place, as I believe the date of publication – when the disseminative power of a text would have been keenest – should take precedence. However, to avoid confusion I have also supplied information regarding when the tour occurred. This information is provided by myself in the header, or is clear from the title, or from the first few lines of the extract. Where no information is available, I have necessarily presumed that the publication date followed soon after the tour and make no further comment. For the most part, these travellers are discussing a particular place or site, and in many instances – from the first line, or title – it is clear what part of the country they are travelling in. Where this is not clear I have indicated the region concerned.

Readers will note that a number of imbalances exist in this anthology: there are more men than women, some parts of the country are better represented than others, there are a greater number of English writers than Americans, and so on. This is simply a reflection of the state of travel writing for this period. More men travelled, and managed to make it into print; Dublin, the West and the South-West were the most travelled parts of the country; Ireland received its largest number of travellers from Britain. Nevertheless, I have attempted, without making qualitative concessions, to provide as much balance and coverage as possible and to show that there was greater diversity among nineteenth- and twentieth-century travel writers than might be presumed. One other, notable, imbalance concerns the greater number of travellers to Ireland in the nineteenth (especially the early and middle decades) century, which contrasts with the declining number of twentieth-century travellers. Unsatisfactory though this may be, there is little to be done, other than delete a number of extracts for the early nineteenth century, which seems more than unhelpful. Besides, if evidence exists indicating how popular the form was during that earlier period then an argument might be made for revealing the extent of that popularity, rather than minimizing or abridging it.

PART I
1800 – 1852

Introduction

The period 1800–1852 witnessed some dramatic moments in Irish history, with the Act of Union, the Repeal Movement, Catholic Emancipation, and the Great Famine notable amongst them. Although not all travellers were actually caught up in these developments, their writing reflected the sense of anxiety engendered by significant change. Several presented Ireland as a place of conflict and uncertainty, seeing the country as resistant to moderate, rational advance. Others travelled in an optimistic spirit, keen to see the changes brought about through the new constitutional relationship established by the Union of 1800. The first writer in this section, George Cooper, came to the country just before this event, and he offered a view of Dublin that was at times critical, focusing on the blatant inequalities he saw around him, and apportioning blame for injustice on the country's rulers. Cooper's sense of anticipated social and political collapse is largely absent from other post-Union travellers, but a number of narratives – the anonymously authored text from 1806 for example – increasingly associate Ireland with political instability. Similarly, Mary Ann Grant remarks on the build-up of troops and the generally agitated state of the country, while another early woman traveller, Anne Plumptre, although much taken with Ireland's antiquarian treasure, and with the sense of optimism afforded by the Union, discovers behind the ideology of parity a level of violence she was unprepared for. Plumptre's distraught ambivalence catches something of the unease concerning Ireland's loyalty, while the tension noted at several points in her text suggests that for even a supporter of the Union Ireland remained a complex, politically charged environment.

In several early nineteenth-century texts an appetite for romantic and picturesque descriptions is clear, but certain specific themes continually recur. Possibly in response to the spread of the Catholic Emancipation movement, the alleged backwardness of Catholicism, Irish poverty, and the unsettled political state of the country are frequent topics for discussion. John Christian Curwen and Thomas Kitson Cromwell, travelling in 1813 and 1819 respectively, both noted the decrepit conditions under which many laboured, their demoralized state, and the sense of impending social upheaval. Cromwell, in particular, wrote of the 'pale if not darkened visages' of the native Irish, and how this contrasted with the 'ruddy open countenances of English rustics'. Like Plumptre a little before him, Ireland was seen by Cromwell as less a happy partner in Union than a discontented element awaiting revenge. Of course, different historical periods created their own trends, and travellers such as Andrew Bigelow in 1819 could describe contrasting, in his case, enjoyable experiences. His tone may also have been determined by the fact that he was commissioned to write 'interesting observations' by several journals, for slightly later travellers, such as Inglis, and the author of the anonymously published text from 1835, occasionally raise the spectre of Ireland's politically uneasy state. Some writers however derived great enjoyment from encountering political controversy first-hand. Charlotte Elizabeth Tonna's eulogistic narrative, which reli(e)ves the Siege of Derry, demonstrates the immediate relevance to Ireland and the Irish of a long-distant conflict. Her approach to the city, her arrival and initial contact, are powerfully conveyed, as is the sense of Protestant and Catholic antagonism. Indeed, the theme of Catholicism runs through several of these texts, and is especially prevalent in the years before Catholic Emancipation in 1829. By 1842 William Makepeace Thackeray chose to make something of a joke of sectarian tensions, although the idea that Ireland was a mere collection of irreconcilable differences had by then firmly taken hold, and his observations of Belfast, referred to by another writer in this anthology some sixty years later, reveal a less than favourable impression.

From the mid-1840s Famine marked many texts, and travellers such as Bennett, East, Tuke, Osborne and Balch all tackled the subject directly, sometimes with sympathy. East's view of the starving Irish as 'sullen' contrasts sharply with Bennett and Tuke, both of whom were appalled by the spectacle of emaciated bodies so close to the heart of the empire. Of the ten 'Famine' writers included here – Mrs West, William Bennett, John East, James Hack Tuke, Spencer T. Hall, Sidney Godolphin Osborne, William Balch, Asenath Nicholson, John Ashworth, and Harriet Martineau – a number are clearly moved by their experiences. However, as Famine receded in the early 1850s there were those who suggested – Ashworth and Martineau among them – that improvement would quickly follow. The after-effects of Famine were still being experienced in 1851 and 1852, but a belief emerged that economic recovery, which for some was tied to greater political stability, could be finally achieved. Indeed, as fast as the first instalments of the 1851 census were published many writers promoted Ireland, particularly in Britain, as a place to which they might emigrate, citing Famine-related mortality and mass Irish emigration overseas as suitable incentives. The publication of John

Ashworth's text is one of the first to move in this direction, suggesting that the worst of it is over, and that Ireland's potential is particularly worthy of consideration. Undoubtedly, the attractions that are promoted relate to a specific region – around Clifden, County Galway, in particular – rather than to all parts of the country. Nevertheless, Ashworth, Martineau, as well as other writers such as Sir Francis Bond Head in his *A Fortnight in Ireland* (1852), imbued the travel-narrative form with a salient promotional rhetoric. Ireland, so the argument ran, could be improved, helped, possibly even saved, but not by the Irish themselves.

The period 1800–1852 saw many narrators attempt to comprehend the complexities of Ireland, a feat just as difficult for American writers as for the numerous British visitors in the same period. Political suspicion, religious strife, social and economic inequality, a variable sense of the country's potential for improvement: many of the travellers who visited in this period attempted to understand Ireland, sometimes against consider-able odds. Several were on business, and a few worked for newspapers, but many were visiting because the country was close to Britain and could be easily reached. But this was in itself a contradiction. Despite Ireland's geographical proximity to Britain, despite even the political Union that existed between the two islands, Ireland remained a conundrum to many travellers: a site of antiquity amidst squalor, of potential insurrection, and of a culture sometimes radically different from their own.

1. George Cooper, *Letters on the Irish Nation: Written During a Visit to that Kingdom, in the Autumn of the year 1799*　　(London: Davis, 1800, pp. 66–75)

Little is known of George Cooper, other than that he was a Barrister at Law, a training somewhat evident from this extract. Like many early-nineteenth-century travellers, Cooper was at pains to 'discover' Ireland, and in his introduction declared that while 'remote corners of the Hebrides have been often explored ... [and] the name of Ireland is most familiar to our ears, yet both the kingdom and its inhabitants have been as little described as if the Atlantic had flowed between us.' A striking narrative, this extract reveals the author's earliest impressions of Ireland, showing Cooper not just exploring the city of Dublin, but offering a set of radical opinions from within the institutions of authority themselves.

You will perceive that I have inverted the order into which I arranged the two grand principles by which I judge of the Irish government, and have taken the liberty of discussing the last of them first. The reason why I have done so was, because the fact which I have measured by it, is of public notoriety. It is not necessary to have travelled into Ireland to acquire the knowledge of it. The existence of an odious aristocracy in it, is known to every man on your side of the water. But to apply the other principle, to observe whether the middle rank does or not abound; a voyage across the Irish sea is altogether indispensable. I proceed therefore to acquaint you with my observations as to that particular.

Here I will be bold enough to assert that the peculiarity which most strikes every stranger upon landing in Ireland, and of which I myself felt the full force, is that face of beggary, misery and starvation which everywhere presents itself. The streets of Dublin are crowded with craving wretches, whose distresses are shocking to humanity, and whose nakedness is hurtful to the eye of decency. With this misery of the lower classes (for in a greater or a less degree it pervades three fourths of the whole people of Ireland,) is contrasted the condition of the wealthy. Their public edifices, their palaces, their squares and the streets which diverge from them, and their equipages, are magnificent beyond measure. In the capital of the kingdom there is to be seen nothing of those groups of moderately dimensioned houses, inhabited by the middling classes of people, and suitable to a mediocrity of fortune, which compose the far greater part of the city of London. The dimensions of all the buildings in Ireland are in opposite extremes. The eye reverts, as in Egypt, from the pyramid to the mud-cottage. The air is either 'mocked with idle state,' or the earth is defiled with more than Cassrarian wretchedness.

I visited the Houses of Parliament, and the Courts of Justice, which constitute two of the grandest piles of building in all Dublin. But neither law nor a constitution can exist in edifices: if they could, Ireland would indeed enjoy them. But what are these boasted terms of freedom and justice, but words and parchment, unless a people have rights and property to be protected? If they are only made the fortresses to uphold oppression, they become a curse instead of a blessing. If they are made the guards of property wrung by the tyranny of a few from the great mass of the people, they are nothing but a monument whose basis is the misery and oppression of the nation.

I looked on the Parliament-house in Dublin with its proud Corinthian pillars, its boast of ancient architecture, its magnificent porticoes, extent of building, glittering cupola, and crowded statues which crown the whole, with delight and admiration. But its semicircular front of Portland stone, only serves to screen so many hundred yards of houses which would otherwise disgust the eye. I next walked to the Four Courts, and surveyed that building from the opposite bank of the Liffey, to that on which the noble edifice bearing that name is situated. I was astonished at the elegance of its exterior, exhibiting all the embellishments which architectural and sculptural science can bestow. In order to take a view of the interior of the building, I then crossed the narrow stream of the Liffey, over a bridge which is the prototype of ours at Westminster. As if making my approach to an Athenian temple, I ascended a lofty range of stone steps. I was soon ushered by an Irish Cicerone into a splendid circular hall, nearly seventy feet in diameter, from which the four courts *radiate* at equal distances. My eye dwelt with pride and admiration on fluted shafts and Corinthian capitals. I enumerated the emblematical devices which adorn this hall; the signing of the great charter of our common liberties by King John at Runnimead, and of those of the city of Dublin by King James, with crowds of feudal knights and barons bold, armed at all points. I looked higher towards the roof of the building, and numbered eight statues as if supporting the dome. There was Liberty and Eloquence, Prudence and Justice, Wisdom and Law, with Punishment, and lastly Mercy, bringing up the rear. Roving thus from ornament to ornament, from the intersecting black and white marble squares of the floor, which seemed formed like a planetarium to revolve round a common centre, up to the cupola where the emulous plasterer had exerted all his skill; I began to fancy myself in one of those fairy palaces which some ingenious romance-writers have described. But, by some accident in coming out, the talisman was broken, and the enchantment vanished in a moment. The visionary fabric melted into air. I found myself as much surprised as many other simple knights-errant have been when they awakened from a similar trance. My olfactory nerve was assailed by the horrid stench which arises from the Liffey, (the *Cloaca Maxima* [Great Sewer] of Dublin;) my auditory nerves were assaulted with the clamourous importunities of a crowd of beggars; and my organs of sight turned away with disgust from every edifice and object within the horizon.

I was impatient to get into the country, for the accommodation which the Dublin hotels (they disdain the name of inns, and have no such thing,) offer to strangers is most execrable and intolerable. An Englishman, who has never travelled out of his own country, can form no adequate idea of their dirt and inconveniences. I had been much better accommodated in the most dreary and unfrequented recesses of North Wales. I could not possibly throw myself on the hospitality of my Irish friends, because at this season of the year they are in the country. I therefore followed their example as soon as I had seen everything which Dublin could offer to the curiosity of a *foreigner.*

In the country, the contrast between the rich and the poor, the lord and the peasant, is as strongly marked as it is in Dublin. But I have endeavoured in my last letter to give you some idea of this class of people. I can only add to my description of this full picture of human misery, that I have read of the bondsmen and villeins of the ancient feudal system, and of the boors and vassals (*glebae adscriptitii*) as they are now seen to exist in the tenures of modern Germany: but I cannot conceive the situation of either to be so miserable as that of the Irish peasantry. I know that the condition of the West India negro is a paradise to it. The slave in our colonies has meat to eat and distilled spirit to drink, whilst the life of the Irish peasant is that of a savage who feeds upon milk and roots. His clothing, if indeed it deserves that name, is a system of 'loop'd and window'd raggedness,' and he lives in a clay-built cottage, such as I have described it to you. I assure you that I have felt for the dignity of human nature, when I have beheld a race of men, in form and motion, in stature and in countenance, were the pride of the species; on whose persons Heaven had lavished all its favours –

> Os sublime dedit coelumque videre
> Jussit et erectos ad sidera tollere vultus
> [He gave to man an uplifted face
> and bade him turn his eyes to Heaven][1]

who are gifted with courage, with generosity, with all the heroic virtues, and with every thing that can give the world assurance of men: to see them, I say, humiliated and degraded to so wretched a condition. I am not the advocate of rebellion; but this I must say, that if such men as these are to be made Helots and Penests of, and chained to the cultivation of the soil without partaking of any of its fruits; if a government fit only for the puny race of Asiatic climes is forced upon the hardy giant sons of the North; their lords and rulers must expect that the avenging thunder will sometimes burst on their heads.

Such are the facts which in this country offer themselves to view; and such is the character of the Irish government, in its practical merits, which the application of these two principles therefore obliges us to make. There is neither balanced power, nor a middle class of people. The country is divided between the disproportionately rich and the

[1] Ovid, *Metamorphoses* (Cambridge: Harvard University Press, 1984; translator F.J. Miller), p. 8

miserably poor. It is ruled by an aristocracy with a rod of iron. As under the despotisms of the East, there is scarce any intermediate station between the sultan and the slave. The free governments of Europe are perhaps distinguished from the despotic ones of the East, by nothing more than the opposite conditions of the great mass of the people. The comprehensive policy of the one produces the peace and happiness of the whole: but in Asiatic monarchies we see a splendid focus collected in the centre, with misery and weakness in all the extremities. Such is the case in Ireland. There is no powerful nobility, no judicial corporation, no mercantile interests to temper and moderate the power of the aristocracy over the people, because these very bodies are themselves the component parts of the aristrocracy.

This is the miserable government which subsists in Ireland. How long it will exist, God alone knows; but, if I may venture to predict, it will not be long. The aristocracies of the world seem to have lived their day. They have perished in most other countries, and cannot long survive in Ireland. This at least I will venture to assert, that not even the plebians of old Rome ever sighed so much for the removal of that patrician power by which they were oppressed, as the Irish do for that of the petty tyrants who rule over them.

2. Robert Slade, *Narrative of a Journey to the North of Ireland, in the year 1802*

(London: Causton, 1803, pp. 32–38)

Robert Slade was Secretary to the Ironmongers' Company in County London-derry, and dedicated his work 'To The Honourable The Governor and Assistants of the New Plantation in Ulster, within the Realm of Ireland'. Although Slade travelled to Ireland with his two sons, who wished to see the Giant's Causeway, he was preoccupied with business affairs for much of the time. This extract, which finds him at the edge of Sheriff's Mountain, just outside Derry, reveals a commitment to the notion of Protestant settlement, tempered by an under-standing of the hardship of people's lives, and the responsibility on the part of the Company to improve their conditions.

These lands, thus held on determinable leases, extend for many miles through a very wild part of the country, as far as the Sheriff's Mountain, which serves as a boundary to the Society's property; I was induced to visit this place at the instance of two brothers, named Steel, who are under tenants, and who mean hereafter to apply for a lease of some of the lands in their own names, in consequence of having an assignment from their landlord, the immediate tenant of the Society, and his having left the country; I must do them the justice to say that they appear to have brought into cultivation the skirts of a dreary mountain, which offers no temptation to industry, and as they bear good characters and are manufacturers, with wives and families, the Society will, I make no doubt, feel disposed to give any proposal they may hereafter make, a favourable hearing.

There being no map of these upper liberties or lands held on determinable leases, it appears to me that the Society would do well to give directions to their general agent, to cause a correct map to be forthwith made, and therein to lay down some roads of communication towards the bog and old road to Strabane on one side, and the lower liberties on the other; also to report whether by erecting a fountain, after the manner practised in Switzerland, and which might serve as a monument to perpetuate the Union, it would not greatly tend to draw the people into a state of society, and ultimately lead to some plan for supplying Londonderry with water, which is much wanted and has been often in contemplation.

There are no turnpikes on the public roads in the North of Ireland, the roads being made in consequence of presentments at the sessions, which if they are proposed by the Society's agent, and supported by their respectable tenants, such as Sir George Hill, the member for Londonderry, Sir Andrew Fergusson, Captain Lecky, Alderman Lecky, and others, cannot fail of being carried into effect; whereby the Society's estate would become infinitely more valuable, their tenants more civilized, and the next generation would probably see fences and inclosures take place in a tract which now appears like a barren waste, hardly accessible even in the summer months, as I found a guide necessary to avoid the bogs when I visited it in September.

These suggestions may appear rather speculative, and so are most improvements in their outset, as every man must acknowledge when he looks back to what has taken place in and about the metropolis of the empire, within these last fifty years; but if the measures recommended are likely to promote the original object of the charter, *that of encouraging a Protestant Colony in the North of Ireland*, the nation at large has a right to demand, and the Protestant tenants a right to expect, from the Society's justice, that every endeavour will be exerted to improve their condition, and make them participate in the benefits of the Union which has recently taken place between the two countries. If such an impression as this could once be made on the minds of the Irish, it would put a stop to that emigration which a contrary conduct, particularly an excessive rise of rent has frequently occasioned. This leads me to question the policy, I might say the justice, of the City Companies in letting their lands on payment of heavy fines, without stipulating for the performance of the relative duties between landlord and tenant. In the instance of the Company to which I myself belong, the Ironmongers', I have discovered, on enquiry since my return, that in the year 1768, they let their estate for 61 years and three lives, on payment of a fine of £21,000, to a gentleman who had acquired a large fortune in India, but who, as far as I could learn, has never seen any part of the Company's Estate. The Irishman who cultivates the soil might with justice observe that he derives no protection by such a line of conduct; and if he were informed that the sum subscribed by all the Companies together, in the Reigns of Queen Elizabeth and King James, amounted only to £40,000, and the Ironmonger's proportion of that sum only to £3,334, he could not be charged with ingratitude if he appeared to feel no obligation to his landlords, in subjecting him to a rent far beyond what can possibly be derived from the product of the soil, and which can only be paid out of the profits of the loom.

3. Anon, *Journal of a Tour in Ireland, performed in August 1804*   (London: Phillips, 1806, pp. 22–24)

The anonymous author of this text states that the 'events which have occurred in Ireland during the last eight years, cannot fail to render any account of the present state of that island highly interesting to the British reader.' What events does the narrator refers to? In December 1796, 15,000 French troops attempted a landing at Bantry Bay, County Cork; in May 1798 a rebellion occurred in Leinster and parts of Ulster; in August of the same year, General Humbert and a French force of about 1,000 men landed in County Mayo; and in July 1803 Robert Emmet led a rebellion in Dublin.

Coleraine is a handsome town, through which we passed on to Bushmills, two Irish miles from the Giant's Causeway. Here we remained all night in a miserable inn, where I considered myself as in no small danger, as the people were moving about the whole of the night, and made frequent attempts to come into my room, as they pretended, for linen for some company who had arrived after they had gone to bed.

Very early, on a dismal morning, Saturday, August 18th, the rain pouring in torrents, we set out with a guide to view the Giant's Causeway. The first place to which we were conducted was a cave, at the mouth of which the sea broke tremendously. It is a sublime cathedral, built by the God of nature himself, and where the elements worship him. We next visited the Three Causeways, one of which is a plain surface of hexagonal stones, more nicely shaped and adapted to each other than the feeble hand of art could effect; and over this we walked as on the level of the sea. In the second, the basaltic columns, rising in different shapes, gave occasion to the guides (of whom another now joined us) to point out the giant's chair, his loom, his well, and his organ; but Pleskin, the last causeway, is the most striking, being that of which drawings are generally taken, and of which there is a model in the museum of Trinity College, Dublin. Here the columns are more numerous and regular, appearing like many rows of elegant pillars rising in clusters over each other: but my curiosity was gratified; and the heaviness of the morning, the call of hunger, and the prospect of the great distance I had yet to travel, prevented me from lingering on the spot. I accordingly returned to the inn; and, after breakfasting and paying an immoderate charge to the guide, set off to walk back to Newtown-Limavady.

This guide was either an United Irishman, or, suspecting me to be one, an artful spy. I asked him whether there were any rebels in that part of the country; to which he replied, 'If there are, they keep quiet; but in the rebellion two companies went from Bushmills to join the rebel army at Ballynahinch, and *fought like men*. Captain McNeven, their leader, had a purse of guineas as long as my arm, and entrusted one to each private, lest he should himself be killed or taken. To avoid being apprehended, he was at last carried through Coleraine in an empty barrel, and is now in America.'

The guide also had a budget of stories relating to the bloody contests betwixt the owners of a neighbouring castle, and the chieftains from the opposite shore of Scotland.

Nothing remarkable happened on the road until we had passed Coleraine about two miles, and were about to ascend the mountain, when a woman, standing at the head of a lane, told us that a farmer the week before was robbed of seventeen guineas and a watch upon the mountains. Although I had not quite so much to lose, this intelligence quickened my pace: and although we met with very few people upon the dreary hills, we, to my great joy, got clear of them long before the close of day; and at a little after six o'clock in the evening found ourselves once more in Newtown-Limavady.

I here met with an adventure which, though unpleasant at the time, will diversify my journal with a curious incident.

While I was at dinner in the parlour, my servant, as I afterwards understood, having gone into the kitchen, found a Sergeant-of-the-regiment. This man my servant found at dinner; and permission being granted to mess with him, they sat down together. Entering into conversation after dinner, my servant, whom I had ordered to conceal nothing, told him my name and object, and the capacity in which he attended me. But the sergeant found it convenient to doubt the narration, and immediately set off to the brigade-major, whom he acquainted that there were two Frenchmen come to the inn, personating an English gentleman and his servant; that they had plans and maps of the country; were going to look at the fortifications of Lough Swilly; with a variety of similar information. The consequence was, that after I had got safely into bed, the door of the room was thrown open, and the major, preceded by the waiter, and followed by a long train of the rabble of the town, whom, with very little delicacy or decorum, he permitted to attend him, entered in uniform, and, after a pompous preamble, demanded my pass. On my informing him that I did not understand a pass to be necessary in travelling through the interior of the country, I was told that it would be necessary for me to remain in the place until I should receive a letter from some friend in Dublin, which should satisfy him in regard to my motives for travelling. Upon this I offered to show him all my papers, which he said he would look over in the morning. He had not retired half an hour when he returned, demanding the surrender of my papers at that time. I accordingly gave him up my pocket-book and writing-case, when he examined minutely every scrap of paper which he found, asking me several questions, which gave me no very favourable impression of his politeness towards a stranger who might possibly prove a gentleman and a loyal man. After satisfying himself, and finding nothing to strengthen, but everything to banish his suspicions, it would at least, I think, have been proper that he should have made some concession; but too proud to do anything that might lessen his authority with the rabble he had introduced, he bade, rather than invited, me to breakfast with him in the morning, ordering a soldier to show me the way; and all this in such a tone as left me to conclude that I was still under an honourable arrest, insomuch that in the morning I rose early and wrote several letters, requesting immediate explanations of my motives from respectable friends.

The soldier came, but went away without me in the morning; so that after waiting till ten o'clock I set out with a young man from the inn, who showed me the way to the house of my friend. There was now no mob to gaze and gape upon his little brief authority, and he was all civility and politeness. I pardon, I praise the vigilance with which he did his duty; but shall never forget the *manner* of executing it, nor the gaping vulgar whom he brought along with him.

4. Mary Ann Grant, *Sketches of Life and Manners, with delineation of scenery in England, Scotland and Ireland* (London: Cox, 1810, pp. 248–254)

Mary Ann Grant appears to be one of the earliest woman travellers in Ireland whose account survives, although it has not been possible to trace any biographical information on the narrator herself. This short extract, from the Irish midlands, depicts a country traumatized by rebellion, yet not quite pacified, despite the build-up of troops and the generally vigilant state described.

Loughrea, June 1805. My last letter would inform my ever dear Mary Ann, that we were on the eve of quitting Tuam, which we regretted very much; I felt a great deal in parting with the amiable family of A; indeed, it is but justice to say, that the polite attentions of every person in the town were uniform to us; and we received such an interesting account of the archbishop and his family, that we lamented that they did not arrive at the palace, before we bid adieu to Tuam. We have been here some weeks, but do not find it near so pleasant, in point of scenery, as our last quarters. The country is not quite so dreary; there is a beautiful lake, near the town, which is a fine object, and the scenery round it is pleasing. I shall not see you so soon as I hoped; G. has been refused leave of absence, in consequence of the state of this country, it seems to cause general alarm, and a second rebellion, it is feared, will be the result of the Catholic Petition being refused, nothing but the military keep the people in any kind of awe; several unpleasant circumstances have taken place in different parts of the country, and a universal tendency to riot seems to evince itself. The most rigid discipline is kept up among the army, and more troops are ordered over. God grant that their power may be able to quell these threatened disturbances; it is fearful to look forward to what may be the consequence, should a rebellion actually take place, and the French take advantage of it to effect a landing; it is generally believed they would experience a too favourable reception: in a case so dreadful, I could be almost tempted to wish for a masculine habit, and proportionable strength to enable me to face the enemy, rather than be left to the mercy of these unhappy, misguided people. I trust, however, that our fears are greater than the danger.

As a slight trait in the character of the lower Irish, and a proof of their disposition to impose, I shall mention two trifling instances. A butcher came, lately, to me, with a kid for sale; I proposed taking a quarter, for which he asked me 4s. 6d.: not knowing the value of the article, but fully aware of the very little dependence that was to be placed on his word, I offered him half of what he asked, which he took; the woman of the house where we lodged, happening, soon after, to come into the kitchen, observed the meat, and asked me how much I gave for it; upon my telling her, she said, was it possible the man could so grossly impose upon me, declaring, that thirteen pence was all that should have been paid for the *whole* kid. The second instance happened to G, who was better prepared to resist imposition; a man came to sell him a greyhound, for which he asked three guineas, and, after a little altercation, took nine shillings! I could relate many anecdotes of a similar nature, but these will suffice to give you an idea of the lower class of people in this part of the country; they are, however, far from thinking they do wrong; the greater number of them are Roman Catholics; they call Protestants heretics, and to cheat or impose upon them, is, in their opinion, no crime; if asked why they told a falsehood, for the purpose of deception, their answer is, that it was to heretics, and that they would do the same by them. Yet, though these people would practise every art, trick, and chicanery, to impose upon a stranger, particularly if a Protestant, they possess genuine sentiments of integrity, were they properly cultivated; their priests have great influence over their minds, and they are rarely known to practise any kind of fraud upon them; why is this? Because reverence for their sacred order, and the strictest deference for their principles is, from their infancy, instilled into their ductile minds. But it is not the interest of these priests to make virtue the creed of their flock, since the most heinous crimes can be absolved by a sum of money, which is usually proportioned to the circumstances of the offender, and becomes the prerequisite of the priest. What inducement is here for virtue? Was it practised, the one party would lose the principal profits of his living, while the other could no longer find a palliative for a vicious course of life: I speak only in general terms; that there are, in this country, many worthy characters, who do honor to the sacred name they bear, and who strive to form the mind and manners of the people consigned to their care, by the standard of excellence, is beyond a doubt;

yet it is also a fact, but too well substantiated, that the greater number mislead the ignorant multitude, who submit themselves entirely to their direction. A person, illiterate in ideas, and penurious in circumstances, confesses to his priest some crime that he has committed; he is not lectured upon the sinfulness of his conduct or, if he is, the proper effect is lost; when he is told, that he can purchase his absolution, to obtain money for that purpose is often difficult, and is it not probable that to remove the difficulty, another crime may be added to the one from which he is to be absolved? Such confidence have they in the power of their priests to grant them absolution, and so much disgrace is attached to the refusal, that when they cannot procure the extorted sum, acts of desperation not unfrequently ensue; a melancholy instance of this kind happened not long since. A poor widow, and the mother of nine children, was refused absolution for want of a certain sum of money; after vainly trying to procure it, she returned to the priest, and conjured him to take all she could give; he ordered her to quit his presence, and an act of suicide was the consequence! She was found by her neighbours, hanging to one of the beams of her wretched hovel.

5. James Hall, *Tour through Ireland, Particularly the Interior and Least Known Parts*

(2 vols, London: Moore, 1813, vol. II, pp. 12–16)

A cautious traveller, the Reverend James Hall (1755–1826) was born in Scotland, educated at St Andrew's University, and employed for a period as an Assistant at Simpson's Academy, Chelsea. Hall's *Travels in Scotland by an Unusual Route* (1807), and his Irish travelogue, constitute the sum total of his published work in this form. Infatuated by Catholicism, as this extract makes clear, Hall travelled Ireland in the belief that this was in itself a remarkably brave thing to do.

From none to whom I had been introduced did I meet with a more hospitable reception than from Mr. Edgeworth, of Edgeworthtown, of whom, and his daughter Maria, to whom I had also letters of introduction, I had heard and read so much.

As the covetous man rejoices in the prospect of adding to his stores, and the pious man at the prospect of those meetings, where the fire of devotion will be made to burn more purely, in hopes of 'the feast of reason, and the flow of souls,' I approached Edgeworthtown, so much, of late, the abode of the Muses.

Mr. Edgeworth and his daughter being about to take an airing in the carriage when I called, which was soon after breakfast, and a very fine day, asked me to accompany them, to which I readily assented; and was much pleased with their remarks on the objects which occured in the course of our ride.

Mr. Edgeworth asked me to make his house my home while I continued in that part of the country; and told me that my boy and pony would also be cared for. With the last part of the request I did not comply, having settled matters respecting them at the inn.

When we returned from our ride, I found the rector of the parish, the Roman Catholic priest, and the Presbyterian clergyman, had been invited to dine; and, that there might be no preference shown to one clergyman before another, at dinner, Mr. Edgeworth said grace himself. In this hospitable mansion, the favourite abode of the Muses, the rendezvous of the wise and good, Papists and Protestants agree. Miss Edgeworth joined in the conversation; and, as may well be supposed, the author of Castle Rackrent, Irish Bulls, the Absentee, Vivian, &c. &c. served much to enliven and improve it. I had heard much of Miss Edgeworth, and knew that she and her father had taken an extensive view of the vast edifice of human knowledge; but found that not one half of her numerous amiable accomplishments had been told me. – Of her it may be said, *Omne quod tetigit, ornavit* [All that she touched, she adorned].

In the evening, when the clergymen were gone, I hinted that, though the Roman Catholic catechisms are clear respecting the forgiveness of sin, and show that a priest cannot forgive it, without sincere and unfeigned repentance; yet that, from nine-tenths of the conversations I had had with Catholics, in various parts of Ireland, I had reason to conclude, the great body of the people believe that, on being simply confessed, priests can, without any condition whatever, if they please, forgive sin. As Mr. Edgeworth was not of this opinion, though Mrs. and Miss Edgeworth were, he immediately rang the bell for John the coachman, who, he said, being a sensible young fellow, and a Catholic, would decide the question at once.

On asking the coachman, among a variety of other things, whether he went to hear mass, and to confession? and being answered in the affirmative, Mr. E. asked him, if he thought that on simply confessing them, the priest could forgive sins? The answer was, 'I think he can.' 'Pray John,' continued Mr. E. 'if you were to take out your knife, and stab me to the heart here in the midst of my family, and run and confess it to your priest, and he should absolve you; would you be really forgiven?' – 'I think I should.' – 'How could that be?' – 'Because (replied the coachman) it is expressely said, by our Saviour to his disciples, and to the bishops and priests, their successors, "Whose sins ye retain, they are retained; and whose sins ye forgive, they are forgiven."' Though the answers of some of the other servants, who were called one after another, did not go quite so far as those of the coachman; yet most of them tended to show, either that priests do not dwell enough on the conditions necessary to forgiveness, or pass them over altogether: and, as this appeared a matter of importance, I had entered into conversation with people in various parts of Ireland, and been at pains to ascertain the fact.

Mr. Edgeworth, who is sole proprietor of most of the houses in Edgeworthtown, and has independent landed property to the amount of some thousand pounds a year, told the priest, next day, when he called, what the coachman had said; adding, that he was sorry such doctrines were afloat. The priest denied such doctrines were taught; called the coachman an ass; and, though we were good friends the day before, I could easily see, from the fury of his eyes, that the priest was now not so fond of me; having learned that what I had said had led to the inquiry. Indeed, his eyes were so furious, and the sound of his voice such, that, being a powerful man, and in a passion, lest he should forget himself, and knock me down, I left the room. Though many of the better sort in Ireland pretend to believe neither in the infallibility of the Pope, nor in the power of priests to forgive sins, yet a large proportion of the common people, to my certain knowledge, believe both.

6. William Reed, *Rambles in Ireland; or Observations written During a short Residence in that Country* (London: Ogles, 1815, pp. 34–36)

William Reed (1770–1813) was a Quaker and philanthropist, and also a great equivocator and fantasist. Although he derived satisfaction from the publication of some of his poetry, his biographer, John Evans, tells us that his main ambition was to travel. He planned trips to Madeira, the West Indies, and Canada, but made none of them, residing in Bristol for most of his life. However, he did manage a visit to Ireland, which began on 16 September 1810, when he sailed into Cork harbour on a Guernsey trader. Although Reed apparently relished his Irish trip, he became melancholy and unwell on his return to England, and retired to Guernsey to see if matters would improve. They did not: 'I have but a very little acquaintance here, and nothing like a companion. I therefore of necessity muse alone, wander alone through the country, and witness the operations of Nature … I don't know how long I can endure this state of things.' Reed passed away on 30 September, 1813.

On leaving Killarney for the banks of the Shannon, I perceived, at no great distance from the town, that I no longer trod upon enchanted ground. Every trace of beauty had vanished, and the county before me resembled one long monotonous piece of beggarly patchwork. Passing through Tralee, the county-town of Kerry, I reached Abbeydorney in the evening. After securing a bed, and requesting the luxury of a little tea, to procure which I found involved no common difficulty in this corner of the world, I rambled into the neighbourhood, to examine the remains of a very spacious and venerable Abbey.

The sun was sinking below the horizon, and threw a melancholy splendour over the walls of the ruin. In wandering among the broken columns and heaps of human skeletons which, to the disgrace of the Irish, are everywhere unearthed and exposed, I roused a number of owls and cormorants from their hiding-places, and was not a little startled by the flapping of innumerable wings, and the shrieks of these funereal birds, as they quitted the monastery. It seemed as though I had trodden with unhallowed feet on that consecrated spot, and excited the anger of the spirit appointed by Religion to guard the sacred place; bringing to my recollection some of those images so forcibly portrayed by the magic pencil of Mrs. Radcliffe, in her visions of Romance.

I now returned to my hotel, which was nothing better than a wretched cabin, reeking with smoke. The members of this humble establishment were the landlord and his wife, the servant-girl (whom presently I shall more particularly notice), the servant-man, a poor idiot, whose employment was that of beating flax, a large sow, and two she-goats. After amusing myself a little with this grotesque assembly, I was conducted to my bed of chopped straw, with a much greater chance of being smothered than of finding a place of repose. When the family had retired, I was rather surprized at seeing the chamber-maid enter my room, with a candle in her hand. She very deliberately walked up to a large coffer, such as is used in farm-houses for holding corn, and after shaking the straw in the bottom, threw over it a coarse piece of sack or blanket. Her whole dress consisted of a serge jacket and petticoat. Neither hat, cap, stockings, shoes, nor chemise, ever enriched, I suppose, the wardrobe of this poor country-girl. Without seeming to feel any embarassment at my presence, on forcing a single button and pulling a single string, her jacket flew from her shoulders, and the petticoat fell as suddenly to the ground as if they had been touched by the fingers of necromancy. When this operation was performed and the candle extinguished, she bounded like a kangaroo into the chest, and thus this extraordinary vision vanished from my sight. As I could perceive several original traits in the composition of this girl, they may deserve some further specification. She was shorter by a head than the generality of women. Her hair was long and black, and stood almost in a horizontal attitude, like the ringlets of a mop frozen into icicles. Her complexion was exactly the colour of a dirty red ochre. There was a roguish kind of sparkle in her dark eye; her nose was remarkably thin, but neither aquiline nor otherwise – her mouth wide, her chin longer, broader, and squarer at the bottom than any that I had seen before. Her neck was unusually short, so short as scarcely to deserve notice, except on account of its resting upon a noble pair of round shoulders,, which would not have disgraced the form of Atlas himself. Her whole person was uncommonly stout without being corpulent, and her limbs were straight and round, and of the same size from beginning to end. Nature certainly had not been at any great pains or expense in finishing this production. It was much more calculated to endure for ages, than to fascinate for a moment by any powers of attraction: I do not recollect to have witnessed in the human form so complete an absence of all those fine flowing lines and graceful curves which, according to the laws of taste, constitute the principle of beauty. In brief, it was like one of those rude unfashioned figures which a common hedge-carpenter, half blind and half foolish, might have chipped with his hatchet from the timber of the black-thorn or crab-tree, to place as a characteristic statue on the tomb of departed symmetry. I rose early in the morning, and found this grotesque nymph milking the goats in the kitchen. She was very civil

and obliging; and after drinking a basin of the milk, I once more, to use
the language of the inimitable Bunyan, 'addressed myself to my journey'.

7. Anne Plumptre, *Narrative of a Residence in Ireland during the Summer of 1814, and that of 1815*   (London: Colburn, 1817, pp. 308–12)

Anne Plumptre (1760–1818) was an author, linguist, novelist and travel writer.
Among Plumptre's works are *The Rector's Son: a Novel* (1798), *Pizarro, or the
Spaniards in Peru: a Tragedy* (1799), and *Narrative of a Residence in France* (1810),
although much of her time was taken up with translating the dramatic works of
von Kotzebue for the London stage. A radical of sorts (she displayed some
sympathy with the French revolutionary cause while resident in France),
Plumptre is more disciplined in Ireland. A text that mixes mineralogical wonder
with oblique political references, Plumptre's *Narrative of a Residence in Ireland* is
one of the most interesting post-Union travelogues. This extract is from her
second journey, in 1815.

To the two former divisions of Limerick a third may now be added, in
the vast additions made of late years towards the south-west, under the
name of Newton-Perry. These buildings were begun about fifty years
ago, by the permission and under the patronage of Lord Perry, a part of
the old walls of the town being thrown down to make way for them.
Here the streets are wide and regularly built; the houses good, but built
of red brick. There are as handsome shops as can be seen even in
London. But the old town is one of the most frightful, the most filthy
places in all Ireland. True, I saw it under every possible disadvantage. The
rain, which had kept off for some hours, began to come on again very
soon after I commenced my walk about Limerick, and the streets were
almost ankle deep in mud: this, however, would not have been if it were
a generally clean town.

My principal object in going into the Old Town was to see the
cathedral. Indeed it scarcely furnishes any other object worth seeing.
This is a fine old building, one of the best Ireland has to show, at least as
far as my knowledge goes. It is a Gothic structure of the thirteenth
century, built by Donat O'Brien, then king of Limerick. It has never
been suffered to fall into a dilapidated state, but has been constantly kept
in good condition. Much were it to be wished that it were better placed;
but it is squeezed into such a poking kind of corner, and so beset with

miserable buildings patched upon it, that the way to it is found with difficulty. The choir is handsomely fitted up. In doing some repairs to the roof, not many days before I was in the church, a cannon-ball was found deep within one of the spars, which must have lodged there in some of the sieges the town has sustained, and was never before discovered. In the time of Oliver Cromwell it was besieged by Ireton, who was repulsed in several attacks, and would in all probability have been compelled ultimately to abandon the siege, had not the demon of discord found his way into the town, and insinuated himself among the inhabitants: – animosities arose among them: some declared in favour of the Pope's Nuncio, some in favour of King Charles, and some were for surrendering to the English army. A house divided against itself cannot stand, – and Limerick fell. Ireton entered and took possession of it: but here ended his career; he died there in a very short time. In 1690 it was besieged by King William; but he found so powerful a resistance, that he was obliged to abandon the siege. The next year General Ginckel succeeded better, and reduced it to submission.

On the quay is a very handsome custom-house, with docks, at which the ships unload their cargoes. There is a house of industry somewhat singularly situated, running as it were into the river. Flourishing linen, woollen, and paper manufactories are carried on here; and a great deal of ship beef and pork is salted. The reputation of this place for gloves is well known; but I found that there are many more Limerick gloves manufactured at Dublin and at Cork than in Limerick. For my own part, I think their reputation is rather, if I may be pardoned a familiar expression, *great cry but little wool*; I could never find in what their great superiority consists. This I know, that at Cork I was asked five shillings a pair for Limerick habit-gloves, while for very excellent ones not so called I paid half that price. There is a great manufactory of gloves at Cork, and most excellent ones; the kid leather very nice, and the work particularly good. I suspected them at first to be French, smuggled into sale in this way; but I was assured by persons of credibility that they were not so.

There were formerly a great many monastic institutions at Limerick. King Donat O'Brien, who founded the cathedral, founded also a convent for black nuns of the Augustine order. Edward the Third took this convent under his especial protection. A priory for canons regular of St. Augustine was founded in the reign of King John by a citizen of the town, Simon Miner. It stood near Baal's Bridge. A sumptuous monastery of Dominicans was founded in 1240 by another O'Brien, King of Thomond, which was endowed with very large possessions in and about the city. All these possessions, at the suppression of monasteries, were granted to the Earl of Desmond, at a yearly rent of five shillings. Another O'Brien, in the reign of Henry the Third, founded a monastery of gray-friars. This stood just without the wall of the town; and, with the priory of St. Augustine, was granted by Henry the Eighth, at the suppression of monastic institutions, to Edmund Sexton a citizen of the town, at an annual rent of two shillings and sixpence. No vestiges of any of these monasteries remain. There is a convent of nuns now in the town, but not inhabiting any of the ancient religious houses. I would have gone to see it, but being Saturday no strangers were admitted. Three other bish-oprics, formerly distinct areas, have been at different times incorporated with this; those of Inis-Catha, Ardfert, and Aghadoe.

Had it not been for the continued bad weather, I believe I should now have gone to Kilmallock, and from thence to Tipperary; it would only have made a circuit of about eight miles in going to the latter place. But such was the morning in which I set off from Limerick, and such had been the weather now for three days, that I began to think my good fortune in this respect had wholly forsaken me, and that nothing remained but to hasten back to Dublin as fast as possible. I accordingly pursued my route this day through a never-ceasing rain from Limerick by Tipperary to Cashel. I will not say any thing of the country; it seemed to me the most dreary and dismal imaginable. At Tipperary I first heard of the disturbances which just now commenced in these parts; only two nights before the Mail had been attacked on the other side of Cashel by a very desperate gang, and a soldier had been killed. I did not, however, from this account at all understand the nature of the attack, but thought its object had been to rob the passengers.

On arriving at Cashel, I found that the attack had been of a much more serious and alarming nature: it took place on the other side of Littleton, which is about eight miles from Cashel; and the object was not so much to get money, as arms. Two guards always attend the mails in Ireland: there were besides at this time two dragoons travelling on the outside of the mail, and two sailors, one of whom was for some purpose, I do not recollect what, charged with a large sum of money. Very different accounts were given of the number of the assailants; the truth was, that in such a scene of terror, tumult, and confusion, it was impos-sible for any one to give a probable guess at their numbers; some estimated them at fifteen or twenty; others computed them at fifty; that they were a strong party was certain. The attack was begun by firing at the leading horses, one of which was so desperately wounded that it fell immediately, and thus was the coach effectually stopped. A desperate conflict then ensued, in which one of the dragoons upon the top of the coach was mortally wounded, and one of the guards very severely. The sailor who had the money about him seeing the leading horse fall, with astonishing presence of mind leaped from the top of the coach, and having an immensely strong clasp-knife in his pocket, cut the traces of the leaders, when, giving a severe lash to that which remained alive, he ran away, dragging after him his poor wounded companion. The coachman, thus freed from the embarassment of the fallen horse, whipped on the two remaining ones and set them into a gallop, by means of which they soon got clear of the assailants. The sailor who had done this important service, amid the scene of confusion stole unperceived away, and lying down in a dry ditch under a hedge by the road side, there remained awhile till the gang were dispersed; when, creeping into a corn-field, he remained concealed there till morning; then thinking himself in safety, he went on to Littleton, having not only saved himself, but all his money. Till his safety was known, the utmost anxiety was experienced by every one on his account lest he had fallen into the hands of these desperadoes, which to him must have been certain destruction. A reward of fifty pounds was afterwards given him by the Government.

It may easily be guessed in what state the whole company in and about the mail must be when they arrived at Littleton, between two and three miles from the scene of action. The wounded dragoon and guard left there, where the dragoon died in a few hours; he had been interred the very morning that I was at Littleton. No attempt was made by the assailants to demand money; they demanded only the surrender of the arms. Such a story was not to be heard unmoved; no one could have heard it with indifference two hundred miles from the spot where it happened, and two years after; but to think of being then but a few miles from it, that I was the next morning to pass over it, that the affair had happened only two nights before, occasioned a feeling not to be described. It was not apprehension for my own safety, I did not consider that as in any danger; I was not to travel by night; I had no arms to excite the desires of those unhappy wretches: – I know not what it was, but my mind was wholly untuned to thinking of any thing else; nothing was present to it but the idea of the shocking scene which had passed, and the inevitable consequences with which it must be attended. That the situation of the lower classes in Ireland, and particularly in this part of the country, was very deplorable, could not be doubted; but who could witness without deep regret the mistaken, the perverted notions they had adopted of the means by which it was to be ameliorated? Such violence must be repelled by violence; and the consequence ensued, which was reasonably to be expected, that *martial law*, that *law* without *law*, was soon proclaimed here. Devoted Ireland! are these things never to be otherwise? – I came to Cashel to see the celebrated rock and the venerable remains of antiquity with which it is crowned, but I could now see nothing except the increased sufferings which the country had prepared for itself; I became indifferent to everything else, and I thought only of quitting scenes which seemed surrounded with nothing but gloom and horror. I saw the rock and the ruins at a little distance, as I entered the town, and as I quitted it they presented but new ideas of devastation, and I passed on.

Yet for one moment I felt an impulse to stop the carriage and ascend the rock. The rain had ceased in the night, the morning was fine, the sun was shining upon the mouldering towers and turrets, and they assumed an air of magnificence which methought ought not to be passed by. The next moment, however, the idea that though the heavens were bright and clear, all was gloom in the moral atmosphere, came too forcibly over my mind to be repelled, and I pursued my route. At present my feelings upon this occasion seem strange to me, they seemed so in a few hours after, but at the moment they were irresistible. I have often asked myself since, why I did not see the ruins of Cashel, – I could never answer the question satisfactorily.

8. J.C. Curwen, *Observations on the State of Ireland, principally directed to its Agriculture and Rural Population in a series of Letters, written on a Tour through that Country*

(2 vols, London: Baldwin, 1818, vol. I, pp. 180–86)

John Christian Curwen (1756–1828), MP for Carlisle, was returned to Parliament in 1786, where he became a noted rural economist. Something of a radical – he approved of the French Revolution, attempted to put down bribery at elections, refused a peerage twice, and took his wife's name of Curwen – he was the author of several agricultural works and reports. A frank and dignified narrator, Curwen displayed a remarkably sympathetic attitude towards the poorer sections of Irish society, when he visited the country from August to October 1813. The following extract finds him just outside Portrush, on 23 August 1813.

Those delightful undulations, that variety of mountain and valley, which had given such peculiar beauty to the portion of the country we had seen, no longer attracted our attention. A regular, almost uninterrupted, and certainly uninteresting, slope from the hills to the sea was here presented to our observation until we reached the village of Lessenaugh.

Unfavourable as were the impressions which the general barrenness, the want of fences, and the rude cultivation of a few spots about the village, had made on our minds as we approached Lessenaugh, these were but preludes to the painful feelings which our further examination subjected us to experience on our arriving within the village itself. A character of such wretchedness was here discernible as to exceed anything of the kind that we had yet encountered; and whilst it arrested our close attention, it impelled a forcible desire to ascertain the extent of the too evident misery under which its forlorn inhabitants were doomed to exist.

On quitting the carriage, I followed a little boy whose curiosity had led him to take a view of us. Dirt and rags could not obscure the health and intelligence which his countenance displayed. He was hastening to announce to his parents the arrival of strangers, and reached the cabin a little before me. As I approached the door, the height of which did not exceed four feet and a half, I was met by the father, bending double to get out of his wretched abode.

In erecting himself he presented the figure of a man muscular, well-proportioned, and athletic. I was so much struck with his appearance that I involuntarily stepped back.

The gigantic figure, bare-headed before me, had a beard that would not have disgraced an ancient Israelite – he was without shoes or stockings – and almost a sans-culotte – with a coat, or rather a jacket, that appeared as if the first blast of wind would tear it to tatters. Though his garb was thus tattered, he had a manly commanding countenance. I asked permission to see the inside of the cabin, to which I received his most courteous assent. On stooping to enter the door I was stopped, and found that permission from another was necessary before I could be admitted. A pig, which was fastened to a stake driven into the floor with a length of rope sufficient to permit him the enjoyment of sun and air, demanded some courtesy, which I showed him, and was suffered to enter. The wife was engaged in boiling thread; and by her side, near the fire, a lovely infant was sleeping, without any covering, on a bare board. Whether the fire gave additional glow to the countenance of the babe, or that Nature impressed on its unconscious cheek a blush that the lot of man should be exposed to such privations, I will not decide; but if the cause be referrible to the latter, it was in perfect unison with my own feelings. Two or three other children crowded round the mother: on their rosy countenances health seemed established in spite of filth and ragged garments. The dress of the poor woman was barely sufficient to satisfy decency. Her countenance bore the impression of a set melancholy tinctured with an appearance of ill-health. The hovel, which did not exceed twelve or fifteen feet in length, and ten in breadth, was half obscured by smoke – chimney or window I saw none; the door served the various purposes of an inlet to light, and the outlet to smoke. The furniture consisted of two stools, an iron pot, and a spinning-wheel – while a sack stuffed with straw, and a single blanket, laid on planks, served as a bed for the repose of the whole family. Need I attempt to describe my sensations? The statement alone cannot fail of conveying to a mind like yours an adequate idea of them – I could not long remain a witness to this acme of human misery. As I left the deplorable habitation, the mistress followed me to repeat her thanks for the trifle I had bestowed: this gave me an opportunity of observing her person more particularly. She was a tall figure, her countenance composed of interesting features, and with every appearance of having once been handsome.

Unwilling to quit the village without first satisfying myself whether what I had seen was a solitary instance, or a sample of its general state; or whether the extremity of poverty I has just beheld had arisen from peculiar improvidence, and want of management, in one wretched family; I went into an adjoining habitation, where I found a poor old woman of eighty, whose miserable existence was painfully continued by the maintenance of her grand-daughter. Their condition, if possible, was more deplorable, and the scene more heart-rending, than that of which I had just taken leave. I now became convinced that, like satiety in pleasure, the human heart can endure pain only to a certain extent. I had not courage to explore further, and became impatient to escape from the repetition of scenes too wretched for human nature to endure, and too multiplied to be within my power to relieve.

The passing of strangers, where there is so little thoroughfare, at all times attracts notice – our stopping created surprise. The whole population of the village assembled – curiosity the inducement. The first group encircling the carriage was composed of children, whose health and vivacity rendered them pleasing in spite of the repulsive state of their dirty persons and ragged apparel. The second circle was composed of young women, some of whom had considerable pretensions to beauty, in defiance of the robes by which they were shrouded – behind stood the elder branches of families, to note what occurred.

A survey of this assemblage produced as sudden a hesitancy in my ideas, as the meeting of two mighty waves, from whose conflict we observe a momentary calm arise. My heart, which had been agitated with an agonizing pity for the calamitous situation in which I was about to leave these poor creatures, to whom mortal existence appeared a grievous burden, became calmed by observing that no one of the numerous damsels present had neglected carefully to put up her hair in papillottes. Could it be possible, in a community where it had just appeared to me despair had so established its empire, that even the extinction of life might be hailed as a blessing, that personal vanity should have influence on any of its members? To what can this be ascribed? Can it be that hope, fondly nursed by a consciousness of attractive charms, diffuses her cheering beams, gilds the opening dawn of life, and promises that the future shall not disappoint! These were strong intimations, however, that every other social perception is here felt and shared by the hearts of the miserable, in alleviation of the wretchedness which they are doomed to endure.

Though somewhat consoled by so unexpected a display of one's pride, and the consequent reflections which it excited, yet my feelings could ill bear thus to contemplate the sufferings of my fellow-creatures and fellow-subjects, without sincerely pitying and sympathizing with their afflictions. Assuredly there must be something radically wrong in this country – humanity proclaims it, and appearances justify the assumption. Where is the proprietor of the place? the traveller exclaims, his presence would soon lighten the weight of misery that presses his dependants to the earth. Though pleasures and wealth from other sources render his interest here unworthy of his thoughts, yet humanity could not fail to exert itself, and meliorate the condition of his dependents. – Alas! vain is the inquiry – unavailing the appeal: it belongs perhaps to some absentee whose utter ignorance of his property here, and complete indifference to the hapless condition of the peasantry on it, paralyzes all efforts of industry, blights the harvest of hope, and produces poverty and misery all over the domain. The waters of oblivion can never wash out the stains which the scenes of woe witnessed this day have impressed on my mind!

9. Thomas Kitson Cromwell, *The Irish Tourist, or Excursions through Ireland: Historical and Descriptive Sketch of the Past and Present State of Ireland* (3 vols, London: Longman, 1820, vol. II, pp. 144–48)

Thomas Kitson Cromwell (1792–1870). Better known as a dissenting Minister than a writer, Kitson Cromwell had an earlier, and possibly more interesting, life as a minor poet and playwright. His *Honour; or, Arrivals from College: a Comedy* was performed at Drury Lane, and between 1818 and 1822 he published several volumes entitled *Excursions through Britain*, a feat which contributed to his election as a Fellow of the Society of Antiquaries in 1838. Kitson Cromwell's text is comprised of twelve excursions, all of which originate from Dublin, and which take place throughout 1819. This extract (ending with a quotation from Curwen, above) finds him just arriving at Navan, as part of excursion eight.

At our Inn in this place, which is good and provides post-horses, we saw a book, apparently placed in the way of the traveller for his entertainment, purporting to be a translation of a *History of the Revolution in France*, the tendency of which was highly jacobinical, and probably afforded a specimen of the works so industriously spread throughout this country during the prevalence of the revolutionary mania. A note appended by the Editor to some violently democratical remark – '*That is true, faith! Bravo!*' – was amusing. Of the present state of public feeling in Ireland, we profess ourselves wholly unqualified to pass a general opinion: political sentiments, particularly if their expression be inimical to the interests, or likely to compromise the personal safety of men, usually lie too deep to be obvious to those who have the most favourable opportunities, and the strongest desire, to become acquainted with them; how much more difficult, then, must their investigation prove to the temporary resident, or general traveller? Besides, the native cunning of the lower Irish would in most cases completely baffle the stranger's inquiries of this nature, however sagaciously disguised by this method of proposing them: yet not by *appearing* to penetrate the veil in which the state partizan might attempt to enshroud himself, would the attack be disconcerted by its object; but, by a refinement of art, the utmost apparent simplicity would conceal the fullest perceptions of the designs of the querist, and the readiest information be seemingly brought forward, where none was actually afforded. Are there then no means of obtaining a knowledge of this point, besides attention to the *language* of the inhabitants? – may be perhaps asked by the inquisitive reader: is not the *countenance,* in most instances, a mirror of the heart? –

and, upon general principles, deduced from the common history of nations, may not the political sentiments of a people be inferred from their actual *state*. There are those – and we believe they are neither the worst logicians, nor the most lukewarm lovers of their country – who would answer these questions tremblingly. For he must have travelled in Ireland with his observation but little directed to this subject, who has not traced even in the features of the peasantry, when *not* illuminated by the animation of discourse, and *not* smoothed by the expression of their natural urbanity, a distinctive character – as marked as ever stamped a national similarity on the faces of a people – which can only be described as speaking a sullen, though patiently settled gloom. Everywhere in Ireland, we meet with lengthened and pale if not darkened visages, the indexes to the minds of men employed in the common agricultural labours, which, contrasted with the ruddy open countenances of English rustics, might appear to the traveller from the latter country those of banditti, of beings detached from civilized society, and ready for the perpetration of any attack upon its legal institutions, rather than of men constituting the far greater portion of a population united under an established form of lawful government. We need scarcely remark, that a general conclusion of the latter nature would be egregriously false; though it must be admitted that outrages too frequently occur in this country, backed by numbers unprecedented in the commission of similar crimes in England. What, then, upon the whole, is to be inferred from these facts? The question is too ample to be discussed in this place; and did we not concieve it one of abstract political economy, rather than as one involving the conduct of the *present* government of the country in any shape, we should perhaps wholly abstain from its consideration. But the present government may do, and we really think has done, much, to remedy the evils which it had no hand in producing: in this light we submit the present remarks; trusting that, it and all who have power and influence in the country, will continue to do more as more shall appear necessary to be accomplished. The national distinction we have just drawn between the peasantry of the two countries – to what is it to be ascribed, if not to national differences in their situation, as respects their domestic comforts, and the relation they stand in to their superiors? The English tourist in Ireland must have indeed shut his eyes, if the use of the faculty of vision alone has not convinced him, that, in both these points of view, (notwithstanding the legal institutions are the same) the condition of the Irish labouring classes is infinitely below that of the English. But long must such a state of things have existed in a country, and grievous, during that long period, must have been its endurance, ere it could have affixed a national portraiture on a considerable body of the people: yet the history of the world teaches, that the continuance of the degradation of a majority in any country cannot be for ever; and who, that really prizes the blessings of order and civil union, but must view with alarm of population rapidly increasing under such circumstances, unless he also perceives the enlightened and the wise of every Christian denomination stepping forward with liberal views towards the *gradual,* but still *unceasingly-progressive* amelioration of their inferiors, rather than attempting to crush the discontents they will use no efforts to prevent, by violent means, the resources only of weak and timid minds, and which the experience of past ages proves are ever ultimately unavailing? 'Privations to the extent endured in Ireland,' says a manly and ingenious British senator [Curwen, *Observations,* vol. II, p. 281], '*must* produce discontent, the parent of disloyalty and dissaffection; and however the great, the glorious work of reform in this most beautiful island may be deferred, it *must* be seriously undertaken, to prevent those fatal consequences which await procrastination. – The inefficacy of force has been manifested by the experience of centuries. Coercion, sustained by an overwhelming military power, by depopulating the country, might produce a temporary calm; but it is the last expedient which ought to be resorted to for the attainment of permanent order, and obedience to the laws and civil authorities.'

10. Andrew Bigelow, *Leaves from a Journal; or Sketches of Rambles in North Britain and Ireland* (Edinburgh: Oliver, 1820, pp. 122–27)

Andrew Bigelow (1795–1877), born in Massachussetts, was a Unitarian minister and author who, in addition to this travelogue, also published *Travels in Malta and Sicily.* Commissioned in early 1819, Bigelow travelled to Europe for the purpose of furnishing a number of journals with interesting observations, some of which found their way to the *Philadelphia Gazetteer,* the *Analectic Magazine* and *The Boston Athenaeum.* In this extract, from 29 April 1819, Bigelow tells of an enjoyable evening at Trinity College Dublin, even if he does rather spoil the effect by including the spectacle of Sir Richard Musgrave, flushed from claret, upstaging the Provost before his guests.

Breakfasting at his rooms this morning, I had the pleasure to meet two or three other very intelligent gentlemen who hold fellowships in

Trinity College. The whole number of these livings in the University is twenty-two; seven senior, and fifteen junior. The salaries of the senior fellows are large; varying from 7 to 900 pounds sterling. Those of most of the junior are as low as 120 and even 100 pounds; but then they have the prospect of rising to the higher form by right of eldership, and they receive in the meanwhile a large part of the avails from tuition. Besides these fellowships, the University has three medical professorships, and five which it owes to royal munificence in the several departments of divinity, common law, civil law, materia medica, and Greek. There are also professors of mathematics, natural philosopohy, botany, rhetoric, and the oriental tongues.

The course of discipline and instruction in Trinity College is modelled after the habits of the English universities. The students are divided into three ranks, fellow-commoners, pensioners, and sizers. The latter are supported, or receive assistance in an eleemosynary manner chiefly, though, in return, they perform some slight services, such as are required of the poorer scholars in some American colleges. Each student, on entering the University, has the liberty of choosing whether he will be a fellow-commoner, or a pensioner. If the former, his necessary expenses are nearly doubled. He sits, indeed, at the same time in the hall with the fellows, and enjoys a few other privileges; but as each student, on becoming a member of the University, is obliged to enter his name with one of the junior fellows in order to pursue his studies under his direction, the fellow-commoner, if the individual chooses to become one, is charged about as much again as the pensioner; that is to say, about 30 pounds annually to the officer instead of 15 or 16 pounds; and this is but one item in the increased expenditure. Sons of noblemen, and of the richer and more distinguished gentry, become fellow-commoners, but the pensioners, as might be supposed, constitute the great body of the students. Evening tea and breakfast are taken both by fellows and pupils in their respective rooms, but dinner is served up in the refectory, or public hall. It is common with the junior fellows to complain of the burden of their duties, and they look forward with considerable impatience to the period when, with their office, they may enjoy *otium cum dignitate* [leisure with dignity]; or rather, to transpose the phrase, *dignitatem cum otio* [dignity with leisure]. But they are subjected to a grievance, of which some are disposed more loudly to complain, although, perhaps, it is but fair offset for the comforts attendant upon academic living. By a special provision in the College statutes, a fellow in the University is doomed to a life of celibacy, unless a dispensation from the inhibition is procured from the King.

It was gratifying to me, to take a still nearer view than I had yet obtained of the manners of the Dublin literati, and this I enjoyed at the dinner-table of the Provost in the evening. The reverend gentleman had requested my company, with a view, as he politely intimated, of making me acquainted with a few men of letters, whom he proposed bringing together on the occasion. Thirty or more guests were assembled, among whom were the most prominent characters connected with the University, and also several eminent city *savans*. Conversation was dignified, but tempered with a proper degree of freedom. It had nothing of that buckram which is often found to mark both the conversation and manners of those, who, devoted to sedentary and contemplative pursuits, prefer a life of seclusion to that collision with the world, which tends to brighten what is solid, and give currency to what is valuable.

If my opportunities for forming an estimate of the polite, as well as intellectual society of Dublin, had been confined to the present, the result could not have failed to be in the highest degree favourable. I recollect, before my arrival here, to have heard a friend, in a panegyric upon the country, pronounce an Irish gentleman to be a finished gentleman. How far this opinion was founded upon an amiable but undue partiality, consequent upon a cordial reception which he had himself experienced, I had then to learn. The result in my own mind has since been, that the belief was in no respect erroneous. The polished inhabitant of Dublin has all that high-toned refinement of manners which characterizes the gentry of the same rank in the English and Scottish capitals; and, from a constitutional warmth and frankness of feeling, superadds an urbanity to his courtesies, which oftentimes the stranger in vain looks for among them. Of the guests who were assembled at the Provost's, there were gentlemen who, to their other information, added the observations which they had made by foreign travel; and I was not disappointed in finding that, while they had thereby shaken off every undue local prejudice, they cherished an unabated, nay, it would seem, a stronger attachment towards the land of their birth.

It would be reasonable to expect that the University should partake much of this pride, which respects the country generally; but a stranger, at least an American, might be surprised on learning the estimation in which it is actually held. In solid science, Trinity College professes to yield to no university in the Three Kingdoms, excepting Cambridge; and with that it aspires, at no distant day, to cope successfully. Less, however, is known of it in America, I am inclined to think, than of the British universities; and even the English scholars have affected, till of late, a Sadduceism in respect to its claims. But, leaving to other hands the decision of these, I would just remark in passing, that the investiture of the gown is by no means thought to preclude the wearer from the privilege of blending with the pursuits of pure learning the art of good living. The Provost's table presented a luxurious display of viands; and the glasses, as they briskly circulated, sparkled with wines of ruby brightness and rarest excellence. The guests who returned to the drawing-room did not separate till a late hour, and it was nearly one before they all took leave. Sir Richard Musgrave was the magnet. His vivid wit and various anecdote render him the delight of the circles which he frequents; and on the present occasion, some favourite recollections being awakened, he threw around him the fine sallies of his humour with an effect which was irresistibly amusing.

The Dublin hours of dining are immoderately late. The four and five o'clock habits of North Britain were sufficiently unreasonable, at least according to my plain Yankee notions; but the good citizens of Dublin prefer to follow more closely the Westminster standard: six, half past six, and seven, are usual hours of appoinment on cards; and I have sat down to dinner as late as eight.

11. Gilpin Gorst, *A Narrative of an Excursion to Ireland, 1825* (London: Skipper, 1825, pp. 17–21)

Little is known of Gilpin Gorst, other than what this narrative largely tells us: that he was Deputy Governor to the Honourable Irish Society and that he travelled to Ireland on Society business. This extract, written during the apparently hot summer of 1825, has a rather quirky, even camp resonance to it, no more so than when Gorst tells us about his visit to the public baths, of his ruined complexion, about the food and drink he consumes, and even when he makes an effort to capture something of the Dublin brogue. Evidently enjoying his trip to Ireland, Gorst is a lively contributor who relates a sense of his day-to-day duties amidst the rhythms of the Irish capital.

Thursday, 16th June. Got up at five – a very hot morning – went down to the sitting room and wrote a couple of letters. At six I sallied out for a walk, and in Stephen's Green, was surprised to find Mr. Schultes at so early an hour. This is one of the largest squares in Dublin, and is a mile round (Is this a Bull?). It is enclosed by a handsome iron railing, with a gravel walk and shrubbery. The lawn in the center, is not very neatly kept, for some large hay cocks were upon it. The square is a very fashionable residence. From thence we went to College Green, and quizzed the Equestrian Statue of William of 'glorious memory'. Some military trophies in the panels of the marble pedestal are painted in party colours, which produce a paltry effect. On the north side of this area, stands the Bank, which, before the Union, was the House of Parliament; it is built of Portland Stone, and is one of the finest edifices in the City. Trinity College fronting the Green, on the east side, presents nothing very striking. Went into a Chemist's Shop, and bought some Cheltenham Salts, Eau de Cologne, and Elder Flower Water, for the Sun had made sad havoc with our complexions. Visited a Bookseller's next, and bought a guide in Dublin; another in Wicklow; and two Litho-graphic Prints of the great Fossil Elk, or Moose Deer, which was found about a year ago in the County of Limerick. The Bookseller told us that the entire skeleton was set up in the Museum Hibernicum, and I made a memorandum to see it. This museum is only open to the public, two days in the week, which I think are Tuesday and Friday. After breakfast, sat down at ten o'clock to investigate the Society's Accounts, and were occupied with them till three. Dressed and walked to the Post Office, in Sackville Street; a handsome building, with a Corinthian Portico. Always put in my own letters, when they are of any consequence. Dinner had been ordered at half-past four, but we waited some time for Mr. Noy, who had been amusing himself in the Four Courts – this excuse was admissable, he being a limb of the profession. The Sauterne and Champagne were as good as the day before, and after dinner we tried the Claret, which was high flavoured, and not '*travaille a l'Anglois*' [fermented in the English style].

We had ordered the Carriage at six, and drove to the Black Rock, a Village about 3 miles distant, on the south side of the Bay; here are a few bathing machines, and it is a place of great resort on Sundays, for the good Citizens of Dublin. There are some very neat Cottages on the road; the thatching of which is the very best work of the kind I have ever seen, and although I had heard much of the neatness of these buildings, they far surpassed my most sanguine expectations. I looked out in various directions for the Black Rock, expecting to see some stupendous mass,

> Huge as the tower which builders vain,
> Presumptuous piled on Shinar's plain.

but could find nothing more than a dark coloured limestone crag, just peeping above the surface, near the water's edge. Went on to Dunleary, to see the new Harbour which is making there, by carrying a mole out into

the Sea, composed of blocks of granite thrown in promiscuously. The
work may now be said to be only in its infancy, and will be enormously
expensive. This place is not now called Dunleary, but Kingstown; in
consequence of His Majesty having visited it, and which event is
commemorated by a trumpery obelisk, erected at the foot of the pier.
The base is a low granitic rock, upon which are placed four cannon balls
of the same material, supporting a square tapering shaft, about twelve
feet high!! surmounted by a regal crown. It is so diminutive, that it looks
at a distance, like a *big* constable's staff, set up to frighten the beggars. I
wish it had that effect; for we were beset by four women, the most
sturdy of the race, that I ever encountered: they were so rude and clamorous, that we vowed not to give them anything; when one of them said,
that they would follow us to Hell, but they would have something. They
hung upon our rear, and annoyed us very much during our walk to the
shore, and we would gladly have given them a *tenpenny* to get rid of
them, had it not been for our oath's sake. Here we observed a large pile
of hewn granite blocks, from the Quarries at Dalkey; intended as we
were told, for the new London Bridge. I collected some specimens of
white granite, with small garnets disseminated, of very perfect form, and
of a good red colour. Mr. Schultes said, he wished they had been at the
bottom of the Red Sea, for he strained his eyes with looking at them
through a microscope. I also procured specimens, with large rhomboidal
crystals of Felspar, of a dazzling whiteness. We returned to tea, after
which, one of the party asked the Waiter if there was a smoking room in
the house. The man appeared somewhat surprised, and said (assuredly
without meaning any offence, for he was the most civil fellow in the
house) that no Gentlemen ever smoked there. Certain it is, that no
Cigars were seen in the mouths of the Dublin Dandies (the Tenth were
not there), and that smoking is confined to the very lowest orders.

Friday, 17th June. Rose at six, and walked into Merrion Square, the
next largest to Stephen's Green, and built with good lofty brick houses.
Returned to the Hotel, and called Mr. Schultes, who accompanied me
to the Warm Sea Baths, at Irish Town. The rooms were very dirty. When
I came out of the Bath, the attendant brought a piping hot towel, as big
as a sheet, and having completely wrapped me in it, stared me in the
face, and hoped I felt comfortable. Paid two shillings and ninepence,
Irish, for the Bath, in the shape of an English half-crown, and returned
in our *outside* Car to breakfast; after which we worked at the Accounts
till two. Mr. Noy then walked off to his magnet, the Four Courts, and
Mr. Drinkald and myself went to the Custom House, to call upon the
Surveyor General, who received us very politely. This is a handsome

building, but is placed so near the River, that you cannot see the upper part of it, without danger of dislocating your neck. It cost upwards of £300,000, and was 13 years in building. It appeared too large for the trade of the Port, as well as the Warehouses, a large portion of which were then advertised to be let by Auction. Saw the Tobacco Warehouse, with an Iron roof, of ingenious constuction; but it makes the place too hot in summer. A West India Ship was unloading at the Quay, where there are no sheds, or shelter of any kind, for the Sugar or other Goods. Hired a Car for half a Crown, and drove down the pier, to the Pigeon House, so called, where there is an Ordnance Depot. Some recruits were practising the great gun exercise. We could not take our Car any further, so we walked down the pier, towards the Light House at the end of it, but the Sun was so scorching that we were compelled to return. The whole length of the pier is 3 miles, and it is a mile and a half from the Pigeon House to the Light House. On our return home, we found cards of invitation to dine with the Sheriff elect, which we declined, having come to a previous resolution, not to accept any dinner invitations during our stay, as it would interfere too much with our occupations. Our walk and drive had given all of us good appetites, and the cookery and the Wines were much approved. Mr. Beresford joined our family party to dinner, and was full of anecdote, which gave a higher *gusto* to the Burgundy. We enquired of Luke, our facetious attendant, if there were any Theatrical Performers of note in town, when he readily replied, 'and be sure, Sir, there is but one, and he is *just gone*, and that is Mr. *Kane*, and the Gentleman was very much noticed by the *quality*, only he is too fond of the Brandy and Water.' Retired to bed at ten, having ordered the Carriage at six in the morning, to go to Lucan Spa to breakfast.

12. Hermann Pückler-Muskau, *The Adventures of Prince Pückler-Muskau in England, Wales and Ireland, as told in Letters to His Former Wife, 1826–29*

(first published 1830, this edn, London: Collins, 1987, pp. 213–18; translator F. Brennan)

Prince Hermann Pückler-Muskau (1785-1871) was born in the principality of Muskau, which was later absorbed within the Kingdom of Prussia. In addition to being described as one of the most spectacular and romantic figures of his age – he had been a soldier and diplomat as well as a talented landscape gardener – Pückler-Muskau was a great traveller who visited the Near East and Africa, as well as many parts of Europe, including Britain and Ireland. Originally published in 1830 in four volumes, and titled *Briefes Eines Verstorbenen* (*Letters from a Dead Man*, though translated into English in 1832 by Sarah Austin as *The Tour of a German Prince*), Pückler-Muskau's travels around Britain and Ireland (in search of an heiress) received plaudits from all quarters. This extract finds him in County Kerry, setting out for the home of Daniel O'Connell, the Liberator, on 29 September 1828.

Derrinane Abbey, September 29th. Beloved friend, yesterday evening I sent off a messenger to Mr. O'Connell, but having rashly paid him in advance, found him back at the inn soon afterwards with no answer and a broken collarbone. As soon as he had felt money in his pocket he had been unable to resist the whiskey, as a result of which he and his horse had fallen down a rock in the dark. He had, however, had the sensible inspiration to send a good friend on ahead and, when I woke up, I was happy to find a very polite invitation from the great agitator.

I have already said that I set out on my way at three o'clock; and although I had to ride for seven hours in heavy rain, with the wind in my face, and in this desert where not once was the shelter of a tree to be found and after the first half-hour not a thread of my clothing remained dry, yet I would not tear this very trying day from the book of my life for anything.

The start of my journey was difficult in every way. At first I could not get a horse. At last an old black carthorse appeared, which had been ordered for me, and a cat-like animal which the guide rode. My toilet was also in disarray – one escaped galosh could not be found and the umbrella had been loosened from its ribs on Witches' Mountain. I replaced the first with a huge slipper of my host's, and tied the second together as well as I could. Then, holding it before me as a shield, my cloth cap covered with a piece of waxed linen on my head, I galloped off – not unlike Don Quixote, and moreover furnished with a real Sancho Panza – to new adventures.

Only a quarter-hour from the town the destructive gusts of wind brought the umbrella, once the ornament of New Bond Street and the bearer of so many hardships with me, to a lamentable end. All its ribs came loose and left only a torn piece of taffeta and a bundle of fishbones in my hand. I gave the remains to the guide, and thenceforth esteemed the weather without care, bearing that which could not be changed in the best of moods.

As long as we were in the neighbourhood of the Bay of Kenmare we rode as quickly as possible, for the path was quite passable. Soon, however, it became more difficult. The entrance to the rugged mountains was signalled by a picturesque bridge 100 feet high, called the Black Water Bridge. Here was a gorge planted with oaks, the last trees I saw from then on. I noticed that my portmanteau, which the guide had tied before him on his horse, was becoming wet through, and I therefore instructed the man to get a cover or mat from a neighbouring hut to spread over it. Later on I had occasion to rue this foresight, for apparently the whiskey also got hold of him there and I was only to see him again shortly before the end of the journey, although I often waited for him to catch up with me.

The path, which was gradually deteriorating, led for the most part beside the sea. All around me the storm was raging in splendour, now over the deserted moors, now through gorges and deep abysses or wild, chaotic tracts, where the rocks were piled so fantastically one upon another that one could only believe that it was here that the giants stormed Heaven. Here and there a petrified cloud formation presented figures like men and animals. Only rarely did I meet a ragged wanderer, and could not avoid thinking how easy it would be for someone to fall on me and rob me in such a place, without a single person knowing it – for all my travelling money lay in my breast pocket of my overcoat, as I was travelling *omnia mea* [all my possessions] with me, in the Grecian fashion. But far from any thought of robbery, the poor, good-natured people always greeted me respectfully, although my costume was less than impressive and in England would have proclaimed me no gentleman.

Many times I was in great uncertainty as to which of the almost invisible stepping stones I should alight upon, but each time I chose fortunately, always keeping as close as possible to the sea, never on the wrong path even if not always on the shortest. Meanwhile time was passing, and when, between long intervals, I met a human being and asked him: 'How far still to Mr. O'Connell's' he never failed to bless the purpose of this visit with: 'God bless your honour!' – but the number of miles seemed to increase rather than to decrease. I only understood this when I realized that I had missed a short cut of several miles, and so had suffered a needless loss of time.

Just as it began to grow dark, I reached a part of the coast which is beyond compare. The Quest for the Romantic would certainly be as unsuitable at this time as it was for Quixote himself, though I was quite pensive as I drove my tired horse at as good a pace as possible. It stumbled at every moment over the loose stones, and I finally brought it to a painful trot with great difficulty. My anxiety was increased when I remembered O'Connell's letter, in which he had written that the proper entrance to his property was to be found on the Killarney side, which carriages could only reach by water, but that the way from Kenmare was the most difficult, and I should therefore have engaged a more reliable guide if I were to avoid any mishap. Also there came back to me, as often happens when one is following a train of thought, a folk story of Croker's I had read recently in which it says: 'No country is better than the coast of Iveragh for drowning at sea or, if you prefer, breaking your neck on land.' I was still thinking of this when my horse suddenly shied and pulled round, with a leap I could scarcely credit from the old mare. I found myself in a narrow gorge; it was still light enough to see several paces before me and I could not understand the reason for this panic of my nag's. At last, it went forward reluctantly, but after a few paces I saw with astonishment that the fairly narrow path ended in the middle of the sea, and the bridle almost slipped from my hand as a foaming wave raced over me like a monster and splashed far up the narrow gully with its white foam. Good advice would have been invaluable here! Impassable cliffs stared at me from every side, before me roared the lake ... only the way back was open to me.

I was at a loss as to what to decide. If I rode back, I could not count on coming across my guide again, and where then was I to pass the night? Apart from O'Connell's old rocky castle, which I could not find, I could not expect any sort of shelter for twenty miles; I was already feverish from wet and cold, my constitution certainly would not stand up to a bivouac on such a night – I had every reason to be disturbed. But all this reflection was of no use; I had to get back, that much was clear, and as quickly as possible.

My horse seemed to have come to the same conclusion for, as if endowed with new strength, it bore me away almost at a gallop. However, would you believe it, once more I was destined to be saved by a sable apparition. At that moment I saw a black form, like a vague shadow, glide across the path and lose itself among the rocks. My cries, my pleas, my promises were in vain – was it one of the smugglers who conduct their affairs on these coasts, or a superstitious peasant who took me, poor wretch, for a ghost? Anyway, he did not seem inclined to venture out, and I had almost despaired of the help I had hoped for when his head suddenly popped out of a split in the stone beside me. I soon succeeded in calming him, and he solved for me the riddle of the path which ended in the sea. It had been constructed only for low tide. 'At this time,' he said, 'the half-tide is already in, a quarter of an hour later it will be impossible to pass. I will try to lead you over it now, for a good tip, but we have not a moment to lose.' With these words he was, with one bound, on the horse behind me, and we rushed towards the sea through the white waves and the rocks, which rose like ghosts in the dim twilight, and had the greatest difficulty with the horse. But the man knew the terrain in such detail that, although soaked in salt water up to the armpits, we reached the opposite shore safely.

Unfortunately here the terrified animal shied once more at a jutting cliff, and broke both bit and saddle girth clean in two. As the damage could not be repaired on the spot, apart from all my other difficulties, I now had the unpleasant prospect of riding the last six miles balancing on a loose saddle. The man had certainly given me excellent directions for the continuation of my journey, but it soon became so dark that you could no longer see any landmarks. The path seemed to lead across a wide moor and was, at first, quite level. After half an hour's bumpy trot, jamming my knees together as much as possible so as not to lose the saddle between my legs, I noticed that the path was again turning right into the higher mountains, for the climb was becoming ever steeper and more difficult to negotiate. Here I found a woman passing the night with her pigs or goats. The path divided into two arms, and I asked which I must take to get to Derrinane. 'Oh, both take you there,' she said, 'but the left is two miles shorter.' Naturally I took the left, but soon found to my chagrin that it was only passable for goats. I cursed the old witch and her deceptive information; in vain the horse exhausted itself scrambling through the blocks of stone and at last, half stumbling, half falling, threw saddle and me off altogether. It was impossible to hold the saddle on by myself, it kept slipping off, and I had to be content with laying it on my shoulders and leading the horse.

Until then I had kept myself in pretty good spirits, and even now the spirit was willing, but the flesh began to weaken. The man from the sea had said: 'Another six miles and you are there', and after I had ridden smartly for half an hour, I remembered that the woman I had questioned had said it was still six miles by the shortest way to Derrinane. I began to fear that this ghostly mountain castle could never be reached, and one goblin would only throw me to the others. Entirely useless, good for nothing, shuddering with both heat and cold, I had sat myself down on a stone when, like the consoling voice of an angel in the desert, a call from my guide rang out and soon after I heard the hoofbeat of his horse. He had taken an entirely different route through the inner mountains, avoiding the sea passage, and, fortunately, had learned from the woman which direction I had taken. In the precious feeling of renewed safety I forgot all abuse, loaded the rescuing angel with my saddle and wet cloak, handed over to him the naked horse and, seating myself on his, pressed forward as fast as possible.

We had another five miles to ride, the guide told me, through a mountain pass hemmed in by precipices. I can report nothing more of the rest of the journey. The darkness was so great that I could only follow the figure of the man before me, like a dim shadow, with the utmost difficulty. At last a bright shimmer of light broke through the dark, the path became smoother, the outline of hedges became visible, and in a few minutes we drew rein before an old building that stood upon the rocky shore, its friendly, golden lights streaming through the night. Eleven o'clock was just striking from the tower, and I confess that I began to be anxious about my dinner when the only living soul I saw was a man in a nightshirt at an upper window.

Soon, however, there was a bustle in the house, an elegant servant appeared with a silver candlestick and opened a side door for me. Inside, I saw with wonder a company of fifteen to twenty people sitting at a long table, at wine and dessert. A tall, handsome man of kindly appearance came towards me, excused himself that he had not expected me at so late an hour, regretted my journey in such terrible weather, presented me for the time being to his family, who constituted more than half the company, and then led me to my bedroom. This was the great O'Connell. A short toilet quickly restored me, while downstairs they were taking care of everything for me, and providing a much needed meal after such a journey.

As I came into the hall, I found the greater part of the company still assembled. They entertained me very well, and it would be ungrateful not to praise Mr. O'Connell's old wine which in truth was splendid. After the ladies had left us he sat down beside me, and Ireland could not fail to be the subject of discussion. 'Have you seen many of its remarkable things yet?' he asked. 'Have you been to the North, to admire the Giant's Causeway?' 'Oh no,' I rejoined smiling, 'before I visit Ireland's Giant's Causeway, I wish to see Ireland's giants.' And thereupon I drank off a glass of his good claret, to him and his great cause. Daniel

O'Connell is indeed no common man, though he is a man of the people. His power in Ireland is so great that, at this moment, he could single-handedly raise the banner of revolt from one end of the island to the other, if he were not much too clear-sighted, and much too sure of his success by far less dangerous means. By legal, openly publicised methods, cleverly using the moment and mood of the nation, he has created this power over the people which, without army or weapons, is yet like that of a king.

13. J.E. Bicheno, *Ireland and its Economy; Being the result of Observations made in a Tour through the Country in the Autumn of 1829*   (London: Murray, 1830, pp. 33–39)

Called to the Bar in 1822, James Ebenezer Bicheno (1785–1851) developed a passion for economic and scientific studies, before becoming enmeshed in futile mining speculations in Wales. Elected a Fellow of the Linnean Society in 1812, Bicheno's earliest writings (later published in more extended form), dealt with the administration of the poor-law system. He served under Archbishop Whately, where he investigated the condition of the Irish poor, visited Ireland again in the 1830s, and was later appointed Colonial Secretary to Van Dieman's Land. Bicheno visited some fifteen of Ireland's thirty-two counties, although this extract finds him at something of a standstill, reflecting on certain aspects of Irish life, rather than actually moving across the landscape.

The tenant of twenty or thirty acres, which is a very common holding, is but little better accommodated. He has probably an additional compartment, hardly divided, for sleeping place, or a dairy; and although it might have been thought that a large family of all ages, and even strangers, lying together in this way would be productive of serious immorality, I must justify the peasantry from the imputations of Arthur Young and some other travellers, and especially from the slanders of the *orange* faction of the country, and declare, that we heard the most unimpeachable testimony in favour of them, and that they are signally chaste in their conduct.

   Yet, after all, these cabins cannot be so unwholesome as theory would lead us to conclude; or how could the inhabitants of them enjoy such plenitude of health, and how could the delicate operation of butter-making be carried on? If the house and its curtilage be dirty, the surface of their persons is more frequently cleansed than in some other places where it is wrapped in fine clothing. At the entrance of a town, the traveller constantly witnesses lustrations which are not performed where shoes and stockings are worn. The cause of fever among them is deteriorated and unwholesome food, arising from a deficiency in their crop of potatoes, or injury sustained from frost, or too mild a winter, which has induced an early vegetation.

Where the habitation itself is so wretched, the ornament of a garden is not to be expected. No rose or woodbine climbs round the door, with some warbling bird suspended near; nor is there the least plot appropriated to flowers. The houses of the more wealthy are remarkably deficient in this respect, although they have a milder climate than England, and might easily preserve the choicest plants. The lady, even, does not indulge in a few pots of rarities at her window. The disinclination of farmers to become gardeners admits of explanation; they are gardeners on a larger scale; but that persons of education, otherwise occupied, should not be cultivators, is less easy of solution.

The clothing of the peasantry is not superior to their habitations. It is as negative, too, as the political virtue of their betters. In the wealthy classes of society, indulgence in dress is usually among the females; in the lowest, it is among the other sex. Passing from a distressed population into an improved district, shoes and stockings are first observed upon men. In England, clothes are the first article which the poor man accumulates. Almost all his first savings, and those of his wife and children, are thus invested. In the winter, they serve as a bank to draw upon, and many of them will be found at the pawnbrokers' before the expiration of this trying season. In Ireland, the peasantry have no superfluity of dress to pawn, for the difficulty there is how to get covered. In Munster, the cotter has his frieze jacket spun at home; his femoral integuments, or a fragment of the same, never buttoned at the knees, and never fitting, bought at the slop shop; and his great coat made of frieze also. In this he works, and, philosopher like, wears it to keep out the heat as well as the cold. His shirt is generally good, as it is spun at home, – *caetera desunt* [everything else is lacking]. The cut of his clothes indicates them to be an imitation of modern dress. King James obliged the peasantry, as far as he could by law, to abandon the dress of their ancestors.

Several districts are marked by the colour of the frieze. In the counties of Cork and Waterford, it is dark-blue and shades of damson; in Kerry, it is grey. The Galway men are fond of a windsor blue, while their wives rejoice in a bit of scarlet. Some of their dyes they obtain from wild plants: alder, the roots of buckbean, and elder. Such peculiarities are worth noticing, as they frequently point out the natural divisions of a country in more important matters than dress. Great quantities of cast-off clothes are imported from England, which find their way into the remotest districts.

In the counties of Waterford, Cork, and Kerry, the traveller witnesses too many instances of the wretchedness of the women, not to be deeply affected by it. If destitution is to be endured, they are the first sufferers. They wrap themselves up in large blue cloaks, with great hoods, summer and winter; and as they do not court the gaze of passengers, the whole country looks as if it was widowed and forlorn. We thought the common people small in stature, and coarse in their features; but as the children are remarkably pretty, the defects of the parents are probably to be attributed to smoke and hard living, and to their exposure to the inclemency of the weather.

If we had credited the representations made to us by *orange* friends very soon after our landing, we should have been dissuaded from attempting to penetrate into some of the remote corners of the west; but as their apprehensions on our behalf arose out of prejudices, working, too, upon them at a moment when they considered their loyalty had been sacrificed to mistaken liberality, we travelled on in spite of their forebodings, and had never the slightest reason to regret our determination, our only care being not to be mistaken for Irish gentlemen. Not a finger was ever lifted against us, but the most cheerful assistance was afforded to us in every difficulty; and although we travelled in the most disturbed districts, and among people who were sheltering murderers, and some of them murderers themselves, I am satisfied they might have been trusted with untold gold; and it is certain, that they are ready to share their scanty meal with the needy, and to relieve one another by acts of kindness, to which the more civilized poor of England are strangers.

An Englishman cannot fail to remark the different behaviour of the peasantry of the two countries in one particular. We never were saluted with a bow or curtsey from any of them, from the beginning to the end of our journey; conduct quite unnatural, and only to be accounted for by the relation in which they stand to the native gentry. I must admit, their nakedness, and shaggy hair, looking like the mane of an untamed colt, give them a forbidding aspect; and that there were occasions, when we met a troop of them on a wild bog, where we were disposed to compound for our safety, by addressing them as the Count Beaujeu did the Highlanders in Waverley, 'Gentlemans Sauvages'.

14. J. Glasford, *Notes of three Tours in Ireland, in 1824 and 1826*   (Bristol: Strong, 1832, pp. 208–11)

James Glasford (d. 1845) was a legal writer and traveller who was born in Dougalston, Scotland. Admitted a member of the Faculty of Advocates in 1793, Glasford became a sheriff-deputy of Dumbartonshire. One of the commissioners of inquiry into the state of education in Ireland, Glasford also published, interestingly, *Lyrical Compositions, selected from the Italian Poets* (1834). In the advertisement to his Irish tour he states that 'the following Notes were written during the course of several journeys undertaken for the purpose of examining the state of education in Ireland'. The text is then divided into three parts: 'Notes of a tour in Ulster in 1824', 'Notes of a tour in parts of Leinster and Munster in 1824', and 'Notes of a tour in Connaught in 1826'. The following extract is from the Leinster and Munster narrative of 1824.

The roads of Ireland are, in general, excellent, formed in many cases of lime-stone; and we found the inns much better than expected. Abundance of material, and, perhaps, abundance of labour, may account for the superiority of the roads, as well as the profusion of them; and to a traveller they are commended farther by the agreeable circumstance, that so many of them, and those, perhaps, the best, are hitherto free from the tax of barriers and turnpike gates. The preservation of the roads must be also greatly aided by the light carriages; all goods conveyed on cars, or small carts – none of the ponderous machines, and enormous teams, under which English roads yawn and shake to their foundation.

Scenery of Ireland sadly defective in wood – not more rich in verdant pasture than wanting in foliage – no contiguity of shade, no umbrageous multitude of leaves. Besides the destruction of woods in so many seasons of disorder and insurrection, or occasioned by the feuds of clans, too many proprietors have cut down, without replacing by new plantations, or, if they have planted, have not always enclosed; perhaps, conceiving it vain to attempt preserving them from lawless hands, or endeavouring to do so by infliction of severe penalties. Thus the same vicious circle is pursued, as in the contest between the government and the absentee; for it is not to be supposed that, in a country where fuel is scarce, and the people poor and untutored, any safety to unenclosed planting will be found in Acts of Parliament which the peasant cannot read, or fines which he cannot pay. Kildare is said to signify the *forest of oak*.

In casting the symptoms of disease in Ireland, too much seems to be ascribed to absenteeism, as it is now called. The activity of *production*, and the demand for the fruits of industry, are surely the important points –

not the place where the commodity is consumed, or money, its representative, expended. Residence of the native proprietor is, indeed, or ought
to be, useful and important in various ways, and from moral considerations; but, with respect to wealth merely, if there is a full and continual
demand for the produce of the agriculturalist, and the fabric of the
manufacturer, it is comparatively of little moment whether these go
abroad in the shape of corn and goods, or are used in the country; they
can only go out in exchange for other commodities, and must form part
of the trade of the country, either in kind or money value; and if, upon
such export, there is called for, still, a new and recurring reproduction,
and further stimulus is given to industry, it is impossible that the country
can be unprosperous. Absenteeism is an evil on many accounts; but the
evil is moral and political, rather than economical.

Much more of excitement and defiance, among the different
religious bodies, is observed in the course of this tour, than in that to
Ulster; except those places, in the latter province, where the Orange
party instigate to violence by their most imprudent display of political
rancour.

Roman Catholic body more powerful as we go south, at least seem
generally so. Education less effective, and knowledge less diffused;
besides, there is not the same leaven of Protestant population as in Ulster
– where so many Protestant settlers were planted, and so much intercourse subsists with Scotland.

The plan of the Protestant Charter Schools, to take Roman Catholic
children from their parents, and make them Protestant men and women,
by immuring them in buildings, and then turning them out to the actual
scenes of the world, without any previous knowledge of life, seems erroneous throughout in its principle, and has been much abused in its
practice; said to have been a scheme of Bishop Boulter, and on his
recommendation adopted by the government of George II. Even if the
plan had been successful in the instances, a very trifling part of the
population would have been *protestantized;* for the expense is very great,
even of dealing thus with a few thousands; but, after all, not successful in
these. The children are unhappy, separated from friends, at the entire
disposal of the masters, who, scattered over the country, cannot be
observed or controlled, and thus become absolute in the government of
their secluded communities, and as naturally indifferent to the task and
labour of teaching. Great errors seem also to have been committed by
the Board of Management, allowing the masters often to contract for the
clothing, transferring the children from one Charter School to another,
allowing the master to employ them in working on his farm, and in

various other ways leaving room for abuses. In some cases, the children are found healthy and cheerful, but much oftener dull, and wanting in intelligence for their years. Frequent elopements take place; and, when finally emancipated, they retain little affection, as may be expected, for their Protestant prisons, and few associations of endearment for their Protestant task-masters; are assailed, too, on returning to their families, or going among the mass of the people, by the usual reproaches and *opprobria* bestowed on the *proselite,* or *parochin brat* – the *vox signata* in Ireland for all in similar predicaments – in short, are marked as a kind of outlaws; and, like animals which are hunted, and *do not know why,* become sullen or hopeless, and run into corners. A great mistake in education to place children in circumstances where their native affections are supplanted and sacrificed, to break their natural ties forcibly, as in these and similar institutions; and an equal mistake to suppose, that religious or moral principles will be rightly planted in their minds, while under such constraint.

As to the character of the common schools in those parts of the South visited, the same difference is still generally marked between the Roman Catholic and Protestant education; namely, that the *plan* and *basis* of the former is more contracted, and the knowledge given much more limited than in the latter. Nor is this owing to their deficiency of funds solely, or principally; for there is an evident indifference, on the part of the Roman Catholic clergy, to extend the sphere of intellectual knowledge among their people. This is the natural operation of the religion; for the *ignorance* of the people is the *power* of the priest; his temporal policy is therefore obvious.

15. Henry D. Inglis, *A Journey throughout Ireland, during the Spring, Summer, and Autumn of 1834*   (2 vols, London: Whittaker, 1834, vol. I, pp. 27–35)

Henry David Inglis (1795–1835) was born in Edinburgh, the son of a Scottish advocate. Although educated for commercial life, he opted for travel and litera-ture instead, publishing *Tales of the Ardennes* (1825), *Narrative of a Journey through Norway, Sweden and the Islands of Denmark* (1826), *Solitary Walks through many Lands* (1828), and *Spain* (1830). A sometime newspaper editor, first in Derbyshire, and later in the Channel Islands, Inglis's *Journey throughout Ireland* was so successful that it had reached a fifth edition by 1838, even though he had passed away within only a year of it going to press.

It was after dark, and on a somewhat chilly evening, when I reached Roundwood; and here, for the first time, I experienced the comforts of a turf fire; the easiest lighted, and therefore, to a traveller, the most agree-able of all fires. For home comfort, commend me to a sea-coal fire! but in travelling, commend me to whatever kind of fire soonest produces the desired results, – heat and cheerfulness. There is nothing to detain one at Roundwood; and I left it accordingly, early next morning, with the intention of sleeping at Avoca, and of resting there a few days. From Roundwood, I passed through a wild but more interesting country; I had the colour and the fragrance of the bright whin blossom, and the companionship of a noisy brook. I made a little *detour*, to glance at Glen-dalough, more commonly known as 'the Seven Churches', – a wild spot, not unworthy of a visit, – and then continued my journey to Rathdrum and Avoca. After passing Rathdrum, the country improves in picturesqueness; and a few miles beyond Rathdrum the attention of the traveller is arrested by the driver of his car turning round, and saying, 'the Meeting of the Waters, your Honour'. But for associations, this spot, I think, would disappoint the traveller. There is a bridge, and the meeting of two streams, and wooded hills, and the handsome residence of Colonel Howard; but to my mind, the character of the valley improves in beauty as we descend. The valley widens; green meadows are left between the river and the more retiring banks; and the feathery birch, then bursting into leaf, contrasted finely with the dark firs, and with those beautiful evergreens, of which, in my journey through Ireland, I shall so often have occasion to speak. Towards evening, I arrived at Wooden Bridge Inn, Avoca. 'There's not in the wide world a valley so sweet.' That, I will not venture to say; but I will say, 'sweet vale of Avoca'; for this I can say consciously.

I remained here three days, walking up the glens and among the mountains; mixing with, walking with, and talking with the people; and allowing the interest which I felt in a fine and romantic country, to be lost in the higher interest, which attaches to the social condition of the people.

The contemplation was a less pleasant one: – for notwithstanding that I was in the next county to Dublin; that Wicklow is a county *orneé*, full of villas and gentlemen's seats; and that the mines in this country, and in the vicinity of the spot which is at present my head quarters, employ nearly two thousand persons; – notwithstanding all this, I found little satisfactory in the condition of the people.

I found rents in Wicklow such as, for the most part, could never be paid by the produce of the land; and the small farmers, as well as the labourers, barely subsisting. High rent was the universal complaint; and the complaint was fully borne out, by the wretched manner in which I found the people – Catholic and Protestant – living. And if the question be put to them, why they take land at a rent which they know it will not bear, – the reply is always the same: how were they to live? what could they do? From which answer we at once arrive at the truth, – that competition for land in Ireland is but the outbiddings of desperate circumstances.

As for the condition of the labouring classes, I found little to bear out the assertions of some of my Dublin friends, to whom Wicklow ought to have been familiar, – that I should find all the labourers employed, and tolerably comfortable. On one of the afternoons I spent here, I walked up a mountain road, and after a short walk, reached a glen with several cabins scattered in it; and three of these I visited.

The first I entered was a mud cabin, – one apartment. It was neither air nor water tight; and the floor extremely damp. The furniture consisted of a small bedstead, with very scanty bedding, a wooden bench, and one iron pot; the embers of some furze burnt on the floor; and there was neither chimney nor window. The rent of this wretched cabin, to which there was not a yard of land, was two pounds.

The next cabin I entered, was situated on the hill side: in size and material it was like the other. I found in it a woman and her four children. There were two small bedsteads, and no furniture, excepting a stool, a little bench, and one pot. Here also were the burnt embers of some furze, the only fuel the poor in this neighbourhood can afford to use. The children were all of them in rags; and the mother regretted that on that account she could not send them to school. The husband of this woman was a labourer, at sixpence per day; – *eighty* of which sixpences, –

that is, eighty days' labour, being absorbed in the rent of the cabin, which was taken out in labour; so that there was little more than fourpence halfpenny per day left, for the support of a wife and four children, with potatoes at fourpence a stone.

I entered one other cabin: it was the most comfortless of the three; it was neither air nor water tight, and had *no* bedstead, and no furniture, excepting a stool and a pot; and there were not even the embers of a fire. In this miserable abode there was a decently dressed woman with five children; and her husband was also a labourer, at sixpence per day. This family had had a pig; but it had been taken for rent a few days before. They had hoped to be able to appropriate the whole of the daily sixpence to their support, and to pay the rent by means of the pig; but the necessities of nature, with the high price of potatoes, had created an arrear before the pig was old enough to be sold. The landlord might not be to blame: he was a very small farmer of hill land, at twenty shillings an acre; and was just as hard set to live, and pay *his* rent, as his humbler dependant was.

I am only beginning my journey: this is but the county of Wicklow; and I was told that I should find all so comfortable in Wicklow, that from the comparatively happy condition of the peasantry there, I must be cautious in forming any opinion of the peasantry generally. While I write this sentence, I write in utter ignorance of what I may yet see; for I write this work almost in the manner of a diary, – noting down my observations from week to week: but from what I have already seen, I am entitled to fling back with indignation the assertion, that all the Irish industrious poor may find employment. But what employment? employment which affords one stone of dry potatoes per day for a woman and her four children.

A labourer in this county considers himself fortunate in having daily employment at sixpence throughout the year; and many are not so fortunate. I found some who received only fivepence; but there are many who cannot obtain constant employment, and these have occasional labour at tenpence or one shilling; but this, only for a few weeks at a time. I found the small farmers living very little more comfortably than the labourers. A little buttermilk added to the potatoes, made the chief difference.

Upon one subject, it is obvious that I must substitute inquiry for personal observation; I mean in relation to the important question, whether there has been any improvement in the condition of the people of late years. I might indeed infer, that no improvement *could* have taken place in the condition of a people whom I find in rags, – living in mud cabins, without furniture and windows, and sometimes without chimneys; and existing upon a scanty meal of potatoes. But I have not contented myself with this inference, and have always anxiously inquired of those most able to give me correct information, – always old persons, and persons of different ranks and opinions; one or two landlords; one or two farmers, both Catholic and Protestant; and frequently the Protestant clergyman and the Catholic priest; – and of Wicklow, I may say, that I found nothing to induce belief, that any improvement had taken place in the condition of either the small farmer of the labouring classes. The number of absolutely unemployed poor has decreased with the active working of the mines at Glendalure, which employ about two thousand persons. But task work, and consequent high wages, have attracted many from a distance; and the miners are a drunken and improvident race. One who had earned thirty shillings the past week, came into the inn while I was there; and I heard him regretting that it was impossible for him to drink the whole of this sum.

I deeply regretted to see at Avoca, a proof of the bad feeling which in that part of the country appears to exist between the Catholic and Protestant population. I was sitting at the window of the inn, one Sunday evening, when a man, in a state of intoxication, came along the road, calling out, 'To the Devil with the Boyne waters, and they who drink them.' Presently three men, who were sitting on the bridge, followed the offender, threw him down, beat and kicked him brutally, and stamped upon his face; ten or a dozen persons were by, and no one interfered; and the men walked away, leaving the other on the ground in a state of insensibility. The explanation is this: there was till lately only one brewery at Rathdrum, the property of Catholics. Another brewery was recently set up by Protestants, in the same town; and the ale brewed in it is called by the Catholics, 'the Boyne waters'. I regret, in the outset of my book, to be obliged to record these facts. I trust I shall not have many such to record.

16. Anon, *Ten Days in Ireland*

(Liverpool: Rockliff, 1835, pp. 32–35)

The anonymous author of this text reflects on how the militarized environment of a village in County Wicklow can contrast so markedly with England, where the local constabulary is seen as even-handed, well-intentioned and, above all, employed to protect rather than intimidate the local inhabitants. The author's remarks – supplemented by later observations on absentee landlords – comprise a radical critique of the government of Ireland.

We returned to Ashford, lunched substantially, and then proceeded on our way for Newtown Mount Kennedy. Before I quit Ashford, let me give its neighbouring gentry, being residents, their due – my warm thanks and commendations to them for staying at home, and dispensing their blessings around them, the beneficial results of which are displayed in one short sentence, "'Tis the only town in Ireland, in which I was never solicited for alms.' Newtown Mount Kennedy, is a neat little town, with a deal of the English character about it. But we were soon beset with beggars, a feature which, in my estimation, speaks little in praise of its neighbouring gentry. They call it seventeen miles and a quarter from Dublin; but I beg to say, they are of the 'mad-dog and woollen-string character'. I wish to appraise my English reader, that there is a police-house in every small town and village, furnished with what are neither more nor less than a standing army. Their number is five at every station, that is, four privates, and what is called a superintendent, alias captain. Their dress is a dark green jacket, white trousers, and cap, black leather belts, with carbine and bayonet; now tell me what they are, if they are not soldiers. There you'll see them stretching about in idleness, with a cane in their hand; swelling with military importance, and ogling the young women. I asked an ostler, at one of these towns, 'What these fellows found to do?' – 'Och, just what you see, sur, and divil a ha'porth more. They take some ramrod sauce to breakfast every morning, and that keeps them too stiff for any kind of work *that* day; without, indeed, they find a job of 'pounding sheep and cattle, or chasing a mad dog, or summit in that way; they're divelish 'cute in that way, sur. But as for any thing else, why, when we go to sleep they go to sleep, and divel a good thing they'll do if they know it, God knows.' Heavens, what a system is this! Looking at the whole nation, what an immense quantity of muscular strength is here unemployed. You'll say it is not unemployed; they are paid by the county, and they perform the duties assigned to them. I say it is unemployed; it is unprofitably wasted, and that is worse than idleness itself, for it bears a semblance, that may deceive many, of their being useful in their generation. Still you will urge that the county pays them, and that you could not collect your tithe without them. I care not who pays them, Ireland is the poorer for so much money as shall be drawn from her for these unproductive services. But if they are really one of the church essentials, inasmuch as they would not be able to collect their tithe without them, abolish the system – pay the church from another source, and then you can dispense with these bayonet collectors. Or if not, charge the church with what belongs to the church. Let them not have odium in the semblance of civil duties, but let proper men have proper names, and instead of being ranked a police force, call them what they are, tithe bull-dogs. It can neither be a fair exaction, nor a good law, that requires a bayonet to extort it, or cram it down your throat. You will tell me that we are obliged to have a local police in England. So we are; and I wish Ireland to have one on the same footing; improve her government and better her condition, and she will have one. I will tell the reader, who perhaps may be misled if I do not, what our local police consists of in England. In country places the constable's situation has to be taken in turns; one man does all its duties, and townships vary in their allowances; it generally runs from £2 to £5. Villages of more importance, particularly in the neighbourhood of large towns, have begun to adopt a plan I much approve of: that is, of paying a man permanently for filling the united offices of constable, overseer, surveyor, and collector of all taxes, rates, and dues, whose salary is from £80 to £150, according to the population of the place, and a deputy to assist him, at a minor salary. These men are useful, and do not eat the bread of idleness. They allow the farmer and the shopkeeper to follow their business, who would have to perform their task, if no such officer had been appointed; and the township has the satisfaction of seeing the business systematically done, without the application of either carbine or bayonet. But of this hereafter. We proceeded about four miles, through lands much neglected; from what cause I know not. A tourist has not always information at hand. It was land rich in its nature, and productive in the extreme, if properly managed, as was proved to me by witnessing neighbouring lands, scientifically cultivated, bloated with fatness, and loaded with luxuriant crops. We arrived at Belleview, the seat of the Latouche family. It is a substantial, plain building, commanding beautiful views, and it has the most extensive conservatory I ever saw. But it is like the rest – all alone, desolate as the swallow's nest in winter. 'Where's your master?' – 'In England.' 'Where's your mistress?' – 'In England.' 'Where's every body that has fine mansions and rich estates?' – 'In England,' may be truly answered. Struck with this remark, I made a memorandum, which I intended to hand over to Miss Laconic, for insertion in her notebook, when I returned to Dublin; it was as follows: – 'Everybody in Ireland who has got money to spare, has gone to England to spend it.'

Though this remark is made here, it does not apply to the benevolent lady of this mansion. I found, on visiting Delgany, which is Mrs. Latouche's own property, situated about a mile from her entrance gate, that she was actually adored by her tenantry; and those are the people to go to, after all, for a landowner's character. She had absented herself for a temporary period, to banish the poignant grief consequent on her recent domestic loss; a loss in which the whole country sympathised; but she is shortly expected to return, and it is hoped she will remain, for the absence from Ireland of so good a lady would be an affliction indeed. Though every facility presented itself for perambulating this princely domain, our want of time compelled us to forego that pleasure for the present, and we returned to the road, which winds along the banks of a mountain stream of silvery brightness, and forms the basement of that romantic scene called the Glen of the Downs. It is short, but bold and impressive; the traveller is filled with a sensation he never can forget; he passes on a road just wide enough to receive him, and, raising his astonished eye to the right and to the left, he beholds two stately hills, towering a thousand feet above his head, clothed with the richest foliage of the forest, whose graceful tops and gently-waving branches seem to give welcome on his glad approach. On the Latouche side, a beautiful effect is produced by an octagon temple, perched like a bird's nest on the side of a well-wooded hill, which seems peeping out of the branches of its luxuriant retreat to detect any wily urchin bent on disturbing its repose. A little further there is a cottage and a banqueting hall, which do great credit to the taste of the distinguished lady of the manor. Killiney Hill is now before us; but having formed a design of seeing Tenyinch, the seat of the successors of the late Henry Grattan, Esq., we left the main road at a place called the Crosses, where a stately ash, with a protecting abutment of stone, conspicuously marks the meeting of four roads. We took the one leading to Enniskerry, on the right of which lies a valley of indescribable beauty; it is of that character which distinguishes Powerscourt from every rival, but more limited, and consequently has less of the sublime. It is Tenyinch, which here lies languishing in loveliness the absence of her lord. How desolate without him seems this splendid theatre of beauty. Though parliament requires him, Ireland wants him; and here, I said, is another proof of Ireland's *cause* of poverty. I never thought myself a repealer, but I have begun to be one, inasmuch as I think Ireland would be better at God's mercy with her gentry at home, than represented at St. James's, and misgoverned as she is.

17. Baptist Wriothesley Noel, *Notes of a Short Tour through the Midland Counties of Ireland, in the Summer of 1836* (London: Nisbet, 1837, pp. 82–88)

Baptist Wriothesley Noel (1798–1873), a Divine, born at Leightmount, Scotland, was educated at Westminster School and Cambridge, before he took holy orders in the Church of England. Although committed to the evangelical wing of the church – in 1846 he visited evangelical missions in France before helping to establish the Evangelical Alliance and, in 1849, being publicly rebaptized – Noel had other interests, notably travelling and travel writing, and he went on to publish a number of non-theological texts: *Notes of a Tour in Switzerland* (1848), *England and India* (1859), and *Freedom and Slavery in the United States of America* (1863).

Leaving Newry, we crossed the southern baronies of the county of Armagh, with Slieve Gwyllan, one of the highest mountains of that part of Ireland, on our left. The road continually ascended for nearly two miles, beyond which the country was irregular and open. With the exception of bog, mountain, and fallow, all the land was under cultivation. Oats and potatoes were, of course, the general crops; I observed, also, flax, wheat, clover, and even peas.

In the parish of Killevy, through which we passed, about one-third of the labourers only are constantly employed. Wages are from 10d. to 1s. at different times of the year; and the ordinary food is potatoes and milk. The average price of potatoes for the last three years has been 2½d. per stone; and oatmeal about 10s. per cwt. Newtown Hamilton, the only town between Newry and Castle Blaney, is a miserable-looking place. Here we watered our horses, and from the door of the public-house at which we stopped, I counted twelve spirit shops almost within a stone's throw. There were ten more in the street by which we left the place. How many there may be on the whole I cannot say, as we had reached the heart of the town before I noticed them. Multitudes of unemployed men were standing in the streets, and many in rags. Few houses, except the poorest cabins, were to be seen along the whole road; and their inmates had all the marks of abject poverty. Butter carts and droves of pigs were on their way to Newry. It is an advantage, doubtless, to the farmer, where an increased rent does not swallow up all his profit, to find a market for his produce; and to the town to have the English trade; but it is also melancholy to reflect, that of thousands of pigs fatted in Irish cabins, not one is ever killed for the use of the Irish labourer; and of all the firkins of Irish butter, few are ever consumed on the farms where they are made. Ireland sees its produce shipped away to strengthen other labourers, and much of the money which that produce brings remitted to absentees. The barony of Fews, though so near to Dundalk and Newry, is still immersed in poverty. The number of labourers is about 1713. Employment has of late years decreased. All the labourers who attended the examination before the Commissioners stated that they got about six months employment in the whole year; wages being 1s. in summer, and 10d. in winter. Michael Farrell said he would take 4s. a week in preference to the present chance. Felix Lamph said that many weeks the labourers could not get two days in the week. John Cullen said, 'I would lie down content at night, if I knew where I was to get work in the morning. It is a very hard thing for a man to run about seeking work, and perhaps not find it.' Patrick Campbell, a stout labourer, stated that till the last eight days he had been idle for ten weeks. Mr. Spence said, if he was willing to work he could not want it. Campbell replied, 'Tell me, Sir, what work there is for a man after the potatoes are shovelled till harvest? Do you think I'd be walking about with my seven children if I could get work?' He was asked how, then, he could live? 'He got potatoes on trust.' John Cullen added, that he had frequently known instances, in time of distress, of labourers being less able to work from insufficiency of food. And yet they marry young; boys of 17 and 18 often come to Captain Atkinson, a magistrate, asking for the loan of a pound to pay the marriage dues. Notwithstanding all this poverty, we met crowds of persons returning from the monthly fair at Castle Blaney, the women, indeed, barefooted, and the men in frieze, but none in rags. The young women wore blue cloaks, with the hoods raised over their heads, or neat caps, and gaily-coloured shawls. But it must be remembered, that these are the farmers.

Several miles before reaching the town, we caught a pretty view of Castle Blaney lake gleaming in the western sun-beams, and lying, like a silver mirror, among the hills. Upon our reaching the town, which was still full of the country people, we were strongly recommended by the civil and intelligent landlord to visit the hall and the lake, for that 'he could not describe its beauty'. It is, in fact, a pretty place. The ash, beech, and Spanish chesnut grow well. The lake is a fine expanse of water, some miles in extent, studded with wooden islands, and the banks are also well wooded. I was glad to hear that Lord Blaney is generally resident, a good landlord, and that the town owes to his father and to him much of its prosperity. Lady Blaney has also a good school for the poor. Our landlord, a thorough Tory, spoke well of the Presbyterians, but said that they were tainted with Whiggery; for himself, he was, in that respect, immaculate. A vast change, he added, had taken place of late years in that neighbourhood for the better, evinced by an unprecedented attention to religious truth among all classes of Protestants. It was pleasing to see that an innkeeper could estimate the value of that change. But he appeared a sensible man, of good feelings: and although he dwelt with much conscious dignity on the recollection that he had entertained at his house the Duke of Northumberland, the Marquis of Abercorn, and I know not whom besides, still he was not, on that account, the less attentive and obliging to his humbler guests.

At Castle Blaney, not without much regret, we turned our backs on Ulster, to hasten by King's-court and Athboy to Ballinasloe. We were not to see the coasts of Derry and of Antrim. We were to leave behind the city of Londonderry, with its steep streets, its commanding ramparts, and fine views down Lough Swilly and Lough Foyle. We were not to hear the roar of the waves in the chasm over which a frail archway conducts to Dunluce Castle. We were not to see the causeway, with its natural mosaic, stretching out into the sea, and its colonnades of clustering basalt; nor the basaltic cliffs of Pleaskin and Fairhead; nor the prosperity of Belfast; nor the magnificent expanse of Lough Neagh, fed by eight rivers through its twenty miles of length and fifteen of breadth; and how could we fail to lament our loss. Sometimes a traveller feels like a hungry Esquimaux, who, when he falls in with good cheer, eats as fast and as much as he can in serious silence, regretting all the while that he cannot eat more and faster. It was with a regret almost as greedy I reflected that we could not travel at the same moment to the north and west, or visit, within the space of a month, the coasts of Ulster and of Kerry, with the counties of Mayo and of Clare.

18. Leitch Ritchie, *Ireland Picturesque and Romantic*

(2 vols, London: Longman, 1837, vol. I, pp. 237–40)

Leitch Ritchie (1800–65) was born at Greenock, Scotland. Originally appren-
ticed to a banking office in Greenock, he moved to London, where, with the aid
of letters of introduction from friends, he launched his literary career. Although
Ritchie published many articles in the leading journals of the day – the *Foreign
Quarterly* and the *Westminster Review* for example – his fortune changed dramatically when he was commissioned to write two series of travel books which
appeared under the titles of *Turner's Annual Tour* (1833–35), and *Heath's
Picturesque Annual* (1832–45), of which the latter series includes this Irish
travelogue.

The scenery of Wicklow, I have already said, is *petite*; and I can only
explain what I mean to the travelled reader, by saying that it resembles in
this character the 'mountains of the Rhine'. The hills, or rocks, or
eminences, which border that 'abounding and exulting river', are mountains to the imagination. They possess the form without the bulk, the
majesty without the height, of the colossi of nature. Their grandeur does
not arise from massiveness, but from shape and combination; and the
whole is steeped in so rich and extraordinary a beauty, that we easily
suppose the effect to be assisted in some measure by an intermingling of
the sublime.

The finest parts of the country come within a single day's ride from
the capital; and the pedestrian, before he has walked an hour, finds
himself in the midst of seemingly interminable wilds, which reminded
Sir Walter Scott of some of that scenery of his own country which his
pen has rendered classic ground. On the road to Glencree, not more than
four miles from the city, there is a desert of 'brown heath, and shaggy
wood,' and naked rock, where the traveller turns round to gaze at the
cultivated country he is leaving, spread with verdant fields, dotted with
villas and cottages, and the horizon covered before him by the roofs, and
domes, and spires of the city, and bounded on the right by the Bay of
Dublin and the open sea. The transition is magnificent; and the distinguished visitor I have mentioned, described the view as, in this respect,
the most remarkable he had ever beheld at a single glance.

The road I have mentioned, however, leads towards Lough Bray;
from which a line drawn to Carnew at the southern extremity of the
county would include, between it and the sea, nearly all the celebrated
scenery of Wicklow. To the west of this line, the country is little known
to the tourist; and, although it has features here and there both of beauty
and grandeur, it is deficient, generally speaking, in the characteristics

which render the other portion a grand Calvary (to use a Catholic metaphor) of stations for the pilgrims of the picturesque. This western part is formed, before the place where I re-entered Wicklow from Carlow, in no inconsiderable part by the barony of Shillelagh, which covers a tract of twenty-seven thousand acres. Here was the grand forest of oak, from which, in former times, great quantities of timber were exported for the purpose of roofing public buildings. In the course of degradation, universal in this country, the name is now associated only with that instrument with which the Irish are in the habit of breaking one another's heads at a fair, or in honour of the birth-day of a saint. Carnew, the extreme southern point of the district, has the remains of a castle built by the O'Tooles, a famous family in this part of the barony. The whole barony belongs to the Earl Fitzwilliam.

Proceeding along the Carlow road, I entered the County Wicklow, and soon after reached Baltinglass, a place which was once a city, and where Dermod M'Murchad, King of Leinster, was buried. Instead of the parliament, which is said to have sat in a castle near the town, the ruins of which are still standing, the assizes were held here in modern times, and gave the place an air of bustle and consequence. But these, too, have now been removed; and the shade of King M'Murchad glides through his old demesnes undisturbed but by the noise of far less offensive instruments than lawyers' tongues, mill-clappers. The name of the place, it seems, may mean either, 'the fire of Beal's mysteries,' or 'the town of the grey houses,' two very different things. The advocates of the former name point to the druidical remains in the neighbourhood, and even assert that Baltinglass was one of the principal colleges of this heathenish superstition. Those on the other side ask triumphantly, if any houses in the world can be *greyer* than the houses of Baltinglass? And, if this is all that is required to settle the dispute, the dispute is settled. The houses are grey, extremely grey; and, therefore Baltinglass is the town of the grey houses.

The Irish are still more enthusiastic in their claims of far descent than my own countrymen, the Scots; a fact which Mr. Moore in his history accounts for, in poetical fashion, by supposing them to cling to the idea of antiquity, as a consolation to 'the wounded pride of a people for ever struggling against the fatality of their position'. This would do very well in the Irish Melodies; but history abhors sentiment. There was no fatality in the position of Ireland at all, and there is none. She was in the position of a country destined, by her very geographical situation, to be absorbed into the body-politic of a greater country beside her. That she did not fall with dignity, and ultimately acquire all the privileges of her conquerors, was owing to there being no dignity in the attitude of her defence. She never opposed herself as a nation to a nation; but as two or three barbarian hordes, each standing up for its own independence, and all ready and willing to betray and sacrifice the rest to the common enemy.

19. Charlotte Elizabeth Tonna, *Letters from Ireland, 1837* (London: Seeley, 1838, pp. 346–56)

Charlotte Elizabeth Tonna (1790–1846) was born in Norwich, the daughter of a clergyman. Although (or because) she lived for a while in Kilkenny, Tonna was hostile to Catholicism and viewed the Protestant presence in Ireland as a necessary check on Romish dissatisfactions. Editor of *The Protestant Annual* (1840), and *The Protestant Magazine*, her historical novel, *Derry* was the text which secured her reputation, and provided her with notable success (originally published in 1833, it was in its tenth edition by 1847). Although the celestial city of Derry is the destination in the following extract, and Tonna is meeting it on more concrete terms, her anticipation of an almost transcendental experience is clearly evident.

The region on which we had last entered was wild and barren; a sort of moorland, swelling and falling; while now and then the indistinct outline of some object of which I could not decide whether it was a cloud or a mountain, appeared on the horizon, overtopping the irregular hills that skirted our left. To the right, I knew we were not very far from the sea; in fact we had enjoyed at one point a fine view of it near Coleraine, and were within a few miles of the Giant's Causeway. On that side, I was watching what I thought a very lovely lake, with a mountain barrier, and hoping every minute to obtain a sight of its boundaries, by passing one end; but in this I was disappointed; the water still kept us at a distance, it was still to the right, a little in front, and a most picturesque crag that abruptly terminated the lofty line of hills on our side, and thus left with a comparative level between us and the lough, receded more and more as we advanced. This showed that we were in some measure following the course of the water, on which I kept my eyes fixed, wondering when we should pass its southern extremity; and conceding to it the palm, as far as a noble boundary went, over all the lakes I had yet seen. The long, regular, undulating line of mountain tops on the farther side seemed endless; and while watching the rippling of its tide, I was startled at seeing a distant sail on their bosom. Could it be? I presently thrust my

head out at the window, and received from the coach-box a confirma-
tion of the half-formed guess – Yes, it was LOUGH FOYLE.

Just then the coach stopped to change horses, and a minute's interval
saw me mounted on its highest seat. None but the coachman, the guard,
and W. remained; and behind the latter, who sat with the coachman, I
chose my station, making little of the shower that impended, while mine
eye truly affected my heart as I looked on the grand liquid thoroughfare
so passionately coveted by Popish James, as a medium of communication
between his Irish adherents and their disaffected brethren in Scotland, so
obstinately withheld from him by the heroic defenders of Derry. Yes,
there was the Foyle, upon which the dying gaze of many a famished
Protestant had been fixed, in vain hope of the supplies cruelly detained
by the inhuman Kirke: the Foyle, whose flowing tide had borne the
Mountjoy upon the boom, and, held in the hand of the Lord, had
broken the fetter of Popery from the necks of three kingdoms. Oh, for a
pen that could write my feelings as my looks devoured that object, and
feasted upon the stately ridge of those Innishowen mountains! At that
time, both guard and coachman were below, and the single horse which
had been put to appeared a little restive: I happened just then to glance
towards it; and the poor ragged fellow who was holding the bit, catching
my eye, exclaimed with a look of most affectionate concern, 'Darling
lady, don't be at all alarmed – he's as quiet as a lamb.' 'Darling Paddy,'
thought I, in return, 'may the Lord, who even here wrought so
wondrously to deliver your hand from the thraldom of Antichrist, shed
the light of his glorious Gospel into your heart, into your cabin, and
through every corner of your own sweet isle!' As to being alarmed, in
the then state of my feelings, they might have yoked wild horses for me,
provided they kept their heads towards Derry.

The road now had become exceedingly good, the country well
cultivated, and numerous vehicles rattled past us, the drivers announcing
with merry cheers that Sir R. Ferguson was elected. Our coachman was
evidently not elated by the news; and as I knew Sir Robert to be what
is called a liberal, I hoped to find his dissatisfaction arose from the same
source as my own. No such thing: Coachee was a staunch Romanist,
and one of the most unreserved character too. He not only communi-
cated to us his religious faith and political creed, but assured me that the
events of 1688 consisted in a rebellion of the English settlers, headed by
Martin Luther, against King James; and that the Irish were defeated by
William of Orange bringing a great army over to help the rebels. I, of
course, gave no direct contradiction, only remarking that I thought
Martin Luther must then have been dead for some time, as he lived in

the reign of King Henry VIII; and with regard to the siege of Derry, that the French rather than the Irish prosecuted it; and the Derry people had done good service to the country by not giving it over to foreign enemies. No, he assured me, there was not a Frenchman in Ireland at the time. Yes, I persisted, I could show him in history books that it was Conrad de Rosen, a French marshall, who drove the poor harmless Protestants from the neighbouring counties to starve under the walls of Derry; and that it very much shocked the Irish army, who were treated quite impertinently by their French allies. 'Oh,' said he, with a most commiserating look, *'you have bad memories'*. A very courteous way, you must allow, of taxing my veracity; but I was not discomfited. 'Sure now,' I resumed, 'it is not my memory I am depending on: how should I, when I was not born at the time, nor you, nor our fathers before us? We have books printed in that same year, and they tell us all about it.' With a very knowing look cast over his shoulder, he observed, 'Them books were written by Luther and his people; but St. Patrick gives a different story.' 'Was St. Patrick there?' 'He was, or else St. Columbkill; I'll show you his chapel presently.' 'Now,' said I, 'if St. Patrick and Luther had both been there, I'll engage it was on the one side they stood; for they taught the same doctrine.' This bold assertion seemed to confound him; but an energetic shake of the head, and another, 'Oh, you have bad memories,' was all that escaped him. I proceeded to relate that when Patrick came over, he found the ancient Irish quite heathens, worshipping stocks and stones; that he brought them the blessed Bible, told them that it was there they would find the will of God made known; and by preaching what was in that book, he brought them to believe in Jesus Christ; and now those who keep the Bible keep the religion that Patrick brought here. 'Oh, it's all wrong!' says coachee, and began to appear sulky. I had kept a sharp look-out right in front, as he told me when I remounted the coach that Derry was straight before us. I now happened to turn to the left, and far away I saw a spire on elevated ground, with one of the sun's last rays resting upon it. 'What is that?' I asked, pointing to it. 'Derry.'

Our road had curved a little, which occasioned this surprise. The broad, beautiful Foyle, grew broader and brighter as we approached, and the sky cleared up. 'Now,' said the coachman, whose pride or something else was gratified by the tone in which I repeated 'Derry!' with some epithet of endearment prefixed – 'now I will show you where the boom was put across the water. You see the fellows laid a great bar of wood, as thick as that horse's body, from one side of the Foyle to the other, to hinder the ships from coming up to the town; but for all that,' he added with much glee, 'they cracked it in two, and the place was relieved'. 'Was not that a great exploit?' asked I. 'Sure it was – you never heard a more wonderful thing.' It was evident that his Derryism was stronger here than even his Popery; and I sighed to think how times were changed in a few years, since the Romish titular himself in his pontificals used to lead his flock in the procession, swell the shout of 'No surrender,' and toss off a bumper to the glorious memory. This is a fact: until the baneful spirit of so-called conciliation roused in their bosoms the hope of recovering their ascendency, vast numbers of the Romanists voluntarily wore the badge which is now denounced, under pretence of hurting their feelings! The coachman pointed out the memorable spot, and on a beautiful little island, just in sight, he showed me the ruins of Columbkill's chapel; then continued his discourse, giving a history of the miracles performed by Columbkill and his successors; with a story concerning a false disciple, that equalled, for the extravagant absurdity of its details, the most open burlesque I ever met with. My heart was moved for this poor Irishman: I longed to enter fully on the subject so important to his peace; but we were almost at the bridge, which lay a perfect level above that noble water; while before us rose the town, covering a lofty hill, on the apex of which stood the cathedral; and just on the bank where we were passing was an old grey stone, pointed out with great eagerness by the coachman, as 'St. Columb's well'. He then, with much feeling, suddenly said, 'It is a pleasure to talk with ye: many a gentleman have I told these things to, and they always laughed in my face, and treated me like a fool. You have not laughed at me – there are few like you.' I was about to make an affectionate reply, but all his attention was demanded to his horses: he wheeled them – we were on the bridge – the firm boards lay beneath us, the noble Lough on the right, the city in front, with the river circling round it, and in a minute I was under the wall – the lofty, dark, impregnable wall of Derry, beneath which we wound for a short space, and then alighted at the Ship Quay, where the vessels landed their welcome stores in 1689. Matters were soon arranged at the office. 'Where is Brown's hotel?' 'Oh, just through the gate: we'll carry your luggage in a moment.' So, after thanking the coachman and guard for their civilities – an accompaniment that in their eyes trebles the value of the money given, – I walked, with as light a heart as ever beat, after the porters, and entered the fortress, passing the Ship Quay gateway, and feeling in every fibre of my frame that at last I was, indeed, really and bodily, within the walls of DERRY.

Brown's hotel is but a little way up the street on the right hand; fully meriting the good character that Inglis has bestowed on it. Here, instead of the friend whom I expected to meet and to escort me eighteen miles further beyond Letterkenny, I found a note, apprising me that he was obliged to start for Dublin, in consequence of the City and University elections, and would not be back for some days: at the same time telling me how to proceed. I bespoke apartments at the hotel, and flew away up the street to the Diamond, but not without encountering on the way a person on the watch, with a warm invitation from the aunt of my truant friend, who lives near it. Thither I promised to repair, but the temptation was irresistible, and before entering her house, I had paced the ramparts half round, and pressed the sod that lies above the heroic defenders in the Cathedral grave-yard. Stranger as I was, every turn of the place was so familiar to me, that I confidently led the way, and named the different objects to my wondering companion, as though I had never been outside the walls. This done, we repaired to the house of the kind old lady, who threw open at once her door and her arms, and even wept a welcome. Oh, these warm-hearted Irish, why cannot I live and die among them.

I had literally reckoned without my host, when engaging the rooms at a hotel: such a thing was not to be named, not to be thought of. My domicile was prepared at the house of one whom I had not yet seen, as he was then engaged in an evening lecture; but he soon arrived, and it did not require much rhetoric to convince me that I must needs remain for four or five days in Derry. You may accordingly look for a journal, for the first day of which this may suffice. We are delightfully housed in the upper part of Ship-quay street, which Inglis truly describes as one of the steepest in Europe. It runs in a perfectly straight line, from Ship-quay gate to the Diamond; the ascent is indeed such that the house-tops resemble a flight of stairs, each being necessarily so much elevated above its predecessor. This is not very far from Brown's hotel, yet I should think the ground-floor is at least on a level with his attics. Of the prospect I can say nothing, for it was dark when I came here: but this I know, I am within the walls of the ancient fortress of Protestantism, and with mingled feelings I review the past, contrasting it with the present, and questioning as to the future. My consolation is that still, 'The Lord reigneth,' even Jesus Christ, 'the same yesterday, to-day, and for ever'.

20. Henrietta Chatterton, *Rambles in the South of Ireland during the year 1838*

(first published 1839; 2 vols, 2nd edn, London: Saunders, 1839, vol. II, pp. 38–42)

Henrietta Chatterton (1806–76), born in London, was the author of *Rambles in the South of Ireland* (1839), *Home Sketches and Foreign Recollections* (1841), and *The Pyrenees, with excursions to Spain* (1843). In later life her attention shifted to lighter work, such as pastoral poems and tales. In 1875 she converted to Catholicism. Despite her varied output, *Rambles in Ireland* was the text for which she was principally known, not least because it was a sell-out success, with the first edition exhausted in only a few weeks. In this extract she has recently departed from Blarney Castle and is now in the vicinity of Passage and Cobh, County Cork.

There are few present enjoyments so great as a pleasant drive on a fine day; and when the drive is through a beautiful country in the soft month of September, along a road commanding a view over every variety of scenery, and yet not ascending a single hill, the delight is complete. Except in the environs of Naples or Salerno, I have never been so enchanted with an excursion through balmy air and smiling scenery as yesterday in our excursion to Monkstown by Douglass and Passage.

Passage is a small, but pretty bathing-place, situtated on the narrowest part of the river, or rather arm of the sea, between Cork and the bay of Cove. A row of comfortable-looking new lodging-houses has been lately built on the side nearest Cork, commanding a lovely view over the broad Loch Mahon, surrounded by its woody villas and parks, and the sloping banks of the Lee, as far as the beautiful vale of Glanmire and Blackrock Castle, with a fine background of distant mountains.

A handsome building, intended for baths, is now in progress; and a good road has been lately made by the water-side between Passage and Monkstown. This road is cut through the rocks, which rise perpendicularly from the water, and are called the Giant Stairs. The arm of the sea which runs through this dark and woody ravine is extremely narrow, and yet so deep, that a man-of-war was lost here, which lay undiscovered, and her tall masts were covered with water, for many years. On emerging from this somewhat gloomy pass, the road winds along the north-west side of the lovely bay of Cove.

At Monkstown I was delighted to see many indications of improvement. Some pretty lodging houses have been built, each surrounded by a flower-garden, with a green lawn in front, sloping down to the sea. The high ground behind these houses is well wooded, and full of beautiful walks. We visited some friends at one of them, who have passed the last three summers at this delightful place: they spoke in raptures of the endless variety and beauty of the walks and excursions of the neighbourhood.

We rambled up the hills, every turn in the walk and opening in the groves of fine trees commanding a view over the broad bay, and distant mountains or valleys, different from the preceding. But the object which most delighted my antiquarian, and somewhat romantic taste, was the old castle of Monkstown. It is situated near the summit of a deep and woody glen, and built of dark stone, of that purplish brown hue which forms such a beautiful contrast to the bright Irish green of the surrounding trees. The walls are still entire, though it has been long uninhabited; and, contrary to most Irish castles, it appears to have been built at the same time. It is a large square edifice, with high gables and chimneys, and those most picturesque projections at the corners of the turrets, called, I believe, machicolations.

When, in former years, I used to sail on the calm waters of the Cove, I never caught a glimpse of this venerable structure without wishing for wealth, that I might buy that beautiful glen and its surrounding woods, repair the old castle, and live and die there.

'Is there no story, no legend of this old castle?' I anxiously enquired, as we scrambled up the rocky path.

'None that I can hear of,' was the reply; 'all that I know is that it was built by the family of Archedeacon in the year 1638, and in the last century was used as a barrack.'

'A barrack!' I exclaimed in dismay, looking up at those beautiful and romantic towers, while many visions of brave knights and fair damsels, stately mothers and tryrannical fathers, were dispelled in a moment by the common-place matter-of-fact sound of the word 'Barrack'. That common soldiers should have exercised and drummed, and gone through their automaton-like evolutions, amid those verdant groves, – that they should have eaten, drunk, and slept soundly in those stately halls, was to me very provoking.

Real warfare, the idea of battles, of castles besieged, and victories lost and won, afford sublime, fearful, or interesting thoughts; but there is something in the drudgery of recruits and barrack-yards, which tells of the back-ground and mechanism of soldiery, and is very anti-romantic. However, I thought of the time when this old place was the residence of the Archdeacons, who had also another castle called Burnakelly, in the days when civil wars were sure to furnish exciting adventures, and chequer the lives of the Irish nobles with many spirit-stirring events. Those were the times of which Campion wrote, when, speaking of

Ireland in the seventeenth century, he says that 'linen shirts the rich do wear for wantonness and bravery: with wide hanging sleeves plaited; thirty yards are little enough for one of them.'

21. William M. Thackeray, *The Irish Sketch Book of 1842*   (London: Chapman, 1843, pp. 508–09)

William Makepeace Thackeray (1811–63), novelist, was born in Calcutta, but sent to England to be educated in 1817. Educated at Cambridge, he trained for the legal profession, but went on to work in journalism, contributing to *Fraser's Magazine*, and *The Times*, and becoming sometime editor of the *Cornhill Magazine*. Although his great works include *Vanity Fair* (1847–8) and *Esmond* (1852), among others, Thackeray was also an accomplished travel writer. Of his Irish travelogue a number of things are noticeable: the wisdom and directness of his remarks, but also the extensiveness of his itinerary, as he journeyed from Dublin to Waterford, then onto Cork and Killarney, before swinging along the coast towards Limerick and Galway, with a final journey to Dublin. A later expedition, from which this is an extract, saw him travel north to Belfast, then north-west to the Giant's Causeway and Derry with, once again, a return trip bringing him south to Dublin.

They call Belfast the Irish Liverpool. If people are for calling names, it would be better to call it the Irish London at once – the chief city of the kingdom at any rate. It looks hearty, thriving, and prosperous, as if it had money in its pockets and roast-beef for dinner: it has no pretensions to fashion, but looks mayhap better in its honest broadcloth than *some people* in their shabby brocade. The houses are as handsome as at Dublin, with this advantage, that the people seem to live in them. They have no attempt at ornament for the most part, but are grave, stout, red-brick edifices, laid out at four angles in orderly streets and squares.

The stranger cannot fail to be struck (and haply a little frightened) by the great number of meeting-houses that decorate the town, and give evidence of great sermonizing on Sundays. These buildings do not affect the Gothic, like many of the meagre edifices of the Established and the Roman Catholic churches, but have a physiognomy of their own – a thick-set citizen look. Porticoes have they, to be sure, and ornaments Doric, Ionic, and what not? But the meeting-house peeps through all these classical friezes and entablatures; and though one reads of 'Imitations of the Ionic Temple of Ilissus, near Athens', the classic temple is made to assume a bluff, downright, Presbyterian air, which would astonish the original builder, doubtless. The churches of the Establishment are handsome and stately. The Catholics are building a brick cathedral, no doubt of the Tudor style: – the present chapel, flanked by the national-schools, is an exceedingly unprepossessing building of the Strawberry Hill or Castle of Otranto Gothic: the keys and mitre figuring in the centre – 'The cross-keys and night-cap,' as a hard-hearted Presbyterian called them to me, with his blunt humour.

The three churches are here pretty equally balanced: Presbyterians 25,000, Catholics 20,000, Episcopalians 17,000. Each party has two or more newspaper organs; and the wars between them are dire and unceasing, as the reader may imagine. For whereas in other parts of Ireland where Catholics and Presbyterians prevail, and the Presbyterian body is too small, each party has but one opponent to belabour: here the Ulster politician, whatever may be his way of thinking, has the great advantage of possessing two enemies on whom he may exercise his eloquence; and in this triangular duel all do their duty nobly. Then there are subdivisions of hostility. For the Church there is a High Church and a Low Church journal; for the Liberals there is a 'Repeal' journal and a 'No-repeal' journal; for the Presbyterians there are yet more varieties of journalistic opinion, on which it does not become a stranger to pass a judgement. If the *Northern Whig* says that the *Banner of Ulster* 'is a polluted rag, which has hoisted the red banner of falsehood' (which elegant words may be found in the first-named journal of the 13th October), let us be sure the *Banner* has a compliment for the *Northern Whig* in return; if the 'Repeal' *Vindicator* and the priests attack the Presbyterian journals and the 'home missions', the reverend gentlemen of Geneva are quite as ready with the pen as their brethren of Rome, and not much more scrupulous in their language than the laity. When I was in Belfast, violent disputes were raging between Presbyterian and Episcopalian Conservatives with regard to the Marriage Bill; between Presbyterians and Catholics on the subject of the 'home missions'; between the Liberals and Conservatives of course. 'Thank God,' for instance, writes a 'Repeal' journal, 'that the honour and power *of Ireland* are not involved in the disgraceful Afghan war!' – a sentiment insinuating Repeal and something more; disowning, not merely this or that Ministry, but the sovereign and her jurisdiction altogether. But details of these quarrels, religious or political, can tend to edify but few readers out of the country. Even in it, as there are some nine shades of politico-religious differences, an observer pretending to impartiality must necessarily displease eight parties, and almost certainly the whole nine;

and the reader who desires to judge the politics of Belfast must study for himself. Nine journals, publishing four hundred numbers in a year, each number containing about as much as an octavo volume: these, and the back numbers of former years, sedulously read, will give the student a notion of the subject in question. And then, after having read the statements on either side, he must ascertain the truth of them, by which time more labour of the same kind will have grown upon him, and he will have attained a good old age.

22. J.G. Kohl, *Travels in Ireland*

(first published 1843; first English translation, London: Bruce, 1844, pp. 154–59)

John George Kohl (1808–78) was born in Bremen, Germany. A student of science, and then law, Kohl worked as a private tutor, before embarking on travel writing as a career, publishing *Travels in the South of Russia* (1841), and *Travels in Istria, Dalmatia, and Montenegro* (1851), among many others. In 1854 he journeyed to North America, eventually publishing a supplemental volume to Hakluyt's work, and later, *History of the Discovery of America* (1862). Kohl began his Irish tour by sailing from Anglesea to Dublin on 22 September 1842, although he had returned to Germany sometime in late 1842 or early 1843, for the first German edition of *Reisen in Irland* was published in Dresden and Leipzig in 1843. The translator for this English edition could not be traced.

As my friend, somewhat fatigued by his journey, retired early to rest, I strolled out, late in the evening, along the strand. Whilst thus occupied, something moved past me; and by the rays of light which beamed from the window of a neighbouring house, I was enabled to perceive the strange attire of flowers which, during the day, I had seen on the head of one of the beggar-women at Bantry. I immediately recognised her as one of those who shut us up in the fish-market, and who had been most zealous in her gesticulations and conduct. In fact, her violence on that occasion afforded strong proof of insanity. She was dressed in a tattered yellow gown, and a large red shawl, completely in rags, which seemed to have been originally intended for a much larger person, since half of it trailed behind her in the dust. She also wore a broad-brimmed man's hat, encircled by a profuse wreath of artificial flowers, and aided by a long stick, which she bore in her hand, she moved along very quickly. Among the beggars of the fish-market she was the loudest, and always held her stick before use to keep us back, whilst whatever she said was spoken extremely quick, and in broken sentences. I have frequently, in Ireland, met with similar half-crazed and comically-dressed beggars, who sometimes reminded me of certain characters in Walter Scott's novels. Mary Sullivan (for she soon confided to me her name) was now proceeding very quietly and orderly along the shore of Bantry Bay. I wished her a good evening, when she thanked me politely. Here business for the day was over; and although she still wore the costume of her part, the play was ended, she had left the stage, and was now returning homewards. As she told me that she lived on the shore of the bay, not far from the town, I offered to accompany her, that I might have an opportunity of seeing the hut of an Irish beggar in the evening. We crossed over some uneven rocky ground, and at last turned as it seemed to me, entirely out of the beaten path; but Mary Sullivan assured me that there was no other way to her sister's with whom she lived, and that if I would give her my hand, she would lead me in safety. These poor people prefer localities somewhat wild, and that the approaches to their dwellings should be somewhat rugged; thereby, as they imagine, securing for themselves greater independence. The labours of the English, in constructing level roads, are, therefore not always regarded with that joyful thankfulness which might be expected. Besides, a stray piece of perfectly bare and barren ground may be procured somewhat cheaper than a more fruitful soil; and on a naked piece of rocky ground of this description, washed by the gentle waves of Bantry Bay, stood the hut of the Sullivans, into which we crept.

The Irish are a very religious people, and have all kinds of pretty pious wishes always at hand, with which they salute each other. Thus, if they pass by labourers at work in a field, they say, 'God bless your work!' to which the answer is, 'Save you too!' They have so strong a desire for the blessing of God that they are fond of adding a wish for it to their expressions on all subjects. In particular you must not neglect to add 'God bless it' to any thing in the shape of praise you bestow on a person or thing; for instance, if you praise a child by saying, 'That is a fine child', you must, if you wish to save the mother the severest apprehensions, immediately add, 'God bless it!' for praise always seems suspicious to the Irish: praise begets envy, they say. It, therefore seems to them that the person praising any thing either wishes to possess it himself, or to deform it by drawing down upon it the envy of the fairies and spirits of the lower world, who take special delight in destroying all that is beautiful on earth. When fault is found, it is not customary to add any thing; and an Irish mother would be less offended, if a person were to say to her, 'Your child is a squalling dirty brat,' than if he were to say, looking at the child, 'What a charming little angel you have there in the cradle', unless he were immediately to add, 'God bless him!' thus warding off the influence of the evil spirits. As they never forget to ask God's blessing, they are also equally careful to return thanks. 'Thanks to the great God!' is an expression continually in their mouths, and I have no doubt in their hearts too. It is customary even to thank God for a misfortune that has befallen them: thus I once heard an Irishwoman, in a melancholy tone and with tears in her eyes, say to another, 'I have lost my poor dear little child, thanks be to the great God!' This reminded me of the Russian 'slawa bogu' which is the customary addition to every story; and a Russian merchant who once told me he had made a very bad speculation, like the Irishwoman concluded with 'slawa bogu'.

When one creeps into an Irish hut, the usual salutation is 'God save you all!' and the answer is, 'God save you kindly!'. Those who now thus replied to our salutation were the sister of Mary Sullivan and her half-grown daughter, who were both sitting at a turf fire boiling the potatoes, with her little son and little daughter, who were lying beside the pig, eating a half-boiled potato which they had taken from the pot. Their father was not at home, for he had been some days on the water, taking up sand. There came, however, another voice, I knew not from what corner of the house, nor did I know what it meant; only it seemed not 'God save you kindly!' I therefore inquired from whence the moaning proceeded. 'It is my eldest son, your honour; he is weak in the understanding, thanks be to the great God! He often moans thus the livelong day.'

The hut was lighted partly by the fire, and partly by a lamp which was suspended from the centre of a crooked rafter. This lamp was a great sea-shell, in which they were burning fish oil by a rush wick. By its melancholy gleam I perceived one of the most miserable and helpless creatures I ever beheld. It was a young man, about twenty years of age, who lay doubled up and groaning in a kind of box which represented his bed, and which was, in reality, the best bed in the hut. Beneath him was some straw, covered with rags; and under his head was a pillow, the only one I remarked in the hovel. His mother showed me some parts of his miserable body. His fingers were quite deformed – two of them had grown together – and his arms were as lean as those of a skeleton. His whole frame seemed to vibrate with a convulsive twitching. His mother said, that this was constantly the case with him. As we were examining his hands and feeling them, he raised himself a little, and looked at us with a vacant stare.

'He has been so from his birth, your honour,' said his mother; 'and we have been obliged to support him for twenty years, without his being able to do the least thing for us.' It occurred to me that the poor creature might not therefore be well treated, as it is not uncommon for poor people to neglect those who cannot help to increase their earnings.

'And yet you love him?' inquired I of his poor mother.

'Love him? Indeed I do, your honour! Why shouldn't I love him? Isn't he my son, my own flesh and blood, God bless him! Eh, mavourneen, look up!' said she to her unfortunate son, while she carefully raised him, supported his head on her arm, and stroked his crippled hand: 'I am the only one, sir,' she continued, 'who understands his language properly. He is always longing for me, and it seems I am the only one he loves. 'Tis I give him his potatoes every morning, and, when I have it, stirabout and milk. You see he has a better bed than any of us. Mavourneen! Don't groan so, my darling!' She smoothed his pillow and laid down his head, which he had again turned away from us.

This woman's affection for her son caused many thoughts to arise in my mind. It appeared to me that as not only the mental but in some measure the corporeal development of her child had remained almost stationary from his birth, so, in like manner, his mother loved him now with the same tenderness, intensity, and indulgence as when, twenty years ago, he was a suckling. She still fed him as she did then; she coaxed and caressed the youth of twenty years of age as she did the infant of a month. Nay, for twenty years she would have kept him at her breast, were it not physically impossible. When we think of the circumstances of people such as these, who have scarcely enough to appease their own hunger, who expect their children to work and to earn money, who usually repel and even imprecate the useless consumer, such affection as I have described may well be called a phenomenon; and it is possible that this poor beggar-woman has shown greater affection for her idiot son than is possessed by a hundred thousand mothers. It is a shame that we travellers so frequently neglect such phenomena, which are so often to be found beneath lowly roofs, instead of seeking them out and making them known to the world.

Mary Sullivan, the old aunt, had meanwhile hung her flower-wreathed hat on the wall, and also laid aside other parts of her costume. She then took from her pocket some potatoes and a fish, which had probably been made a present to her; the former she placed on that corner of the fire which she seemed to consider as her own, and the fish she suspended over it by a wire. She next took out her pipe and began to smoke. She told me, in answer to my inquiry, that her smoking cost her at least a halfpenny a day, or upwards of fifteen shillings a year, exclusive of the many little fragile clay pipes which she must use in that time. This was no inconsiderable sum for a beggar-woman; and as in Ireland a large piece of bread can be purchased for a halfpenny, it is to be wished that another Father Mathew may arise, to wean the poor Irishwomen from tobacco, and induce them to expend in bread, for themselves and their children, what they now lay out on this useless weed.

Tenderness and hospitality are qualities generally possessed by the Irish. All classes are likewise much at their ease in their intercourse with strangers; and in this respect the higher ranks resemble the Parisians. In many countries, when a stranger visits the huts of the poor, he must undergo a long and scrutinizing stare before they feel comfortable in his presence. With the Irish it is quite the reverse. Poor and half-naked though they may be, such accommodation as they have is instantly offered to their well-dressed visitor without embarrassment; and though they never forget to address him politely, as 'your honour,' they always appear to consider him – what he really is – their equal.

When I took my leave of the Sullivans, more than one 'God speed ye!' accompanied me to the door, with the most sincere thanks for the honour I had done them by my visit, and for the sympathy which I had shown for the unfortunate brother and son. The two little ones had in the meantime lighted a couple of dry splinters of wood for torches, and accompanied me over their rough, rocky path. When at last I drove them back, and bade them good-bye, I saw them for a long time standing above on the rock, lighting my way with their torches, while with their pretty little voices they continually called out, 'Take care, your honour, take care! God speed ye!'

23. J. Grant, *Impressions of Ireland and the Irish*

(2 vols, London: Cunningham, 1844, vol. II, pp. 186–91)

James Grant (1802–79) was born in Elgin, Scotland. A devout Calvinist, Grant was a journalist and novelist who published *The Great Metropolis* (1836), *Sketches in London* (1838), and *Paris and its People* (1844) amongst others. In 1827 he founded the *Elgin Courier*, but moved to London in 1833, where he joined the staff of the *Morning Chronicle*, and later the *Morning Advertiser*. Grant sailed to Dublin in early August 1844, although this extract sees him at his tour's end, when he has returned to Dublin and appears to be composing himself for his trip home. Grant returned to London, either by the end of October or early November 1844, and ensured his manuscript almost immediately to press.

The political condition of Ireland has for centuries been the subject of deep anxiety to England, but never at any period was there cause for regarding the condition of that country with deeper anxiety than there is at this hour. Ireland is in a most critical state. I am aware that there is, for the moment, a lull in the repeal agitation, by which Ireland has been violently convulsed for some years past, but that lull is only for a moment. To what is the temporary tranquility to be ascribed? To the growing indifference of the people of Ireland to repeal? He who would come to such a conclusion must be wholly ignorant of the real state of the country. The people are as resolutely bent on repeal as ever. The temporary cessation of the agitation for the restoration of a domestic legislature, is entirely to be attributed to the wishes of Mr. O'Connell. He deems it prudent that there should be a brief pause in the career of agitation. He has his reasons for this; he knows what he is about. He is desirous of bringing over as many Protestants as he can to the modified measure of repeal, known by the name of 'Federalism'. He is charged by his enemies, and suspected by some of his own friends, of virtually betraying the cause of entire repeal, by the course which he has adopted in avowing a preference for federalism to a total disconnection of the two countries. They are not so far-seeing as Mr. O'Connell himself who reason in this way. He feels assured, and there can be no question that he is right in his conclusions, that if he were to coax over the great body of the Protestant population of Ireland to the adoption of federal principles, they will not end there. They will find no resting-place for the sole of their foot until they have landed on the shores of entire repeal. Federalism is but the half-way house to total and unconditional repeal. Besides, the government and parliament that will grant the former, will not withold the latter. The principle is the same in both cases. Let federalism be only once conceded, and the concession of entire repeal inevitably follows. With federalism conceded to them, the Repealers will be in a condition to wring entire and unconditional repeal from the Ministry and the Legislature. Mr. O'Connell's conduct, therefore, in avowing his willingness to accept federalism as an instalment – for though he is too good a tactician to make the admission, there can be no question that that is all he intends – is a master-stroke of policy. It is an ingenious device – a piece of consummate tactics.

But will the Repealers ever succeed in achieving their object? Will they ever be able to wrest the restoration of their domestic parliament from the government and legislature of this country? The answer to the question depends on the circumstances. If immediate and ample justice be done to Ireland, they will not; if that justice be much longer with-held, they will. There is one way, and only way, of crushing repeal. That is by rendering Ireland in reality what it is nominally – an integral part of the British empire. There is no denying that hitherto the union has been a mere fiction. There has been a parchment connection between the two countries, but nothing more. Ireland has been treated not as an essential part of the empire, not as being on a footing of perfect equality with England and Scotland, but as a conquered province. The union between Great Britain and Ireland has been on the principle of Irish reciprocity: the advantages have been all on one side. See how different the union between England and Scotland. What a contrast does that union present to the union between Great Britain and Ireland! Scotland, since her union with England took place, has been, in all essential respects, one with this country. It has been an integral part of it. Who ever hears of Scotch grievances? Nobody. Why? Because they have none of which to complain. If they had, there is not a people under heaven that would make a greater or more incessant noise about them, than my countrymen. They will furnish, before the coming session has passed away, a memorable proof of the outcry they would raise were they in any way insulted or injured. Sir Robert Peel has given notice of his intention to assimilate their banking institutions to those of England. They conceive that this will be inconvenient, perhaps slightly injurious to them. Well, then, let the reader remember my words, as to the stir they will create in the approaching session on this subject. They will make their mountains echo and their valleys resound with the roar of their indignation. Poor Ireland is so accustomed to insult, to injury, and to injustice, that the threat of a similar measure to it would scarce have caused a whisper of dissatisfaction among her people.

24. Theresa Cornwallis West, *A Summer Visit to Ireland in 1846*   (London: Bentley, 1847, pp. 155–61)

In her preface West states that her 'object in travelling through [Ireland], was to satisfy myself of its actual condition, through the medium of my own senses, and to exhort my English countrymen to "go and do likewise"'. In the summer of 1846, when West travelled through some of the more destitute parts of the country, she was furnished with ample evidence of Ireland's 'actual condition', especially the extent of Irish suffering, much of which she reports. Nevertheless, this extract, with its closing image of regimental parties and fêtes in the shadow of Birr Castle, shows that a different response was possible and that the effects of hunger were not universally experienced. At this point West has just departed from Mount Shannon, and is making her way through Nenagh and Roscrea, and onwards towards Birr, County Offaly.

Emerging from the little hamlet, we crept up a steep hill and suddenly came upon the fag end, as I then supposed, of the great bog of Allen; with its pyramids of turf and deep black trenches full of water, so dreary and unlike everything else. How very curious it is! The road has a raised causeway across it, and rather dangerous in places, as it was undergoing repair. In the distance we saw the mountains of Slieve Philim, Arra, which rise from Lough Derg, and Slieve Bernagh. The outlines of all the Irish mountains are very soft, and wear that tender blue tint so observable in Sorante; an effect of the atmosphere, as they seem to melt away into it.

At Nenagh we halted, and in spite of the Assizes were made very comfortable. I never tasted anything so excellent as the mutton cutlets placed before us by the civilest and most active of waiters. The town was alive with people marketing, and attending upon the courts. They pressed upon the carriage, and a tall, clean hostler in a brown holland blouse indefatigably kept them at arm's length. Mr. West remarked an order and cleanliness in the inn-yard we had not met with since quitting England; and every department of the hotel bore testimony to the vigilant eye of a painstaking landlord.

Our start was as smart as a crack turn-out for Ascot or Epsom. A good-looking, cheerful-faced boy in a spic and span blue jacket with bright buttons, velvet cap of hunting cut, top boots and doe skins, bestrode as shining and well-conditioned a pair of well-groomed little horses as heart could desire. The harness glistened like gold; he brandished, without using, a hunting whip, and looked occasionally over his shoulder to see what impression he made upon us. Be sure his fee was doubled as well as the hostler's, and we complimented him upon the cleanest stabling, and best posters in Ireland, when we reached Roscrea.

While eating their dinners at Nenagh, our servants fell in with a respectable English bailiff who was journeying to the seat of his employer. He said he knew the country well, that the people dreaded each other as much as the extortion of landholders, and often affected a poverty to which they were in reality strangers, like the Jews of old; and for this reason, that they could be pillaged by all down to the hundredth cousin were their prosperity made manifest to the needier claimants of charity. He knew farmers 'well to do' who could afford to give their daughters £400 or £500 a piece, who yet lived on potatoes and butter milk solely, and suffered the females of their family to go clad in rags, shoeless and stockingless, and went about themselves like the meanest vagabonds.

All this tract of country is pretty and fertile, diversified with country seats, and not in such apparent misery. Near Toomavara, the mountain called the Devil's Bit rears itself. There is a curious cleft in it like the gap of Dunloe, indeed several Irish hills have this peculiarity, just as though a piece were bitten clean out of them.

Between this and Dunkerrin we left the corner of Tipperary we had been crossing and got into King's County; but at Roscrea, we found ourselves in Tipperary again for a few hours.

Roscrea is a dark, dilapidated town, with a horrible pavement, all round stones and mud. It lies between Slieve Bloom and the Devil's Bit, and is watered by the Brosna. I noticed the ruins of one of King John's many castles; and that of the Butlers, a fine remnant of antiquity, commands the town.

Just above the posting-house, I perceived the architecture so common in Irish ecclesiastical structures, with the pointed arch and chevron moulding. It forms a portion of the ancient abbey, which has been converted into the present church. Exactly opposite to it stands the Round Tower.

This was what I had come some miles out of the direct road to look at, so I got out of the carriage and pattered up the wet street to take a nearer survey. The people were rude, and would hardly make way for me to pass; I thought want had hardened their hearts, poor souls! It is quite hemmed in by habitations of one sort or another, so as to present a very imperfect view from the street; but in crossing the bridge as we left Roscrea, I looked back and gained a good view of it, with its triangular topped window, and the door whose remarkable double hinge is noticed by Petrie. Behind it the castle rose very proudly; this is used as a barrack. The Brosna flows past the base of the Round Tower, and altogether it forms a curious and pretty picture.

Our drive this evening was quite delightful the whole way nearly to Birr. The land undulates charmingly, and presents a greater variety of wood and tillage than almost any we had passed through. The slopes of the hills were covered with promising crops, and I saw haymakers still at work in the lowlands. Their mode of carrying hay, strikes the English eye as both uncouth and slovenly; but an Irish gentleman who Mr. West met, assured him *he* was so alive to what he thought a defective system, he had used every endeavour to introduce the English plan of immediate stacking, but he found it of no avail. The quality of the grass differs; that of Ireland is so much more succulent, and the climate altogether so much moister, they are in a manner compelled to adopt a means different from ours and longer in its process, with a view to allowing the grass a longer period for drying. His stacks, he said, were sure to catch fire when the hay was exposed to the sun only the time necessary in England. It is raked up into numerous pointed cocks which are made and re-made, and left days, nay weeks to dry. When nearly ready to stack, they throw two or more cocks into one, and casting a rope over and under the mass, a man lies flat on the top to give weight, and a horse drags the burden after him to the yard, or to a corner of some field where two or more stacks are formed. By this means the ground is strewed with hay all wasted, and under every cock a yellow rotten spot is left, which of course spoils the look of the field for some time. In many places I saw men mowing down grass absolutely under water, which could only be used as litter I conclude; and hay-making was not over, though reaping was begun when we left Ireland.

Portions of the road were repairing, and being cut down a great depth, the narrow line left for passengers was anything but agreeable, or safe for a loaded carriage.

It was ten o'clock when we drew up at Birr, or Parsonstown in King's County. Just outside the town I caught sight of a beautiful Catholic chapel, alias church: for they call all their own places of worship chapels, distinguishing those of Protestants by the term church; a sort of enforced modesty that always jarred painfully on my feelings.

There is but one inn, the general appearance of which was very comfortable. We had a good sitting room, and a very spacious bedroom. The old woman who officiated as housemaid, told me it was a gay place, for a regiment was quartered here, and balls and parties were never ending.

25. William Bennett, *Narrative of a Recent Journey of Six Weeks in Ireland*   (London: Gilpin, 1847, pp. 127–35)

William Bennett (1804–73) was born in London, the son of a Quaker tea merchant. Although his interests, and subsequent publications, reveal a catholic taste – *Extracts from the Spirit of Prayer* (1836) and *Joint-Stock Companies and other Associations* (1861) – Bennett was a true liberal, with especially tolerant views on education. An acquaintance of Wordsworth and Coleridge, Bennett, like many Friends, became concerned about the level of Irish suffering during the Famine years and decided to make a visit to the country, to supply small seed, and to present proposals for the improvement of Ireland. His narrative is composed of letters, written principally to his sister, and describes certain events from the spring of 1847. The proceeds from the sale of the book were directed towards Irish relief.

It was late in the evening when we arrived at Kenmare, – tired, and a good deal exhausted. I had looked upon our painful mission as now completed, not having any idea of the awfully wretched condition of this town and neighbourhood, until accounts had begun to reach us, the last day or two, on approaching its vicinity. We were beset immediately with the most terrific details of the want and sufferings of the people: indeed it could not be concealed. The sounds of woe and wailing resounded in the streets throughout the night. I felt extremely ill, and was almost overcome.

In the morning I was credibly informed that NINE DEATHS had taken place during the night, in the open streets, from sheer want and exhaustion. The poor people came in from the rural districts in such numbers, in the hopes of getting some relief, that it was utterly impossible to meet their most urgent exigencies, and therefore, they came in literally to die; and I might see several families lying about in the open streets, actually dying of starvation and fever, within a stone's throw of the inn. I went out accordingly. In the corner of an old inclosure, to which my steps were directed, on the bare ground, under the open heaven, was a remnant of three. One had just been carted away who had died in the night; the father had died before; the rest could not long survive. A little further, in a cask, placed like a dog-kennel, was a poor boy, who had lain there some time, in high fever, without friends or relatives. I proceeded down the main street. In the middle of it, on a little straw, under an open erection, made by placing two uprights and a board across them, were two women, horrible to behold, in the last stages of consumptive fever, brought on by evident starvation. The town itself is overwhelmed with poverty; and the swollen limbs, emaciated countenances, and other hideous forms of disease to be seen about, were innumerable. In no other part of Ireland had I seen people falling on their knees to beg. It was difficult to sit over breakfast after this. Two clergymen, hearing of our being there, came in, along with Captain Herbert, the Government Inspector, who had just come down under the new relief measures. With one of the former, I immediately went to visit a family he had just come from. The house itself was not so completely wretched; but the scene within was the counterpart of what we had witnessed in Erris. He could have shown me many such. At his earnest request and representations, I engaged to visit his additional parish of Tuosist, lying along the southern shore of the Kenmare estuary, which I had previously heard described as in the most awfully destitute condition. The other clergyman, who officiated in Tuosist and Kilcatterin, still further down, was returning home. We all started together, the first-mentioned clergyman accompanying us about two miles.

A handsome suspension-bridge leads out of the town, and is a work of great public utility. The passage was often difficult, and liable to much detension, especially to the poor, before its erection, – to which the Marquis of Lansdowne, the principal owner of the town, and of the property in the neighbourhood, contributed liberally. But his influence does not extend to the welfare of the peasantry on his estates in the parish of Tuosist. We took the car as far as Kilmichalog, about ten miles along the coast. It is a wild alpine region; the inhabitants being mostly self-dependent, and in ordinary times holding very little communication with the rest of the world. The clergyman depicted their present state and condition in the most affecting terms. He could think but of two persons at all in the condition of gentlemen residing in the whole district. He declared it to be his belief, that out of a population of upwards of 30,000, there were 10,000 who had no other means of subsistence, at the present moment, than seaweed and shell-fish from the rocks. There existed considerable remains of clanship among these mountaineers. He described them as a highly moral, a careless, but a peaceable and contented race, with great kindness and simple hospitality, and strong family attachments; but now the bonds of natural affection were fearfully broken and destroyed, under the pressure and sufferings of their present calamity. Their cattle, as in other places, had almost wholly disappeared. Cows had been parted with for 20s. to 25s.; sheep 3s.6d. to 5s., being brought in by the poor people to sell for anything they would fetch. At parting I handed him £5 for immediate urgency; and ordered to Kenmare two small bales of clothing I had remaining in Dublin. The Central Committee have since responded to an application on behalf of this district.

From the spot where we parted with the car we struck directly up the mountains. There was a new road making under the public works, and a truly magnificent one it will be; requiring not a little first-rate engineering to carry it in the best way over the mountains. We pursued its yet only rough-hewn course with considerable difficulty – carried a great height above the lovely and secluded, but little known Lough Glenmore, until the works and work-people disappeared in the ascent, and we could no longer track it. We then made a short cut over the crest of the mountain somewhat arduous, and down a tremendous defile to the junction with the new line on the other side; which – after some noble vistas into deep, abrupt-looking valleys, alive with the voice of waters, and the motion of many graceful white-threaded streamlets coming down from the heights – brought us out at Adragool, one of the sweet secluded harbours on the north side of Bantry Bay. The boundary line between the counties Kerry and Cork is passed on the summit.

We were deceived in the distances, and found the walk along the coast long and toilsome, though very fine. It is needless to caution the experienced traveller against the length of the Irish miles. They are in proportion to the English, as 11 to 14, but in the rural unmeasured districts they know nothing of real distances. The people along this line are poor and distressed. The want of clothing is as great as the want of food. The wan, aged, and sunken countenances, and the silent beseeching look, without a word spoken, of some of the women and girls, is what enters into the heart deepest, and is the most difficult to bear. To describe properly the state of things in some of these wretched districts, is a vain attempt. It is impossible, – it is inconceivable. STARVATION, – a word that has now become so familiar, as scarely to awaken a painful ideal, – is NOT being two or three days deficient of food. It is something quite different; and the effects of dwindling and insufficient nourishment upon a whole population, – upon the mass of men, women, and the little children; the disease, – the emaciation, – the despair, – the extinction of everything human beyond it, – are utterly past the powers of description, or even of imagination, without witnessing. I am in possession of details beyond anything that has appeared in print, or, I believe, in private circulation; in fact, for the sake of poor humanity, unfit to communicate. My mind was at times so struck down, that for days together the pen has refused its office; the appalling spectacles have seemed to float between, whenever I attempted it, and to paralyze every effort. The loss of a parent, of a child, we know what it is in any one of our families. If the causes are, or appear to have been, in any way within the reach of neglected assistance, or of human control, we know how manifold the agony is increased. Multiply this into all the cabins, the populous way-sides, the far-off solitary mountain hamlets, – vivify the details of famine and pestilence, by thousands and tens of thousands, throughout the length and breadth of Ireland, – and we may have some idea of the voice of anguish and lamentation that now ascends from her whole land.

We had to regret the darkness overtaking us in the latter part of this walk. After losing sight of the bay and the opposite mountains, it was a very long ascent, and then it seemed an almost endless descent; in the course of which we first looked down upon, and then rounded the foot of a most romantic mountain-locked lake. Ravines were crossed, that looked fearful in the twilight, with the rushing sound of wild waters below; and the last forms of the mountains that were visible were truly grand.

We had no time left to investigate the beauties of Glengariff. To all appearances it was a most delightful spot, combining perhaps the lovely and the grand, the mighty rock and the secluded bower, the sweet cove and the majestic mountain, in the highest degree possible. The remainder of the journey was a rapid return through Bantry, where we heard the distress was very great; Skibbereen, where distress and fever had much abated – we were informed, that in the barony of West Carberry, comprising the south-west corner of the island, out of a population of 97,000, probably one-fourth had been carried off; Roscarberry, Clonakilty and Bandon, to Cork. In this great city fever was much on the increase, and ascending in the scale of society. There were stated to be 22,000 extra paupers in the city at that time. From Cork we proceeded by Watergrasshill and Rathcormuck, through the handsome town of Fermoy by Clogheen to Clonmel. Here we had the satisfaction of attending the Quarterly Meeting for Munster, and of visiting, in company with a very kind friend, the soup-kitchen, jail, auxiliary poorhouse, additional fever-hospital, and the lunatic asylum, all which appeared to be under the most efficient management. I must here acknowledge the kindess of C. Bianconi, in forwarding the various parcels of seeds to the far west, free of expense, on application. I think it right to mention the terms of esteem and gratitude in which, throughout this whole journey, I heard the efforts of England and Englishmen towards Ireland everywhere spoken of, under the desolation which has been permitted thus mysteriously to sweep over the land.

26. John East, *Glimpses of Ireland in 1847*

(London: Hamilton, 1847, pp. 93–97)

John East was a clergyman of the Church of England who published *Sabbath Meditations in Prose and Verse* (1826), as well as other religious texts. In 1828 he was preferred to the rectorship of Croscome, Somerset, and in 1841 became one of the curates of St. Michael's Church, Bath. From the early 1840s, East belonged to the evangelical wing of the church and frequently appeared, at public meetings at any rate, as an advocate of the cause of Missions. East began his journey from Dublin on 14 April 1847.

My departure from Dingle, on the bright morning of the 3rd of May, was marked by two or three circumstances painfully indicative of the existing state of things. Our road lay through the two, and my car-driver stopped in the middle of it, leaving me to be quickly besieged by a force of clamorous applicants for relief. He went in hope of purchasing a few oats for our horse, for a feed by the way, but in vain. Not an oat was to be had for money. The wife of the owner of my vehicle, also came and solicited, as a favour, that I would leave with her a part of the hire, as they were without money in the house. Nor were we more successful on the whole thirty miles of road to Tralee, in our application for food for our poor steed. He had to run the entire weary distance unfed, and I was truly astonished at the patient endurance of an animal which had cost his owner only three pounds. Of the miserable crowd around my car, as it lingered by the bridge of Dingle, one individual was so preeminent in wretchedness, that it appears to me, that her form can never fade from my remembrance. She even seems to meet my eye, whenever I revert in thought to that morning or that place. She was a woman of apparently between forty and fifty years of age, on whom the deadly disease of the season had laid its hand. Her person was like a moving death. She said little, but came with faltering step close to me as I sat in my car, placed her staff on the stop at my feet, and leaned on it over me, as though she would make it impossible for me to resist her appeal for aid. Her whole aspect was loathsome in the extreme, and her breath seemed the very breath of the famine plague. Independently of my willingness to give a mite of relief to a degree of misery, which defied all efficient help, I was glad to purchase my release from her by a dole, on the receipt of which she retired. If, however, such are the appearances of physical evil, what must sin itself be in the sight of holy beings, especially in his eyes, 'who is of purer eyes than to behold iniquity' without inifinite abhorrence? Yet to that pitiable creature, and to multitudes resembling her, Romanism denies the knowledge of pardon, life, and health, through the blood of the Lamb. It is not the sight of even such horrors of misery, that overwhelms the soul, while contemplating their moral and spiritual condition in the light of holy Scripture. It is the reflection, that they are chained down in ignorance, superstition, and crime, by the most abominable system of doctrinal corruption that ever palmed error upon man in the guise and name of truth. Could I have believed that the priests who exercise unlimited spiritual power over the masses of Ireland's famished and implagued population were exerting their great influence to lead the willing mind to the Saviour of sinners, and to the hope laid up in heaven for them who through faith in Him 'have received the atonement', I should have looked at those masses of human suffering with a totally different feeling. Tears must fall at the sight of miseries so intense and so widely spread; but hope would gleam through those tears, and lead the soul's expectations brightly onward to where 'there shall be no more death, neither sorrow, nor crying, neither shall there be any more pain, and there shall be no more curse'. But Romanism, like all false religious systems, inspires fear and darkens every hope. Its votaries are either plunged into the lowest depths of spiritual ignorance, or they are, to a certain extent, intelligently the subjects of the 'fear which hath torment'.

With my civil carman and his serviceable equipage, I pursued my way up the lofty range of hills which divide the noble scenery round Dingle bay, from that which expands northward over the bays of Brandon, Ballyheigue and Tralee, the waters of the Shannon, and the counties of Kerry, Limerick, and Clare. I had heard much of the pass as one of the finest in Ireland, and I was not disappointed. The road is cut through and along the edges or sides of gigantic rocks, beetling over the traveller's head in threatening attitudes. The bold and picturesque cliffs of Connor hill rise majestically on the right hand; and on the left, the mighty Brandon rose to the height of 3,126 feet, in a succession of precipitous rocky slopes, sheltering in their hollowed glens many lovely tarns, supplied by perenial springs and streamlets, the latter often falling in graceful silver cascades from the rugged heights. Large bodies of poor men were employed in improving or making good the road, or in raising a frail rampart of turf or uncemented stones, between the road, and precipices of awful depth and perpendicular steepness. The aspect of these bodies of men was little encouraging to a tourist or a rambler. Scarcely was there a solitary act or look of passing civility, which I had found common in other parts. They were working as machines, evincing no interest in their labour, and they eyed the stranger in a manner most repulsive. There was among them at least an appearance of more savage-ness, than I had ever yet seen in my fellow-men. I wished I could believe that the heart would have spoken more kindly than did the dark, sullen countenance. As a general remark upon the natural character of the native Irish Roman Catholics, I most cordially enter into the observa-tion of one who knows them well: – 'Their first thought is one of kindness – exuberant, if not even romantic kindness. It is the second thought – which they imbibe from a mental reference to their despotic priesthood, or to their political leader and agitator, it is this that infuri-ates them against all who differ from them in religion or in politics.' Only a few months have elapsed, since, in the western part of Ireland, no labourer could, with personal safety, have gone eastward, even in search of work, unless he could exhibit his passport as a repealer or a teetotaller. For the temperance movement itself has been made grossly subservient to the schemes of the Romish Church, and Conciliation hall.

27. James Hack Tuke, *A Visit to Connaught in the Autumn of 1847*   (London: Gilpin, 1847, pp. 19–27)

James Hack Tuke (1819–96), a Quaker philanthropist, was educated at York, and entered the family tea and coffee business, before becoming a partner in a banking firm. He worked with the Friends Asylum in York, visited the United States, supported many charitable institutions, and travelled around Ireland in 1846 and 1847 with William Edward Forster to distribute relief funds subscribed by English Friends. In 1848 Tuke suffered from a dangerous attack of fever, contracted when visiting sheds provided by his father for starving Irish who had sought refuge in York. He returned to Ireland in 1880 to distribute funds, and then again in 1881, publishing *The Condition of Donegal* in 1880.

The enormous size of the Unions of Connaught is also a subject which deserves attention; I have before mentioned that Leinster, which contains nearly the same area and population, has nearly double the number of Unions, and, of course, Union-houses. The Union of Ballina (county Mayo) is about 60 miles in width by 30 in breadth, or nearly three times the size of Middlesex, containing an area of 509,154 acres, with a population of 120,797 persons, and a net annual value of £95,774. Let us suppose an Union stretching from London to Buck-ingham or Oxford in one direction, and from London to Basingstoke in another, with a poor-house at St. Albans, and we shall have a good idea of the extent of the Ballina Union. A consideration of these facts, or a glance at the map, will convince any one how impossible it is for the wretched paupers of the extreme or even central portions of this mammoth Union to receive the relief which, by law, is designed for them. Look to the parish of Belmullet in the barony of Erris, itself as large as the county of Dublin, and conceive for a moment the hardships of those who travel 50 miles or more to the poor-house at Ballina. The barony of Erris alone is clearly large enough for one Union, and ought to have its poor-house at Belmullet.

I must be allowed to dwell at some length upon the peculiar misery of this barony of Erris, and parish of Belmullet, which I spent some days in examining. Afflicting as is the general condition of Mayo – fearful as are the prospects of the province in general, there is here yet a lower   · depth in misery, a district almost as distinct from Mayo as Mayo is from the eastern parts of Ireland. Human wretchedness seems concentrated in Erris, the culminating point of man's physical degradation seems to have been reached in the Mullet. It may seem needless to trouble you with particular descriptions of the distress I have witnessed; for these descriptions are but repetitions of the far too familiar scenes of the last winter and spring; although the present seem aggravated by an earlier commencement; nevertheless, such a condition as that of Erris ought, however painful, to be forced on our attention until remedies are found and applied.

This barony is situated upon the extreme north-west coast of Mayo, bounded on two sides by the Atlantic ocean. The population last year was computed at about 28,000; of that number, it is said, at least 2,000 have emigrated, principally to England, being too poor to proceed to America; and that 6,000 have perished by starvation, dysentery, and fever. There is left a miserable remnant of little more than 20,000; of whom 10,000, at least, are, strictly speaking, on the very verge of starvation. Ten thousand people within forty-eight hours' journey of the metropolis of the world, living, or rather starving, upon turnip-tops, sand-eels, and sea-weed, a diet which no one in England would consider fit for the meanest animal which he keeps. And let it not be supposed that of this famine diet they have enough, or that each of these poor wretches has a little plot of turnips on which he may feed at his pleasure. His scanty meal is, in many cases, taken from a neighbour hardly richer than himself, not indeed at night, but, with the daring of absolute necessity, at noon-day.

On entering the houseless and uncultivated region of Erris, the traveller is reminded of the wilds of Canada: for some miles hardly an

acre of cultivated land or the appearance of human residence greets the
eye. Yet this district is reported by the Waste Land Commissioners as
peculiarly capable of improvement. After some miles ride I found a
resting place for my horse, and leaving him to bait, explored, in the
mountains, a village upon the property of Sir R. Palmer, a non-resident
proprietor, who is said to have an income of many thousands from this
county, but is doing nothing to improve his estate, or to give employment to this starving portion of his tenantry. Most of the inhabitants of
this village were owing a year and a half's rent, for their 'sums' of land
(uncertain quantities), for which they generally paid from £3 to £8 per
year. The condition of the people was deplorable; and the last year had
not left them the means of meeting this demand. The landlord's 'driver'
was pursuing his calling, seizing almost every little patch of oats or
potatoes, and appointing keepers whose charges, amounting to 45s. for
the fifteen days allowed between seizure and sale; are added to the rent,
and unless the tenant can raise a sum sufficient to satisfy the landlord
and his bailiff, his whole crop is liable to be 'canted' and himself and
family to be evicted.

One poor widow with a large family, whose husband had recently
died of fever, had a miserable patch of potatoes seized, and was thus
deprived of her only resource for the ensuing winter. What could she do?
The poor-house was thirty miles distant, and it was full. Though many of
these ruined creatures were bewailing their cruel fate, I heard nothing
like reproach or reflection upon the author of their misery, and the bailif
told me that he had no fear of molestation in pursuing his calling.

In this village fever was terribly prevalent, and the food such as
before described, but wanting the sand-eels and sea-weed. Advancing
further in Erris, the desolation and wretchedness were still more
striking. One may indeed at times imagine oneself in a wilderness abandoned to perpetual barrenness and solitude. But here and there scattered
over this desolate landscape, little green patches appear unexpectedly
where no other sign of man presents itself to you; as you walk over the
bog, and approach nearer to the spot, a curl of smoke arises from what
you suppose to be a slight rise on the surface.

To use the graphic language of a late European visitor, 'Let the traveller look where he is going, however, or he may make a false step, the
earth may give way under his feet or he may fall into – what? Into an
abyss, a cavern, a bog? No, into a hut, a human dwelling-place, whose
existence he has overlooked, because the roof on one side was level with
the ground, and nearly of the same consistency, – if he draws back his
foot in time, and looks around, he will find the place filled with a

multitude of similar huts, all swarming with life.' Of what is this human dwelling-place composed? The wall of the bog often forms two or three sides of it, whilst sods taken from the adjoining surface form the remainder, and cover the roof. Window there is none, chimneys are not known; an aperture in front, some three or four feet in height, serves the office of door, window and chimney – 'light, smoke, pigs, and children, all pass in and out of this aperture'. The moment a stranger is observed, the inhabitant retreats within the dwelling; and if you would converse with its occupant, or explore its interior economy, it is needful to follow him. Do not be afraid, however, for although the only decently-dressed man who may have visited him before is the landlord's driver, the inhabitants of these bog-holes are a quiet harmless race. Stoop low enough, or you may carry away the door-post; it is perhaps safest to enter on all-fours, as I have had to do – the darkness and stifling turf-smoke for awhile prevent the use of the eyes, and unable to distinguish whence comes the welcome which accosts you, of 'God speed your honour,' you instinctively grope forward; beware, however, of too suddenly regaining an erect posture, or your hat may appear through the roof; for in no part does the height exceed five or six feet. Accustomed by this time to the darkness, which the inmates in vain endeavour to dispel, by lighting small reeds or the pitch of rushes, you are able to discern the size of this human burrow: and in a space from seven or ten feet square (I have measured them even less), you may find a family of six or eight persons, men, women and children, in this filthy stinking hole, kneeling or squatting round the peat fire, or lying on the damp ground. As for furniture there is none – one or two broken stools and the 'boiling-pot,' and in some a slightly raised space, upon which is spread a little damp dirty straw, oftener upon the cold ground, and a ragged coverlid, constitute in many cases the whole. Surely, then, the inmates must be clothed in skins, to protect them from the cold and damp. Alas! No – rags and tatters are their only garments, and nakedness even is the portion of some, who are obliged to remain indoors or borrow from their neighbours. I asked a poor inhabitant of one of these hovels near Belmullet, whose dropsy-swollen body showed the effects of 'the hunger', what he and his family, six or seven in number, had to subsist on? In reply to my question, he pointed to some withered turnip-tops lying in the mud, at the door of the cabin, 'upon these'. 'And what else?' I asked. 'Yonder's one of the family, seeking for sea-weed, on the beach,' said he, stretching out his skinny arm in that direction, where his daughter was busily engaged. 'And are there many so badly off?' 'Yes, worse, aback in the mountains; they are dying there every day.' How could worse be, when he seemed to be enduring a daily death? But indeed I knew that there were many worse off 'aback in the mountains', and that deaths from starvation had actually occurred.

At Bangor, through the kindess of your correspondent, W.T. Campbell, I obtained several accurate particulars relative to the state of the barony, from the police returns. In one district, 'where last year 650 families existed, there are now only 500, half of whom are existing upon the small turnips' before described; and of this food 'not sufficient to last the whole for two months'. In one town-land, 'there are eighty-five landholders, and but two stacks of oats, hardly any potatoes, and but few turnips'.

In another parish, there are 'whole villages depopulated', 'whole town-lands uncultivated', 'scarcely 400 families remaining out of 587 last year'; and, on an average of the whole barony, it would be safe to say, 'that one acre is not this year cultivated to forty in ordinary seasons', and that 'there is not food for the whole for six weeks'.

From Bangor to Belmullet, a distance of twelve miles, the same dreary waste of uncultivated and neglected land extends. In only one place did I observe any sign of improvement or superior cultivation. This was upon an estate of a proprietor named Atkinson; and as this is the only instance in the barony of any attempt to adopt a perfect system of drainage, it is the more observable, presenting, as the land does, a pleasing contrast to the desolation around it. I never saw what appeared to me more complete or excellent work. It has been executed under the super-intendence of a Scotch steward. The earnings of the labourers, indeed, were low enough, barely 6d. per day, but this employment was a great boon to them. It may safely be said of the landlords of Erris generally, that there appears as much want of willingness as of ability on their part to do anything for the benefit of their starving tenantry or wasted estates. Erris affords one of the most perfect specimens of the mischiefs connected with that vicious system, by which landed property remains in the hands of those who are wholly unable to discharge its duties, or even to open the door to allow others to perform them.

At Belmullet, the capital of the district of Erris, a crowd of almost naked perishing creatures were congregating in the streets, in a state of 'perfect destitution', as the landlord of the inn assured me; they had no homes, no shelter, no land, no food; they slept at night in the streets, and begged for support during the day, of neighbours hardly richer than themselves. He told me also that 'six persons had died in the streets in the few previous nights'; and I am sure that several whom I saw there are now beyond the reach of earthly calamity. The ghastly smile which momentarily played on the countenances of these living skeletons, at the prospect of a little temporary relief, I cannot easily forget. It rendered still more painful the expression of intense anxiety and bitter misery which was exhibited in their livid and death-set features.

Although so much has already been said about evictions, I can hardly omit to mention one instance connected with that system of extermination which many Irish landlords think themselves justified in adopting. The extreme western portion of Erris is a narrow promontory, called the 'Inner Mullet': upon this wretched promontory a proprietor named Walsh, residing in another part of the country, has an estate, from which he was desirous of ejecting a number of tenants. As no less than one hundred and forty families were to be turned out, and cast forth to beg or perish (for the poor-house was fifty miles distant, and could not have contained them), it was natural to expect some resistance, even to the preliminary process, from persons with such prospects. The landlord, therefore, summoned the sheriff to his assistance – the stipendiary magistrate was requested to call out the police: but a maddened tenantry might overcome a handful of police; and as it was thought the 'kindest' way to prevent bloodshed by showing a superior power, fifty soldiers, headed by the commanding officer of the district, were added to the force. Surely to the minds of these poor ignorant people, law, police, military, magistracy and proprietary must have seemed alike confederated against them.

I have no particular information respecting the character of these tenants, and it is of course not improbable that some of them may have been far from 'fulfilling their duties': be this as it may, it is impossible for an Englishman to contemplate one of these wholesale evictions without feelings of the deepest pity for the sufferers, and indignation towards the inflictors.

28. Spencer T. Hall, *Life and Death in Ireland, as witnessed in 1849*   (Manchester: Parkes, 1850, pp. 43–48)

Spencer Timothy Hall (1812–85), printer and bookseller, was sometime editor of the *Iris* newspaper in the early 1840s, before he published his *Mesmeric Experiences* in 1845. Although he published the later *Homeopathy; A Testimony* (1852), clearly maintaining an interest in quasi-medical issues, his interest in local travel literature appeared to occupy him increasingly, and he embarked on a series of guidebooks of Lancashire, Worcestershire and Yorkshire, as well as a collection of verse, *Upland Hamlet and Other Poems* (1847).

It was in the last week of April, that I accompanied the chieftain and one of his sons (who was then on a visit from England) in an excursion to an estate, comprising an entire electoral division of the county of Limerick, and bordering on the county of Tipperary. We went by train to the Pallas station, where a car was in waiting to convey us forward to the little town of Cappermore. A few of the tenants, on horseback, had met us at the station. Others, meeting us on the way, drew to the side of the road, and paying the customary compliments of recognition as we passed, fell into the rear and followed on. The commencement of the estate was marked by a little hamlet, clustering about some ancient ruins near the road, and a wild scattering of rocks somewhat further on, with here and there a wayside cabin, sending out its inmates with inquiring looks, (and this on one of the loveliest mornings of the spring,) made the ride peculiarly pleasant and exhilerating. Nor will it need telling – the appearance of a genuine landlord among his Irish tenantry being so rare – that on arriving at the town itself, the turn-out of the populace was very numerous, and as grotesque a scene as could well be imagined, fraught for me with a manifold world of interest.

The best saddle-horses the neighbourhood could supply were now at our service; and alighting from the car and mounting these, we were soon further on our way; every man on the estate who could raise a horse or mule joining the cavalcade. Crowds who were not rich enough for that, acompanied us on foot, – most of them having some congratulation, petition, or complaint, which they were anxious should reach their landlord's ear. Many of their requests would have struck our ordinary proprietors in England with consternation – their object being, perhaps, not only to obtain forgiveness of two or three years' rent, but to get some bonus besides, sufficiently large to pay the passage of a whole family to America! And, in truth, there was no dispute about a landmark, – no wrong between relative and relative, or neighbour and neighbour, though smothered up for years – no hope delayed – no service, real or imaginary, unrequited – no want of any kind – that they did not seem to think could now be satisfactorily settled, so unlimited was their faith in the influence of their returned landlord!

Wishing by personal observation, to learn the state of his lands in these parts, and unable to attend with the slightest advantage to such a mingling of ejaculations and supplications – fearful, too, of his horse treading upon some of the old widows or others who came imploring and catching at the bridle or stirrups – he commissioned me to make such notes for him of what was said, as might aid him in his after consid-erations. No sooner had I taken out a little book for this purpose, than it was a signal for the poor creatures to rush from him to me, with such force and confusion of language as made it exceedingly difficult to select from the whole a single cogent story. A few memoranda, however, I had managed to pencil down; but so fast did the crowd around me increase, and their intreaties so multiply, as to convince me that it would take, not minutes, but weeks to hear them all, and at length I had to hurry after our party, now out of sight. Yet, even when I had put my horse to a rapid trot, two brothers (who wanted the settlement of some family differ-ences, arising out of the terms on which their mother rented her holding,) clung to my stirrups, and thus ran by my side, reiterating their plea for a considerable distance.

By this time we were drawing towards the mountains, and the interest of the scene was increasing every moment. For a few miles the road became steeper and steeper, bringing us at last to a point which, to the right, lay a deep, wild, streamy valley, the boundary of Tipperary; while down to the left, lay cultivated fields, and cabins from which came relays of people, to make up for those who from fatigue were unable any longer to keep pace with us, and many of whom might now be seen in small knots, left far on the winding road behind us.

On arriving in a glen, where a natural fountain of clear water was gushing from a rock, the chieftain suggested a halt, and we dismounted to lunch – a supply of refreshments having been brought for the purpose. Here we had scarcely been at rest a minute, when the two brothers I had left so far below on the road were with us again, and continuing, or rather renewing their story; and men, who spoke so little English as to need an interpreter, had several of them some suit or other to urge, arising in almost every case out of long arrears of rent, for which they wanted to beg time or entire forgiveness.

Scenes thoughout the morning, so novel and stirring, appealing as they did to such a variety of faculties, had given my heart an unusual impulse. The acquaintance into which, for the moment, I had been brought with the mind and wants of these suffering people, and which, for aught I then knew, might continue for some time; together with the warmth of their temperament, the quickness of their wits, their loyalty towards, and trust in their landlord, and many other engaging qualities, had already obtained a strong hold of my affections. A conviction, too, of what the Irish generally *might have been,* had those qualities been properly cultivated and respected as long as they had been mistrusted, or despised, or forced into inferior courses of action, made my soul begin to yearn towards them with a sympathy that longed for expression. Thus animated, I snatched up a glass, and catching a draught of water from the fountain, drank to 'Ould Ireland', in a tone and manner that were instantaneously echoed from nearly all who heard me. A short time afterwards, when we were again on the move, across the breast of the Guanavan mountains, one of the tenantry rode up to me, touched his hat, and looking calmly in my face, said, somewhat inquiringly, 'I think your honour's an Irishman?' Why do you think so? I asked him, in reply. 'Och, sure it is because you spoke so kindly about Ireland, where we waited by the water.' Well, said I, but do you not think that an Englishman can speak as kindly about Ireland as one of yourselves? 'Not so naturally as your honour spoke there.' Yea, I replied, you may take my word for it, that there are some Englishmen who would lay down their lives for Ireland, if by so doing they could redeem her from her great distress. 'They may say so,' was his quiet, though incredulous rejoinder, 'but the past would not make one think so'. Yet, see — I again remarked — how much some of them contributed to the famine relief funds. 'Yes,' he answered, 'but in what way was it disposed of? — and what was it that made us need the relief at all?' There will not be time, said I, to reason that question out, even if we could; though I should certainly like to hear what you, as an Irish farmer, would say upon it. 'At any rate,' cried he, suddenly brightening up, 'your honour's face is not that of a man who would mean us any harm?' No, certainly, I replied, you may rely that I will do you no harm if I can do you no good. — The drift of all he had said was to draw that assurance from me, and in half a minute he was talking in Irish to some of his neighbours behind, telling them what I had said, with an effect that set their eyes a-gleaming. Of these men I shall have again to speak, as they appeared the week following at the rent table, in Limerick. It is probable that at this time, from my taking notes, they thought I was going to be in some way officially connected with the estate, and so took an early opportunity of sounding out my feelings towards them.

It was now past noon, and there was a dash of the romantic in the landscape itself, and in our relation to it, irresistibly charming. Backing out of the procession, I lingered somewhat apart, the better to catch and retain its character. Still winding upwards, the cavalcade kept on its course – the chieftain himself at its head, and with the ample framework of his person, inherited from a race of reputed Irish giants, yet inlaid by some of the more conspicuous qualities of the old English squire, well suiting his position. But how unlike was all the rest of the scene to anything ever beheld in England! The farmers, nearly all in their long cloaks and capes, and their slouched hats, wanting little to make their costume completely Spanish; and many of them talking loudly in their native language, so different, too, from ours! The eager pedestrians in their motley dress, some of them walking with, and others shouldering their shillelaghs; at one time spreading out from, and at another closing up with and running alongside the horsemen; and women and children, in costume equally picturesque, gathered or running here and there, both on the heights above and the plains below, to watch the passing spectacle! Such was the scene at one instant, yet changed the next. For now we had all come to a pause on a lofty natural platform in the bosom of the mountains, were resting our horses, and gazing with its owner, (not without emotion,) on the vast and variegated expanse, all glowing as it was, beneath as soft and bright a sky as ever ravished the heart of an Italian painter. Would that I were able of that picture to give but an outline! Uncoiling itself in the middle of the plain was a shining river, and on its banks the little town through which we had come, dwindled in the distance to a tiny hamlet. Here, comparatively near to us, crumbled low the ruins of an abbey. Yonder, afar, were the towers of old castles, with fields around them diminished in that perspective to the size of diamonds. The smoke of white cabins in the mid-view curled up in slow and graceful columns, while that of those in the distance cast a filmy haze, scarcely more dense than is often occasioned by the intense sunshine of a summer-day. The bright peaks of some mountains beyond all, completed the prospect. And there, in the position I have described, sat the owner of his steed, with his peasantry around him, o'ergazing the whole! Reader, do you envy him? If so, let me further tell you that he had the credit of being as good a landlord as any in the neighbourhood; and he was also considered to have on that estate as good a tenantry. For the greater part of that land he had himself to pay a specific sum for tithes, according to law; and, for no inconsiderable portion of it, poor rates too. Yet, mark. There were scarcely half-a-dozen persons upon it that were not one, two, or three years behind in the payment of their rent; and on our descending again to the town in the afternoon, the implorings of the poor for a trifle of money to buy food with were so general and heart-rending, that we were obliged to tear ourselves away to escape them!

29. Sidney Godolphin Osborne, *Gleanings in the West of Ireland* (London: Boone, 1850, pp. 74–80)

The Honourable and Reverend Sidney Godolphin Osborne (1808–89) was a philanthropist who wrote on diverse matters: education, sanitation, women's rights and cholera, and whose publications include *Hints to the Charitable* (1856), and *Letters on the Education of Young Children* (1866). In 1849 he visited Ireland, an experience that left an impression of the suffering endured by the destitute Irish poor: 'In these pages, [readers will] find a ready source of reference to those facts, on which I ground my appeal for the consideration of all who love mercy and justice, to the oppression, and the suffering, of the people of this part of the Queen's domininons.' This book is the result of two trips made by Osborne to Ireland, the first in the summer of 1849, followed by a second trip of a month's duration in 1850. At this point in his narrative he is passing through Clifden, during part of his second journey and is making a visit to one of the local auxiliary houses.

There was a yard, with a day ward in it, of about 30 ft. by 15 ft., with open roof, in which were about 160 small children; in one corner there was a child with the small-pox out upon it; at least 30 of the others had not been vaccinated; there were 24 with caps on, with bad heads. The state of these children's clothing was quite shameful; if possible, they were in this respect worse than the same class at Limerick. Many of them were mere skeletons. They were walked out into the yard for me to see them better; as they passed us, one child actually, whether of herself, or by order, put her hand across to hold the rags together in front of the poor thing who walked with her, that we might not be more shocked than she could by such ingenuity prevent; they looked in the yard so cold, so comfortless, so naked, and such a libel on humanity; that I was glad to have them called in again to the close and infected atmosphere of the crowded day room; they were, I believe, all girls, though such is the nature of pure rag attire, that the dress often ceases to be any guide, as to the sex, amongst the young.

There were two underground places, which the architect meant for lumber rooms, which we, however, found inhabited; they were damp and chilly, unventilated, and utterly unfitted for the purpose to which they were applied. There were some adult women in one of them, crouched upon the cold floor, looking just as such beings, so starved, so clad, would look in such a place; they were new admissions. There was little about the whole house out of keeping with what I have described; want of space, want of clothing, in a refuge crowded by those who come in starving and naked, must defy anything like the order and decency which should characterise every public establishment professing to be under the guardianship of the laws.

We now went to an Auxiliary, just occupied by a class of able-bodied women, called the 'Police Barrack'. The day rooms of this wretched building had no sashes in the ground-floor windows; they were, however, covered with iron lattice; immediately under them was a mass of stinking filth of the most miscellaneous character. Passing through a narrow dirty passage, we turned out of a confined yard, in which some masons were at work building up a wall, into two day rooms, i.e. what had been two rooms; the partition door, however, had been removed, though the division walls, or some of them remained. The rooms were measured in my presence, and the result, on a drawing in my notes, records, that the area of both inclusive of 21 ft. by 12 ft.; in this space, we found 32 women in the inner room, 35 in the outer, being 67 adult women in a space of 21 ft. by 12 ft.! the ceiling was not, I believe, nine feet from the ground. In another small room, 9 ft. by 11 ft., twelve grown-up women lived, i.e. existed. In a loft, of dimensions not larger than the first-mentioned rooms, the roof coming down at an acute angle to the floor, twenty-six adult women were said to sleep; I believe more did sleep.

No power of pen can describe the state of the clothing of this seething mass of female pauperage; there were some, that the others, for shame's sake, would not let stand up before us; some I felt ashamed to ask to do so, though with more rags on. The smell of the rooms was intolerable; that of the yard, from an unmistakeable source, no improvement on it. I can hardly conceive anything more thoroughly brutalising, than the herding of this mass together at night; for if they do not sleep in their dirty rags, they must at all events, I presume, be disentangled from them when they lie down, in the place where they lie down; this rag heap, then, redolent of many days or weeks' wear in this confined space, must add its share to that offence to every sense, which, without it, the masses so herded on the floors would produce.

There were altogether 150 inmates in this house. The day rooms look through the lattice into the public street; how such a place, for such a number of persons, could ever have been sanctioned, I cannot understand; if they escape a pestilence, which shall destroy life, they cannot escape an amount of moral disease, which must so brutalise, as to painfully affect it.

We now went to another Auxiliary, in which were between 40 and 50 infants, with their mothers, many of these small morsels of misery were absolutely naked; their mothers, generally speaking, clothed only so far as a small allowance of filthy rags, can be called clothing. Of course they were crowded far more than was in any way justifiable. In another auxiliary, there were 2 or 300 able-bodied females; still the same want of dress, or rather the same insufficiency of rags; packed closely at night in two or three dormitories; by day, their only shelter was one room, of the same area as any one of the said dormitories; but its size reduced by the tables for dining; they were sitting in heaps, in idleness, about the yard. The auxiliary for the boys was some miles off, so that I did not see it; I can only hope it is no worse than those I did see, though that were scarcely possible.

This Clifden Union had poor rates in course of collection at the end of the quarter, terminating 30th of last March, to the amount of £2,287, it had received relief from the rate-in-aid in that quarter, to the amount of £2,115, its net liabilities at the same period, over balance at the Bank, were £6,292. The weekly average mortality per 1000 inmates, for the four weeks ending March 30th, 1850, was 8:1!

It is awful to contemplate, as in the case of this Union, to what one's fellow creatures can be exposed, when the scene of infliction is in one of these out of the way corners of her Majesty's dominions. There is a chance, in a place like Limerick, of some stray traveller, or some local party of sufficient courage and humanity, rising up, to publicly protest against such treatment of our fellow subjects, in establishments, supported under legal enactment, and supposed to be under official supervision; but here, I believe, anything might be done, and the chances of exposure be small. The people of all ranks are so now accustomed to scenes of misery and tyranny, that they have ceased to be shocked or roused by them; they say, 'the potato rot' brought it about, 'potato plenty' will heal it. The intermediate misery is counted as a small thing for humanity to notice; humanity, I fear, has been so taxed, that it has become blind to anything, which might increase its burden.

I know no justifiable excuse, however, for such wanton contempt of life and decency; I do not know why the 'rate-in-aid' Bill was passed, but to obtain the efficient working of the Poor-law, in bankrupt Unions; it is folly to call this make-shift, make-shame system, Poor-law administration.

In England one-fiftieth part of such conduct, would so rouse the indignation of the public, that a speedy end would be put to the abuse, and I have no doubt, pretty severe rebuke dealt on all who connived at, or promoted it. I have yet to learn, that Ireland is not an integral part of Great Britain; I have yet to learn, that doings so disgraceful can exist in Ireland, and not be a shame and disgrace to England.

My friend here again indulged himself in large investments in bread, to feed the poor wretches he found in the street, and with the customary result; he soon being forced from the pressure, to make a retreat at the rear of the shop. I cannot wonder at the perseverance he displayed, he was new to Ireland; less hardened than myself. From a window we got an opportunity of seeing, ourselves unseen, some of the bread he had given consumed; there was no deceit in the way it was devoured; more voracious reality, it would be hardly possible to conceive; to see the fleshless arms grasping one part of a loaf, whilst the fingers – bone handled forks – dug into the other, to supply the mouth – such mouths too! With an eagerness, as if the bread were stolen, the thief starving, and the steps of the owner heard; was a picture, I think neither of us will easily forget.

Benevolence has its drawbacks; if Mazeppa had been bound to an Irish car in Connemara; in a year of famine, with a few loaves of bread tied to him, he would have had a scarcely less lively experience of one wolf hunted, than he had on his wild horse, after the fashion in which his perilous ride is handed down to us. No sooner was our car under weigh, than a pack of famished creatures of all descriptions and sexes, set off in full chase after us; the taste of fresh bread, still inflamed the spirit of some; the report of it put others in hot hungry pursuit; the *crescit eundo* [it grows as it goes] is ever realised in the motion of an Irish mob. Our driver did his best, but our pursuers had us at advantage; for our road was up a very steep long hill; they gained on us, and we were soon surrounded by the hungry pack; the cry of the regular professional mendicant, the passionate entreaty of the really destitute – the ragged, the really starving; the whining entreaties of the still more naked children, still more starved, – in a famine the weakest ever suffer soonest. The quickness and volubility of Irish national mendacity, sharpened by hunger, and excited by the rare chance of appeasing it, all combined to give voice to the pack. No two luckless human beings were ever so hunted; no ravening wolves ever gave more open expression of their object – food. A little coaxing – my friend's; a little violence – my own; a little distribution of copper coin from both of us, at last rid us of the inconvenient, but natural result of an

Englishman, with money in his pocket, and a baker's shop near, wishing in Ireland to feed some starving people.

30. William S. Balch, *Ireland as I saw it: the Character, Condition, and Prospects*

(New York: Putnam, 1850, pp. 161–65)

The Reverend William Balch was an American Universalist minister who travelled to Ireland at a time when the effects of the Famine were still raging. He arrived by ship at Cove, County Cork, on 17 May 1848, although within a week he had moved on to Tralee from where he offers the following impression. In this extract Balch experiences tremendous despair, something he finds all the more difficult to accept given the relative affluence only a few miles away. A powerful witness to the effects of Famine, Balch is moved by the simple incomprehension of what he saw around him. He later published *Peculiar People; or, Reality in Romance* (1881).

Tralee is situated in the bottom of a delightful valley, about a mile from the head of a small inlet, which sets in from the bay of the same name, with which it is connected by a ship channel of recent construction. The hills on the north rise in gentle undulations; but on the south, stretching off to the west, is a range of abrupt hills, covered with brown heather, and dotted with white cabins and patches of tilled ground far up towards their summits. The town itself shows many signs of thrift I had not expected to see, in this part of the country. Some of the streets are spacious and regularly laid out, and many houses are new and handsome, and the grounds about them are tastefully decorated. A fair proportion of the inhabitants are well dressed and genteel in their manners.

I noticed many very handsome women sitting by their windows, reading, walking in the streets, or present in the church. I was surprised at such marks of refinement, so unlike the character of the people we have seen since leaving Cork. I am sorry to be compelled to add, however, that we also saw specimens of destitution, and misery, more horrid than any before described.

In one place we saw an old woman lying on a sort of bed, which had been made of old rags, upon some boxes, by the side of a yard fence. Two sticks were stuck in the ground, on the top of which was placed an old door, the other side resting on the fence. This formed her only shelter. A ragged quilt was spread over her, which she wrapped closer about her as we came near. A dirty cap was on her head, beneath it her shriveled, cadaverous face, faintly tinged with a hectic fever, one hand, withered to a skeleton, lay by her cheek on the coarse pillow of straw, which must have been gathered from the stable near by. Close to her sat a middle aged, and more decently dressed female, who might have been her daughter. She begged of us, in the name of God, of the blessed Saviour, and the Holy Virgin; in strong words which seemed familiar to her, bartering freely the rewards of heaven, for one poor ha'-penny, for the sick, and dying woman. The old lady muttered some words in answer to our inquiries, which were scarcely intelligible; indicating, however, that it was the 'will of God', and apparently trying to submit, as well as she could, to what she seemed to regard a dire necessity. One or two younger women, and some small children, gathered around us, perfect pictures of destitution, the most abject and loathsome. It was impossible for us to contemplate this scene of misery. We had not nerve to listen to their tale of woe. What we saw was enough – too much almost, for human credulity.

It was more, by far, than we believed possible in a Christian land; in a town of twelve thousand inhabitants, and the capital of Kerry county, close by the elegant mansions of opulent merchants and landholders, where fashion and luxury make a fair display; and only a few rods from churches of various denominations, where God is professedly worshipped, in the name of the merciful Redeemer, who gave it as a witness of the divinity of his mission, that 'the poor have the Gospel preached to them', and made the standard of acceptance to the honors he came to bestow, 'I was hungered, and ye gave me meat; thirsty, and ye gave me drink; naked, and ye clothed me; a stranger, and ye took me in; I was sick, and ye visited me'; assuring them, that inasmuch as they had done it unto one of the least of his brethren, they had done it unto him.

Mark our further astonishment, when, as we turned away from this place, we saw posted up, close by, and in many other places about the town, notices of a sermon and a collection for that day, to take place in the Methodist church, in aid of 'Foreign Missions'. My God! Thought I, is it come to this, that these poor creatures – thy children – are to be laid on boards in the street, and left to starve, while Christians are called upon, in the name of religion, and the hopes of heaven, to give their substance to help convert the heathen? How strangely is the Gospel of thy Son interpreted! How singularly are its commands applied! Is this the evidence of a living, saving faith? The working of that charity without which we are nothing? Why will the wise in their generation be sticklers about dogmas and forms of worship, while the masses pine in ignorance, and die in beggary, for lack of true knowledge? Here is a prolific soil, a genial climate, and every physical ability which a bountiful God could bestow; and yet what heart-rending scenes of starvation and misery! What wails of oppression! What appalling horrors; what stoic indifference on the part of the better — some times the religious, portion of the community; what inhuman neglect on the part of government, which pretends to exercise royal protection over her colonies!

We turned from this horrid picture, and went away to seek some object to divert our minds, and relieve us from the painful feelings which had overwhelmed us. We did not succeed. The elegance of some of the public buildings, the court-house, the church, the Catholic chapels, the meeting houses of Presbyterians and Methodists, the hospitals, the Union work-house, the infantry barracks, the Green park, the fine bay — nothing could eradicate the impressions of that wretched family, which inhumanity suffered to remain in the open street, under circumstances which appealed so forcibly to every generous and Christian feeling for sympathy and relief. More than once I turned to go back and cut short my means of travelling, by contributing sufficient to make them all comfortable. But then I felt what an insufficient thing is individual charity, where there is so much poverty and suffering. I cannot avert the evil, turn back the tide, or check the streams which are swelling constantly the flood of pauperism already spread so widely over this land. The root is deeper than I can reach, and useless is the effort of a stranger to do more than give a drop of comfort as he passes by.

So I tried to stifle the breathings of what little benevolence had not been steeled to indifference by the shameless beggary we had already been subject to. The effort was vain, for that and other like pictures haunt me still; and by no other principle than that a man's own is at his disposal, and judgment does not justify an indiscriminate bestowment of his temporal possessions. Of course, the history of the past, the philosophy of our political and social economy, the doctrines and precepts of our pulpits, the conduct of Christians, the judgment and prudent calculation of our heads, all join in this opinion upon this subject; but still the heart demurs — it will not rest satisfied. There are deep feelings which come welling up at the sight of such miseries, which relax the tight cords of all our systems, and make us pitiful and sad — unless we have the means and disposition to afford relief. And this feeling is not relieved by the fact that one is in the possession of every desired comfort himself, which he claims as the reward of his own industry and prudence. The heart will be satisfied by no such logic, but continues clamorous for the exhibition of sympathy, and a willingness to share an other's woe, and help, by every practical means, to obtain relief.

The traveler's soul is often embittered by such scenes of degradation and misery. The splendid palaces of kings and noblemen, the exquisite beauty of royal galleries of art, the bibliotheques of wisdom, and even the grandeur of natural scenery, the most powerful antidote of all, are inadequate to erase from the memory such pictures of misery as one sees in Ireland. While I write, the endearments and comforts of home, the general prosperity of friends and country, and the reflection, in the most favourable light, that I gave some small expressions of sympathy, can not still the warfare in my soul, that there is a wrong, a great and crying guilt some where, for which a fearful requisition shall be made. The responsibility can not rest on the mere passer-by; and yet, as one among men I feel it. I had not means to give, nor power to correct; but I had a heart to feel – but what is feeling, to hungry mouths and grieving hearts? It is bread and clothes they need and a chance to do, more than prayers! Still there is a power in sympathy, a virtue in prayer, which blend with those deeper wants than worldly famine can reach, or any phase of abstract theology satisfy.

31. Asenath Nicholson, *Annals of the Famine in Ireland, in 1847, 1848 and 1849*

(first published 1851; 2nd edn, M. Murphy (ed.), Dublin: Lilliput, 1998, pp. 136–38)

Asenath Nicholson (1792–1855) was born in eastern Vermont, USA. A teacher, writer and traveller, she first journeyed throughout Ireland between June 1844 and August 1845, then returned and spent a further twenty-eight months, from May 1846 until September 1848, visiting the Famine Irish in many of the most remote districts of the West. A bible reader committed to the conversion of the Catholic Irish, Nicholson was no crude proselytizer, but a conscientious figure struck by the misery of what she saw around her. At this point in her narrative – 17 April 1849 – Nicholson is in the vicinity of Louisburg, County Mayo.

April 17th. With a sister of Peter Kelly I went to 'Old Head', and was first introduced into one of the dreadful pauper schools where ninety children received a piece of black bread once a day. It was a sad sight, most of them were in a state of rags, barefooted, and squatted on the floor waiting for a few ounces of bread, with but here and there a fragment of a book. The clean schoolmaster, on a cold day, was clad in a white vest and linen pantaloons, making the last effort to appear respectable, labouring for the remuneration of a penny a week from each family if by chance the family could furnish it. These ninety all belonged to Mrs Garvey's tenantry, and there were others looking on who had come in likewise, not belonging to her lands, who wishfully stood by without receiving one morsel. I looked till my satiated eyes turned away at a pitiful sight like this. Neither the neat cottage, the old sea, nor my favourite Croagh Patrick could give satisfaction in a wilderness of woe like this. When will these dreadful scenes find an end?

Naught but desolation and death reigned; and the voice of nature, which was always so pleasant on the sea-coast, now united with the whistling of the wind, seemed only to be howling in sad response to the moans and entreaties of the starving around me. The holy well, where the inimitable drawing of the blind girl was taken, is near this place. In years gone by this well was a frequented spot where invalids went to be healed. It is now surrounded by stone, covered with earth, and a path about gives the trodden impress of many a knee where the postulant goes round seven times, repeating a Paternoster at every revolution, and drops a stone which tells that the duty is performed. A hole is shown in a stone where the holy St Patrick knelt till he wore the stone away. A poor peasant girl, in the simplicity of her heart, explained all the ceremonies of the devotees and virtues of the well, regretting that the priests had forbidden the practice now. A company soon entered the churchyard and set down a white coffin, waiting till the widow of the deceased should bring a spade to open the grave; and while the dirt was being taken away she sat down, leaning upon the coffin, setting up the Irish wail in the most pathetic manner. She, by snatches, rehearsed his good qualities then burst into a gush of tears, then commenced in Irish, as the meagre English has no words to express the height of the grief, madness or joy. The ground was opened but a few inches when the coffin of another was touched. The graveyards are everywhere filled so near the surface that dogs have access, and some parts of the body are often exposed.

A debate was now in progress respecting good works and the importance of being baptized into the true church. Mrs G., who professed to be a papist, disputed the ground with them, till the contest became so sharp that I retired, for their darkness was painful. It seemed like the valley and shadow of death, temporally and spiritually.

The little town of Louisburgh, two miles from Old Head, had suffered extremely. An active priest and faithful Protestant curate were doing their utmost to mitigate the suffering, which was like throwing dust in the wind; lost, lost forever – the work of death goes on, and what is repaired today is broken down tomorrow. Many have fallen under their labours. The graves of the Protestant curate and his wife were pointed out to me in the churchyard, who had fallen since the Famine in the excess of their labour; and the present curate and his praiseworthy wife, unless they have supernatural strength, cannot long keep up the dreadful struggle. He employed as many labourers as he could pay at four pence a day, and at four o'clock these 'lazy' ones would often be waiting at his gate to go to their work. He was one day found dining with the priest, and the thing was so novel that I expressed a pleasant surprise, when he answered, 'I have consulted no one's opinion respecting the propriety of my doing so. I found,' he added, 'on coming here, this man a warm-hearted friend to the poor doing all the good in his power, without any regard to party, and determined to treat him as a neighbour and friend, and have as yet seen no cause to regret it.' This same priest was not able to walk, having been sick, but he was conveyed in a carriage to Mrs Garvey's and most courteously thanked me for coming into that miserable neighbourhood, and offered to provide some one at his own expense to convey me into the Killery mountains, to see the inimitable scenery and the wretched inhabitants that dwell there.

In company with the wife of the curate and the physician, I went there. The morning was unusually sunny, but the horrors of that day were inferior to none ever witnessed. The road was rough, and we constantly were meeting pale, meagre-looking men, who were on their way from the mountains to break stones and pile them mountain-high for the paltry compensation of a pound of meal a day. These men had put all their seed into the ground, and if they gave up their cabins they must leave the crop for the landlord to reap, while they must be in a poor-house or in the open air. This appeared to be the last bitter drug in Ireland's cup of woe!

'Why,' a poor man was asked, whom we met dragging sea-weed to put upon his potato-field, 'do you do this, when you tell us you expect to go into the poor-house, and leave your crop to another?'

'I put it on, hoping that God Almighty will send me the work to get a bit.'

We met flocks of wretched children going to school for the bit of bread, some crying with hunger, and some begging to get in without the penny which was required for their tuition. The poor little emaciated creatures went weeping away, one saying he had been 'looking for the penny all day yesterday, and could not get it'. The doctor who accompanied us returned to report to the priest the cruelty of the relieving office and teacher, but this neither frightened or softened these hard hearts. These people are shut in by mountains and the sea on one side, and roads passable only on foot by the other, having no bridges and the paths entirely lost in some places among the stones. We left our carriage and walked as we could; and though we met multitudes in the last stages of suffering, yet not one through that day asked charity, and in one case the common hospitality showed itself, by offering us milk when we asked for water. This day I saw enough, and my heart was sick, sick.

32. John H. Ashworth, *The Saxon in Ireland: Or, the Rambles of an Englishman in Search of a Settlement in the West of Ireland* (London: Murray, 1851, pp. 92–97)

The Reverend John Harvey Ashworth was born in Yorkshire in 1795. Educated at Oxford, he moved to Ireland immediately after the Famine, buying an old castle at Craggan, Co. Clare, which he apparently restored. It is not clear how long Ashworth stayed in Ireland, but he was possibly back in England by the end of the 1860s, for he held the position of Vicar of St Mary's, Stateley-in-Cartmel, from 1874 until his death in 1882. One of the better-known settlers to the West of Ireland, Ashworth presents the country as an untapped source, capable of untold, indeed unimaginable wealth, with salvation – as in this extract – deployed as a useful metaphor for the emigrant experience. His later works include, *The Young Curate, or the Quicksands of Life* (1859), and *Rathlynn* (1864).

When we left Cong, nothing could be more promising than the state of the atmosphere on a fine morning; and when I looked at the small and ill-constructed boat in which I was called upon to embark, but few misgivings at the moment crossed my mind, seeing all so calm above and below. But I would advise all future travellers not to launch themselves on these waters except in a stout four-oared boat. I had given no orders on the subject, and the result was, my setting forth in a kind of cockle-shell concern, manned by two boatmen only. We had not left the seven islands behind us more than a quarter of an hour, when a low wailing sound like distant wind, and suspicious gusts, began to creep over the water, and ruffle its hitherto serene surface. Surprised, and perhaps a little startled, I cast my eyes westward, and saw heavy clouds like those of the preceding day, when I was at Ross Abbey, advancing in masses from the heights of Benleva and that lofty range which divided the Maam district from the distant Glen Inagh. It had been a halcyon calm, as was soon proved. Having resided occasionally among lake scenery, I was well aware of the often dangerous nature of the navigation of these loughs, and how frequently sudden squalls from the mountains have overwhelmed the incautious adventurer, and consigned him to a watery grave. It was not, therefore, without anxiety that I looked ahead, and saw, but at too great a distance for affording immediate shelter, the large island of Inchagoil. Another island, Cleenillaun, was to our right; but the boatman said, if the squall came down, we could not face the waves so as to make good our retreat thither. Our only chance, therefore, was to make Inchagoil. And verily the squall did 'come down' in right good earnest. Thinking and conjecturing were now useless; it behoved us to be stirring and active, for the wind gains to blow in fearful and fitful gusts, and the angry rippling of the surface of the lough, increasing into yet more angry waves, promised, ere the storm was over, a too close resemblance to the ocean swell. Our little bark was tossed on the now rolling billows; one side rising high out of the water, while the other seemed as if it would dip below it. The men, nothing daunted, stripped to their shirts, and, rolling the sleeves over their elbows set right earnestly to work. Anxiously I looked upwards, perchance any break in the clouds might give promise of the storm abating: but no; sullen, leaden-coloured masses hurried along, and, as I cast my eyes around, not an island, not a distant mountain, not a vestige of the shore was soon to be seen, but all was as wild and cheerless, as if we had been tossing in the midst of the far Atlantic. Hark! What an awful peal of thunder was that bursting on the heights of Benleva, and resounding through all its precipices and glens! The storm now rages above us. Oh! When shall we reach Inchagoil? It was indeed an awful scene, and one I cannot easily forget. There we were, tossing helplessly, in the centre of that wide expanse – the waves below greedy, as it were, to swallow us – the wild war of the elements above eager to overpower us. Our only chance was to keep the boat close to the waves; but then the surf, which now began to curl the tops of the billows, often broke over the bow of our boat, and caused us to ship large quantities of water. My office it was to bale this out as quickly as I could; and, in truth, I was not sorry to thus occupy myself, as it diverted my attention from the confusing scene around us.

The heavy rain too now began to pelt us bitterly; but I had so well provided myself with 'patent appliances' for these emergencies, that so far I was scatheless. I was thus also enabled to cover the clothes of the boatmen with my ample cape, so as to secure the poor fellows the comfort of a dry jacket when the turmoil was over. 'Hurroo!' said Mike,

turning round for an instant, and directing his gaze over the bow of the
boat; 'by the 'mortial, there is Inishannagh Cliff, and that is but a stone's
throw from Inchagoil. Arrah Pat, darling, pull strong on your side, and
we shall be under Berry Island in the strike of a minute.' It was a long
minute certainly; but everything is this lively land allows for exaggeration. Thus an Irish mile and an Irish acre are both on an enlarged scale.
It was a lovely little bay which we were now entering, and so protected
by a small island to the westward, called Berry Island, that the water was
comparatively smooth, and we now felt in perfect security. The clouds,
too, began to break away; the rain ceased; the sun darted his warm and
cheerful rays once more upon the scene, and my thoughts were lifted up
in thankfulness to the Most High, and mentally with the Psalmist did I
exclaim, 'Give the Lord the honour due unto His name; worship the
Lord with holy worship. It is the Lord that commandeth the waters: it is
the glorious God that maketh the thunder.' The island of Inchagoil, on
which we now landed, near some ruined cottages, has no bold or prominent aspect from the lake. It stretches along, as you view it at a distance,
as one continued ridge of low elevation; but, on exploring it, I found
that it was not strictly so. At the eastern and western extremities it rises,
in the latter almost perpendicularly, to an elevation of nearly eighty feet
from the level of the water. Though the cottages seemed deserted, yet
occupants there were, certainly, on the island; for, as usual in Ireland
when a stranger approaches, some persons engaged in a distant field left
their labour and came to give us the greeting. On inquiry, I found they
were persons employed by the Lessee, Mr. L., to till the lands and watch
the stock. Not being able, however, to extract any information from
them, I declined their services, and proceeded alone on my tour of
discovery. This island of Inchagoil was one of those taken possession of
by the early Irish saints, and is supposed to have been honoured by the
actual presence of St. Patrick. To him, certainly, the church existing here
in ancient times was dedicated, and the ruins still bear his name. Leaving
the shore, and proceeding into the interior, I soon arrived at some ruins,
inconsiderable as to size, and rendered more so in appearance by the
rank luxuriance of briers, weeds, and nettles by which they were half
concealed. Making my way as well as I could through these obstacles, I
entered under a small but perfect archway into an enclosed area, about
eighteen feet long by thirteen wide. What this has been, whether the
outer entrance to monastic buildings, or a portion of a church, I could
not decide; but the former is probably the case, as I found the scanty
remains of St. Patrick's church about a stone's throw from the building I
was now examining. Opposite to the first archway is another, but

smaller, which doubtless led to other buildings, as considerable foundations are visible, and heaps of dressed stones are scattered about the
adjoining ground. Both these doorways are circular.

Climbing without difficulty the highest portion of the walls, which
are fortunately held firmly together by the clinging ivy, I contemplated
from thence a magnificent prospect. Not a cloud was in the heavens, the
atmosphere was clear and bright; and the eye wandered with delight over
a scene, the vastness and the lovely combinations of which it is difficult
to conceive. To the south-west, mountain towered above mountain, peak
above peak; deep valleys perforated their recesses, and the arms of the
lake were seen penetrating far inland, till lost in distance and gloom. To
the south and east the waters of the lough stretched far away, and sometimes it was difficult to trace the low eastern shore on the horizon.
Many islands varied the now placid bosom of the lake and immediately
before me rose the hill of Glan, on the western shore; below which, and
stretching over a bold promontory, was the wood of Annagh; and far
away in the same direction was visible the smoke of Oughterard; rising
from its lovely vale. But the attempt to describe such scenes is vain: I
know I must have wearied you with such frequent, but very imperfect
details; but to travel through such a country as this, and altogether to pass
by its picturesque beauties, would be unjust. Besides, I feel that persons
of warm imaginations would never think of settling in the flats of
Holland or Lincolnshire, though the richness of the land and the pecu-
niary benefits to be derived therefrom are most manifest. Beautiful
scenery will have its influence on the mind of an emigrant, and I do not
therefore think that my frequent notices of the general aspect of the
country will by any means be lost. There is a freshness, a cheerfulness, a
constant variety, a union of softness and grandeur about the scenery of
the West of Ireland, that, to my mind, make it one of the most desirable
places of settlement in the world.

33. Harriet Martineau, *Letters from Ireland*

(first published 1852; 2nd edn, G. Hooper (ed.),
Dublin: IAP, 2001, pp. 90–93)

Harriet Martineau (1802–76) was born into an old and distinguished Norwich family. Her earliest work – a number of essays published by the Unitarian Society – enabled her to visit Dublin first in 1831, where she resided with her brother James. There she planned her highly successful *Political Economy* series (1832–34), which she followed with many others, several of which showed her to be a great traveller and social observer: in particular, *Society in America* (1837), *Retrospect of Western Travel* (1838), and *Eastern Life, Present and Past* (1848). In 1852 Martineau, accompanied by her niece, visited Ireland again. Her letters, originally published by the *Daily News* (whose correspondent she was), were published in full in 1852. In this extract she is in the vicinity of Clifden, which she approves for the number of its English settlers and their revitalization of the Irish economy.

September, 7th 1852. These western wilds are the region for English settlers. The further we proceed, the more of them we find; and we must say that, as far as our observation goes, they seem to be heartily welcome. In old days we used to believe (and we find that some residents think so still) that the peasantry, all over Ireland, had a strong dislike to working for wages; and that the one good thing in life, in their estimate, was to have a bit of ground on which they might be independent. We now find indications of a very different feeling wherever Englishmen have settled. Mr. A. is a very fine man, who employs sixty people or more, who would be starving but for him. Mr. B. is a gentleman who has a very fine wife, who has so many people come that they keep much company, and spend a good deal of money. Mr. C. has a very fine place and garden, and it employed plenty of people for a long while to raise it and get it into order. Mr. D. has a very fine mill; and it is a fine thing for the place – it employs so many people. Mr. E. has a very fine farm, and the people are sure of work and wages all the year round. And so on, from one county to another, in the west.

Mr. Robertson, the agent on the Martin estates, now the property of the Law Life Insurance Company, has lived in the country for many years and is much esteemed and trusted by his neighbours. It is he of whom we used to hear that he had no locks and bars on his doors, as there was nobody to be afraid of. He is the lessee of the Martin fisheries, and he employs fifty persons, on the average of the year, on the salmon-fishery near the Martin's Castle. His bog reclamations answer well, and employ much labour. There was some discontent about the 196,000 acres of that property being all transferred to one company; but there was nothing else to be done, as the company had claims exceeding the value of the whole estate. It is not yet divided, to be sold in portions. It has been so laid out that the saleable parts could not be disposed of without throwing away every chance of making anything of the more unproductive. Time will remedy this; and the management of the estate will proceed with a view to a future division and sale. Meanwhile, there is no necessity for a forcible clearance, nor even for the company to enable the people to emigrate. Some have earned the means, and are gone; and more employment is found for those who remain. The other great domain, the D'Arcy estate (about a fourth the size of the Martins'), is divided, and has been sold in portions, of which two or three are bought by Englishmen. Our guide at Clifden told us that the castle and lands belonging to it are bought by a 'Mr. Eyre, the head banker of London'. Mr. Scully, his agent, now resident at the castle, is gratefully spoken of throughout the neighbourhood, for the pains he takes to improve the people's ways and promote their welfare.

On leaving Clifden for the north, we see, on the first water-power, and at the foot of a little wooded ravine, a large mill, with a dwelling-house beside it. A new settler lives here – with a Scotch name – and he is evidently the great support of the population round him. After ascending the swelling moorland above, we see, far off and away, the lovely coast, with its bays, promontories, valleys, and islands – as sweet a scene as ever basked in autumnal sunlight. The driver points out what he calls the light on yonder hill: this 'light' being a clearing where green fields and stubble shine amidst the surrounding moor. This is Mr. Twining's, of Clegan – too far off for us to visit; but a letter of Mr. Twining's has been published, in which he speaks hopefully of the capability of the district. We turn down to the right, and see a church, a large expanse of drained bog and of advanced cultivation; and a large, eccentric-looking abode. This is Mr. Butler's, a settler of many years' standing. Some way further on, amidst a scene of remarkable beauty, there is a handsome house, with its roof-tree just laid, and workmen busy about it. In the sloping fallow before the door, two men are harrowing. There is a pleasant and cheery look about the place. It is Captain Fletcher's. Then follow immediately half-a-dozen or so of brilliantly clean dwellings, some gardens, really verdant fields, a post-office, a shop, a school-house, up the hill on the left-hand side; and on the right, charmingly seated on its green bank, and with garden sweets about it, the grey stone house of James Ellis, whose name is his sufficient eulogy. This Quaker family lives among an exclusively Catholic peasantry, on terms which it would do the conflicting zealots elsewhere good to witness, – if they could go to hold their tongues and learn, instead of preaching mischief where all is now peace. This Friend, who values his own faith as much as any M'Hale or Dallas, employs a large number of labourers, who are all Catholics; and they find they can all be religious in their own way, without any strife.

Somewhat further on, towards Kylemore Lough, in a solemn seclusion, at the foot of dark mountains, stands the abode of Mr. Eastwood, another English gentleman, who is improving a large estate there. After that, there are no more dwellings for many miles, except the little Kylemore Inn, and some cottages beyond. The moorland is too wild for settlement, and the misty mountains allow too little sunshine to encourage tillage. The singular and glorious Killery follows, with its admirable road, one of the benefits left behind by the lamented Alexander Nimmo. Then comes the Jumper village I told you of, with its new church and pretty parsonage at the extremity of the fiord. Further on, when the Connemara mountains are left behind, and the moor looks as if nobody had ever crossed it before, we come upon the plain, domestic-looking Catholic chapel, and, almost within sight of it, the national school-house of Carrekenedy. That school-house is a pleasant token of English care to light upon in the wilds.

We are now approaching Lord Sligo's property. The road continues most excellent to within five miles of Westport, where Lord Sligo's 'demesne' skirts the town. This young nobleman seems to be much beloved, Protestant as he is, by his Catholic neighbours. In the morning, one may see him handing round the plate in his own church in the park for contributions for Protestant schools, – the police of the neighbourhood being on the floor of the church, and the soldiers in the gallery; and in the evening you may hear from his Catholic neighbours how good he is, – how just and kind to his tenantry and labourers, how generous as a family man, how self-denying under the reduction of rents and increase of burdens that he has to bear for his share are no secret, and should be none. There is no disgrace in the fact; and there is honour in the way in which it has been met. From Westport, for some miles on the road to Newport and beyond it, the aspect of things is more dreary than anything that had before met our eyes in Ireland. We need not describe it. Those soaked, and perished, and foul moorlands, relapsed from an imperfect cultivation; those hamlets of unroofed houses, with not about one or two roofs in sight; little bridges, with their centre-stones tumbling out; graveyards overgrown with thistles, while cattle go in and out over the crumbling earthen fence; signs of extensive former habitation, amidst which we may see two or three human beings moving about like chance survivors of some plague, – these features of a lapsed country are understood at a glance; and here we found them. But presently we met a gentleman, riding a fine horse, and looking as if business carried him on so briskly. He touched his hat; we inquired who he was, and found he was another English settler – Captain Houston – who is gratefully spoken of for his excellent and extensive farming; and he is only one of seven or eight settlers who have large farms near Westport.

P A R T II
1852 – 1921

Introduction

From 1852 to 1921 Ireland witnessed increasing political unrest, the awakening of a national consciousness, a literary revival and rebellion. Fenian activity, as far afield as Canada in 1866, and more dramatically in Britain the following year, registered with some writers, although the Land League and Home Rule increasingly dominated Irish, and Anglo-Irish, political life towards the end of the nineteenth century. The first extract in this section, by John Forbes in 1852, follows in much the same mood as those above by Ashworth and Martineau: extolling the wonders of the new 'English colonists' who are transforming the dreary bogs and wastes of Ireland's Western seaboard into a 'green smiling island amid the dark desert of moors and bogs'. But thirteen years later, when William Whittaker Barry, a barrister from Wiltshire visited, changes had taken place. Soldiers, artillery, constabulary, panic: these are just some of the items Barry raises during his walk into the city of Cork in 1865. It is not clear how far the optimism of many travellers in the immediate post-Famine years was just that – optimism – and how much was a reflection of real and significant change. But whatever the truth, the confidence of those few years, when some imagined Ireland reborn after the calamity of Famine, was quickly extinguished.

The Home Rule movement was founded in 1870, the Irish National Land League in 1879, and the Irish National League in 1882. Not surprisingly, because this period of Irish history is associated with social and political upheaval, many travellers wrote of political events throughout the 1870s and 1880s: demonstrations, troop movements, speeches and rallies. James Hack Tuke reports on the highly militarized state of Mayo and Galway; Bernard Becker writes of boycotting in Ballinrobe; William Sime awaits the arrival of Charles Stewart Parnell in Athlone; William Henry Hurlbert visits Wicklow, the site of recent evictions; Arthur Bennett travels to Belfast, where he hires a guide to take him around the Falls and Shankhill Roads, the scene of recent disorder; Marie Anne de Bovet attends an Irish National League meeting in Waterford. However, not all of these extracts are so relentlessly political. In some a lighter note prevails, as in Marietta Lloyd's encounter with servant girls in a Big House near Fermoy, who put on the garb of their masters and take to chasing one another around the house, screaming and laughing, until finally exhausted. Yet even here something is amiss; the fun is too edgy, possibly even parodic, although the nuances of the encounter appear lost on Lloyd herself.

In large part, the rising tide of political violence is reflected in these extracts, with an increasing desire to experience events as they unfold, rather than report on their after-effects. As with many Famine narrators, travel writers to Ireland in the nineteenth century appeared keen on writing to the moment, and it comes as no surprise to know that many of them were journalists, in some instances contracted to visit Ireland on behalf of newspapers: James Macaulay, Bernard Becker, William Sime, Henry Spenser Wilkinson, Paschal Grousset and William Hurlbert all worked at some time as journalists, and of these we know that Becker and Grousset travelled specifically as newspaper correspondents, for the *Daily News* and *Le Temps* respectively. And it is not difficult to see how certain encounters would have appealed to readers outside the country: Becker's description of the notorious Captain Boycott, armed with his double-barrelled shotgun, and presiding over a dragoon of Orangemen, for example, must have made for great copy. If travellers to the Orient went in search of exoticism, or to Africa for adventure, then many came to Ireland for the simple pleasure of politics as an unfolding, almost theatrical experience. Everything, it would appear, was on offer; everything they had heard, especially how intractable the place was, seemed true. If travel writers journeying in other countries needed occasionally to enliven their narratives, travellers to Ireland had only to write up their experiences, like anthropologists on a field-trip.

As far as these extracts are concerned, a change may be discerned towards the end of the century. The above-mentioned Lloyd, actually travelling in the 1880s, conveys a domestic interest and studiously avoids politics, while Alfred Austin, journeying in the early 1890s, writes very much as a tourist addressing other tourists. Although these were also politically charged years, Lloyd, Austin, even Kate Douglas Wiggin, who visited Ireland possibly in the late 1890s, opted for a lighter touch. Not until we meet up with Burton Egbert Stevenson, an author and librarian who travelled around parts of Ireland in 1915, do we begin to see the re-emergencé of the older patterns of confrontation and violence. Stevenson arrived at a time of especially heightened political tension: in 1913 the UVF and the Irish Volunteers had both been formed, with both groups gun-running the following year to Larne and Howth respectively. Nevertheless Stevenson attempted to show something of the complexity, even the 'charm' of Ireland to his readers, although the prophetic nature of his words is certainly chilling: 'Those political adventurers who have preached armed resistance so savagely, without really meaning a word of it, may have raised a Frankenstein which they will find themselves unable to control.'

As in the early nineteenth century, those who visited the country between 1852 and 1921 displayed similar preoccupations and interests. Motivated by the country's reputation for easy friendship one moment, by its internecine conflicts the next, Ireland appealed to a wide range of travellers. On 24 April 1916, Irish Volunteers seized central Dublin buildings, initiating what would be known as the Easter Rising, and on 29 April they surrendered to the British authorities, and saw their leaders executed between 3 and 12 May. This year marked the start of a concerted period of unrest, moving from the 1916 Rising, through the War of Independence, and on into the Civil War. The two closing extracts in this part, from Douglas Goldring and G.K. Chesterton, give impressions of Ireland in 1918 and 1919 respectively, impressions that for all the elegance and sophistication of their commentary, reveal a country at something of a crossroads: at odds with Britain, and increasingly at odds with itself.

34. John Forbes, *Memorandums made in Ireland in the Autumn of 1852*

(2 vols, London: Smith, 1853, vol. I, pp. 259–63)

John Forbes (1787–1861) was born in Banffshire, Scotland, and educated in surgery at Edinburgh. A founding member of the British Medical Association, one of Forbes' principal interests lay in the medical topography of England. A sometime editor of the *British & Foreign Medical Review*, Forbes was so highly regarded in his field that he was appointed Physician to Queen Victoria, and later, Physician Extraordinary. He received a knighthood in 1853.

We left Clifden in the forenoon to pursue our journey through the northern districts of Connemara to Westport. The weather still continued fine, and enabled us to see, now at a distance, now nearer, during the first half of our journey, our old and dear friends the twelve peaks of Binabola. The whole tract through which we passed, a distance of at least thirty Irish miles, may be generally characterised as moorland, bog, and mountain, the general wildness and barrenness being only broken here and there by isolated patches of cultivation; and yet it is here, strange to say, that so many of the English colonists have chosen to settle as if they were ambitious of showing that resolution, when aided by money, can triumph over every disadvantage both of soil and climate.

Perhaps I ought to except from this general charge of barrenness a portion, at least, of the first six or seven miles out of Clifden, which were not only better cultivated, but were pleasingly diversified with views of the inlets or bays, along whose heads we travelled. This locality may be now regarded as partly 'planted' by Englishmen. First we passed, close on the left-hand side of the road, the new house and new farm of Mr. Butler, with its neat new church opposite, and where fencing and draining and bog-paring were seen going on all around with much activity. Immediately beyond Mr. Butler's are two or three more settlements, on one of which a new house is still under the builder's hands. Then, after an interval of bog, we came to a sort of straggling village, containing a grand new shop, built and endowed by Mr. Ellis, and which is the wonder and the comfort of all the country round. It is a perfect storehouse of all kinds of necessaries, – all I believe, of the best sort, and all transferable to the uses of the community at the lowest possible scale of prices. Further on we came to Mr. Ellis' own demesne; and as his house and school are only a very short distance off the road, we paid them both a visit, the schoolmaster informing us that Mr. Ellis is surrounded by moors and barren hills, and was, indeed only four year since, nothing but a barren moor itself. By indefatigable and continuous exertions, and a great expenditure of money, Mr. Ellis has converted this wild spot, if not to a paradise, certainly to a cultivated, fertile-seeming, English looking homestead, – a green smiling island amid the dark desert of moors and bogs around it. In accomplishing this great work, this benevolent and noble-minded man, a worthy member of the Society of Friends, – achieved a triumph of another kind, and yet greater: he saved a whole population from utter ruin, nay, from death itself. I was told by a gentleman on the spot, that but for the constant employment, and its accompaniment, constant and liberal pay, scores of the poor people in these secluded valleys must of necessity have sunk from mere starvation. Even now, Mr. Ellis' works supply the staple support of the labouring class in the district, as, at this very time he constantly employs about sixty persons on his farm, and in breaking up fresh moors to add to it.

Mr. Ellis' own abode, a neat house in the English cottage style, is prettily situated on a gentle elevation at the mountain's base, and commands, what cannot fail to be a delightful view to himself, the whole of the conquests achieved by him over his wild and stubborn enemy, the primeval bog.

To complete his bounties to the poor of this valley, Mr. Ellis has built a school at his own expense, and pays the whole outlay for keeping it up in full efficiency, including the salaries of an English master and mistress. It is a neat building of two stories, the one floor being set apart for the boys' and the other for the girls' school. At the time of my visit there were nearly 60 boys in the school and 32 girls, the whole number of girls on the books being about 40. There was not one Protestant in either school.

The boys' school is conducted precisely on the principle of the British and Foreign schools in the Borough Road, London. The girls, in addition to book-learning and writing, are carefully taught sewing and the other mysteries of the needle; and for this purpose remain at school from half-past nine in the morning to half-past five in the afternoon, an interval being, of course, allowed for play and food.

I remarked that the boys were more ragged, and altogether less neatly dressed than in most of the National Schools I had visited, and was told that this was the result of principle on the part of Mr. Ellis, he deeming it unsuitable to hold out any mere physical lure to attract children to the school, and wishing to encourage the parents to make an effort to clothe their families out of their own earnings. Ragged as they were, however, they were fully a match, in point of learning, for the boys of any school I had yet seen in Ireland. Their feats in mental arithmetic were really alarming to men accustomed to do their little reckonings in pen and ink; and were enough to frighten from their ancient haunts, if any still lingered there, all the elves and fairies and brownies of the Malloge Mountain, at whose base they were performed.

The aspect of the girls' school was very different, and seemed to whisper the secret that the womanly care that presided here was not so rigid, at least, in the matter of political economy, as was the masculine authority; the girls being all extremely neat and well dressed, with a great array of charming white pinafores. However, it appeared, that even Mrs. Ellis was not altogether regardless of social economics, as she made the children buy the main parts of their dress out of their own earnings with the needle, she only supplying, from her own private stores, the pinafores aforesaid. On the whole, looking on this scene in all its varied relations, I doubt if I found anything in Ireland more delightful – more especially as there was added to its intrinsic attractions the enhancing charm of unexpectedness.

If I might be forgiven for touching, however slightly, on what ought always to be sacred in a traveller's eyes, the cares of the kind hosts who receive and succour him, I would add that I was almost as much surprised and gratified at what met my eye and ear in the interior of Mr. Ellis' cottage, as I was by the metamorphosis which his enterprising philanthropy had worked on the scenes around it. In the crowded haunts of civilisation, whether in town or country, we are prepared for and expect all the high conditions of social and intellectual refinement; but 'in deserts where no men abide', as may almost be said of this locality, such things strike us with a sort of wonder: unreasonably, no doubt; for men and women of cultivated minds, and long accustomed to the elegancies of civilised life, cannot leave behind them, with change of scene, what has in fact become a portion of themselves.

35. William Whittaker Barry, *A Walking Tour Round Ireland in 1865, by an Englishman*   (London: Bentley, 1867, pp. 272–76)

William Whittaker Barry (d. 1875) was born in Wiltshire, qualified as a barrister in 1853, and published one other travelogue, *A Walking Tour in Normandy*, in 1868. At this point in his Irish narrative – dated 27 September 1865 – Barry is approaching Cork city, but so overwhelmed is he by the fear of Fenian activity that he is able to discourse on little but anticipated Irish violence. Barry's narrative point of view, especially his reluctance to employ direct speech, reinforces his outsider status, and creates the impression of a fearful and inhospitable environment. Barry began his walking tour in Belfast, on 11 August 1865, from where he departed a little over two months later, on 17 October.

The county of Cork had been, for some little time, proclaimed under the Peace Preservation Act, and much alarm prevailed just now in the south, lest there should be an immediate rising of the Fenians. I saw little of the newspapers, but from such of them as came in my way the account was, that Cork was in a state of panic. All I observed in my route today seemed to confirm this view. In the villages I pass through, there are groups of people, evidently discussing the all-absorbing events of the day. Any respectable-looking man coming from the Cork direction is surrounded and eagerly appealed to for the latest information, and one who says he saw nothing new in that morning's paper is looked upon as quite an authority. From the terrified appearance of the people there are evidently ominous rumours afloat along the countryside, whether or not they have any foundation in fact. I hear one woman as I pass say, 'There's a gentleman going on; I wonder he is not afraid of being killed!' This was pleasant, certainly. As I approached nearer Cork several public cars and other conveyances full of people were coming away from the city. There was scarcely a vehicle of any kind going to Cork. This circumstance, in an opposite manner, was certainly almost as ominous as the footsteps to the lion's cave, which the fox, in the well-known fable, saw on his way to pay an intended visit to the king of beasts. Whether there was a country fair going forward today, or these people were really leaving the city through fear of remaining there, or they were Fenians escaping from probable arrest, or it was a mere coincidence, I never had the means of ascertaining, and therefore never knew. I only note down the facts as they actually occurred.

Long before I reached Cork it was nearly dark, and there was no moon. I am ashamed to say that, for the first and only time during my travels in Ireland, I was afraid of encountering some undefined danger. I felt very much like a child in the dark. I find myself carefully scutinising, so far as the little light will allow, the countenances and appearances of the different men who pass. Now three men abreast come along the road. Surely they are Fenians. Then I hear steps coming stealthily behind me. This certainly must be a Fenian with accomplices in the rear, and about forcibly to administer the Fenian oath. I look back and see a little girl with naked feet, carrying a huge loaf. Away with these childish fears! But they do not vanish. I still find myself scanning the countenances of the different people. At length I meet a soldier, a non-commissioned officer, walking alone. This is the most assuring sign I have yet met with, for, brave man though he may be, and accustomed to face danger, he would not thus stroll out of the city alone if there were an insurrection raging there; besides, he would be with his regiment. However, to make assurance doubly sure, as they say, I stop, and have some talk with the soldier. He, probably divining my fears, for I did not state them, was most civil and obliging in answering my inquiries. He said the city had been in a state of panic, but was now quite tranquil. One night in particular, an order came to the barracks at Ballincollig, near Cork, for a troop of soldiers. They immediately got ready with artillery, and men took off to protect the battery, and marched into the city, where they took up their quarters in one of the principal streets until four o'clock in the morning. It appeared that, on the night in question, the constabulary were going to make a number of arrests, and feared a rescue. No doubt such a course, though probably prudent under the circumstances, was calculated to create alarm, and hence the panic. Even in calm, quiet London, of all cities in the world the one least liable to panics, I apprehend that, if troops were required to take up their position in Belgrave

Square or the Green Park, that those of the Upper Ten Thousand who reside in these neighbourhoods would suddenly discover that their presence was required at their country seats, or that the sea-side air of Brighton would do the children good, and be off by the morning trains in different directions.

At any rate my own panic was now allayed, and I walked leisurely on. An appearance of fire startled me for a short time, but it proved to be the light of a large manufactory. As I walk along a main thoroughfare in the outskirts of the city, there is an aspect of unmistakable quiet. The men resume their usual characters – that of workmen going home, or persons moving about their lawful business. Lovers, too, are here, or those who ought to be such, sauntering up and down, or sitting billing and cooing on the banks. When I enter the city I ask a gentleman the way to the Imperial Hotel; he starts aside like a frightened deer, but recovers his self-possession almost as quickly as he had lost it, for he is strong and healthy-looking, and in the prime of life, and gives me direction. This gentleman, catching sight of my knapsack, probably mistook me for a Fenian with some companions in the neighbourhood. By the aid of another inquiry from three young gentlemen, who seemed surprised at my not knowing such a well-known place, I reach the locality of the Imperial Hotel. In the principal streets near here groups of young men are pacing up and down, with anxious looks, and hurried and exciting conversations; but there are no police about, except two or three here and there.

36. Nassau William Senior, *Journals, Conversations and Essays Relating to Ireland*

(2 vols, London: Longmans, 1868, vol. II, pp. 156–59)

Nassau William Senior (1790–1864) was an economist called to the bar in 1819, and later appointed first Professor of Political Economy at Oxford in 1825. An ex-student of Archbishop Whately's, he published several texts on political economy, but was also the author of several travel and related works: *A Journal kept in Turkey and Greece* (1859), *Essay on Fiction* (1864) and *A Journal kept in France and Italy* (1871), among others. This extract is from his two-volume memoir, and is entitled *Journal of a Visit to Ireland in 1862*.

Bilton Hotel, Dublin: Monday, September 1, 1862. – We (that is, my daughter and I) reached Dublin yesterday morning by one of the steamers, the 'Connaught'. She is the best boat that I ever was in. Though there was much wind, she was perfectly steady.

Finding that the Archbishop of Dublin was at his new house, called 'Roebuck', we drove over to dine with him. But there are many Roebucks. We drove to Roebuck Villa, and to Roebuck Hall, and to several other Roebucks in vain. We enquired everywhere for the house of the Archbishop of Dublin, but no one knew it. At last, one man said, 'Is it Mr. Whately you mane? Then I'll show you his house.'

It was near some of the houses at which we had enquired; but it seems that the population of the Roebuck district is Roman Catholic, and no one chose to admit the existence of a Protestant Archbishop of Dublin.

Glassdrummond: September 10. – We have been at this place for the last ten days. We have employed all our mornings in driving about the country. This district, called Morne, is a strip of land about thirty miles long, and from two miles to one hundred yards wide, between the Morne mountains and the sea.

The most interesting object is Dundrum Castle, finely situated on a hill above the little town. It was built by the Knights Templars. Extensive outbuildings surround an inner court, containing perhaps a couple of acres. In the middle of this court, unconnected with any other building, rises a solitary round tower, about fifty feet in diameter, and sixty or seventy feet high. One floor of it probably contained the chapel, always circular in the buildings of the Templars.

Dunderave, Bushmills: September 15. – From Glassdrummond we proceeded, on the 10th, to Dunderave. It is a very pretty place, about a mile from the Giant's Causeway, created by Sir Francis Macnaghten, and by his son, Sir Edmund Macnaghten, the present baronet. The house built by Sir Edmund is on a bold unusual plan. It consists of a hall, about forty feet square and fifty-six feet high, lighted from above. Round it are the sitting-rooms on the ground-floor, and the bedrooms on the first floor – the latter opening into an open gallery, running round the hall at about half its height. The vast body of air contained in the hall keeps the temperature equable, and gives perfect ventilation. It is therefore the usual sitting-room. The park is belted round by woods, now about fifty years old, which, though kept low by the sea-winds, are yet high enough to give considerable shelter.

The Giant's Causeway is rather curious than beautiful; but the head-lands on each side of it, running into the sea, along a line of twenty miles of bold coast, forming deep bays covered above with turf, and presenting their columnar faces to the sea, afford a succession of striking and peculiar scenes. The finest of these promontories is Pleaskin, about 370 feet high. The little valley below it receives much seaweed in rough weather. It is accessible only by a path worn on the face of the cliff. While we were there, two men and a woman, loaded with seaweed, climbed up it. The woman had fallen, about twenty years ago, while ascending it. She was injured, but not enough to prevent her continuing her terrible trade. Farther on the coast is Carrick-a-rede, a small basaltic island, connected with the mainland by a rope-bridge, which we none of us ventured to cross. The promontory commands a fine view of the Causeway headlands to the west, and Fairhead, 636 feet high, to the east.

Carrick-a-rede was our most distant excursion towards the east. To the west, we reached Portrush, a watering-place on a peninsula of sand-hills, fringed with rocks, and forming, with the cover of the Skerry Islands, about a mile from the shore, an imperfect natural harbour, which might easily be made a very good one.

The cottages on Sir Edmund Macnaghten's estate are good, but in its immediate neighbourhood are villages, one of which, called Ballintoy, is as bad as any that English travellers in Ireland have ever described. Some of the cabins in Ballintoy seemed to be without windows or chimneys, the smoke coming out at the door. The population, as far as we saw it, consisted of half-naked children, and half-starved dogs. They followed the carriage for miles, and hung on us when we left it to examine Carrick-a-rede. The explanation is, that these wretched villages are the property of a good-natured careless landlord. He never comes near them, does nothing, and forbids nothing; so that the over-population natural to the Irish has followed, with its necessary concomitants – idleness and misery. The evil influence of the priest does not exist, for the villages are exclusively Protestant.

37. James Macaulay, *Ireland in 1872: a Tour of Observation, with Remarks on Irish Public Questions* (London: King, 1873, pp. 154–57)

Little is known of James Macaulay, other than a few basic details: that he was born in 1817 in Edinburgh, and that he studied medicine at the city's university. Although Macaulay appears to have practised for a number of years, by 1850 he had made a radical shift into journalism, a field in which he was to have some success. From 1858 until 1895 he was editor of the *Leisure Hour*, and in 1885 he published a short biography of General Gordon for the Religious Tract Society. This extract finds Macaulay choosing to evaluate what he terms Catholic and Protestant 'contrasts', rather than providing details of the actual experience of Irish travel.

The contrast between different provinces or districts of Ireland is not so marked as between countries wholly Catholic or Protestant, or as in the Swiss cantons. It is a country of mixed population; not merely mixed in the sense of partly the one and partly the other religion in different localities, but so intermingled in the same provinces as to make the contrast not at once evident. Add to this that in Protestant countries the Roman Catholic Church is so modified in its outward aspects, as to be scarcely recognizable as identical with the Church of the dark ages and dark countries. In Ireland the people can no longer be kept in ignorance, for 'the schoolmaster is abroad'. Even Sunday-schools are becoming common among Roman Catholics, – a thing unheard of at no distant time. It must be remembered also that to Protestants the Catholics are chiefly indebted for these educational advantages, the national schools being mainly supported by a parliamentary grant. Nearly all the charitable schools also, before the national system commenced, were supported by Protestant contributions; the Kildare-Street schools, the London Irish Society, and others, as well as the Irish Church Mission schools of the present day. In the face of all these educational appliances, the Catholic people cannot be kept in ignorance, as in former times, or as in countries where Protestants do not stir them to emulation. Their bishops cannot check this flow of knowledge, though their effort is to obtain the control and guidance of it.

Yet, making all due allowance for the number of Catholics in the north of Ireland, and of Protestants in the south, and for the modified character of Popery in the presence of the reformed faith, the contrast between Ulster and the other provinces is notorious. Here is the testimony of a Catholic traveller: 'I left,' says M. Prevost, 'the industrious colonies of the north, and suddenly the scene changed, and I found again the deserts, the bogs, the hovels, in which live the miserable people.' The same traveller in another part of his journal says: 'Kilkenny was an important town when Belfast was only a village: it had several factories, eleven water-mills, and such a carpet factory that its English rival, to avoid competition, demanded the repeal of the Union. In 1781 Belfast was an unimportant place, with a poor harbour, and the revenue of the port only £1,500.' The statistics of population alone will suffice to show the progress of the northern borough. In 1782 it was 13,000; at the Union about 20,000; in 1821, in round numbers, 37,000; in 1831, 53,000; in 1841, 75,000; in 1851, 100,000; in 1861, 119,242; and in 1871, 174,394. Kilkenny at the last census had 15,609. As an inland town it could not be expected to increase largely, but it had the elements both of mining and manufacturing prosperity, if the people had the energy to use them. With far greater advantages, the city of Cork need not have allowed its northern and modern rival to get so far ahead. The population is about half that of Belfast.

To any one who has travelled or resided in Ireland it is a waste of time to tell of the contrast between the Catholic and Protestant provinces. But a few statistical facts will be understood by strangers. Of the 25,000 troops usually stationed in Ireland scarcely 3,000 are in Ulster, and these chiefly in the border counties. Of the 13,000 constabulary less than 2,000 are in Ulster. Of committals for crime not one-sixth are in the north, though in other places the difficulty of obtaining evidence on conviction, from conspiracy and connivance, makes the proportion less than actually exists. During the famine-time, out of £10,000,000 relief money not £1,000,000 went to Ulster; and of this a large part was for the poor Catholics, who flocked thither from less prosperous parts of the country. Everywhere throughout Ireland at that sad time, the great mass of the relieved were Catholics, of the relievers Protestants. With one-third of the whole population, Ulster's share of the police, jail, and poor-law expenses is not above one-eighth. Its pauperism, its crime, its poor-rates are all less; its education, its wealth, its industry, its benevolent and religious institutions are all more, in proportion to the numbers of the people. In short, there is a condition of social and moral health, and an atmosphere of prosperity in the north, utterly diverse from the south, with its filthy cabins, swarming beggars, decaying villages, and its Catholic faith. The contrast is the more striking when we remember that in some of the northern counties the Catholic population is large, and also in some of the towns, especially Belfast and Derry, where a considerable portion of the lower labouring class is from the south; but notwithstanding this mixture of population, the contrast between Ulster and Munster is almost as marked as between the Protestant and Catholic cantons of Switzerland.

38. James Hack Tuke, *A Visit to Donegal and Connaught in the Spring of 1880*

(London: Ridgway, 1880, pp. 84–89)

Written almost thirty years after his first Irish visit, this account of Tuke's travels to Donegal and Connaught shows the same determination, and the same sense of political purpose as before. Just as outraged by what he perceives to be basic inequalities, Tuke effectively conveys the differences between Britain and Ireland by drawing attention to the impoverished state of Ireland. This extract finds him attempting to draw many strands and places together, with the emphasis mainly on Counties Mayo and Galway.

The return of Mr. Parnell from America was signalised by a general illumination in the town, and even in remote villages and hamlets, where the police supposed no strong political feeling existed. In the towns, speeches more or less violent were made on the Sunday evening after his return, and bands and tar barrels caused a great stir among the people. At Ballinrobe a drunken orator commended Charles Stuart Parnell, as 'the only honest man in Ireland'; and at Westport several speakers addressed a large and excited audience from the window of our hotel.

But this is of slight moment compared with the deep seated sense of discontent which pervades many districts of Mayo and Galway. At Westport the agent for the largest proprietor, who also acts for others, rarely if ever leaves his house unless guarded by two policemen armed with double barrelled guns loaded with slugs; and his son, who is equally protected, is thought to be a special object for vengeance. This is in consequence of his having shot a man who was one of a party that fired upon his father and himself whilst driving on the road. At Ballinrobe again I noticed two armed policemen walking up and down the town together. 'That is how we do it in Mayo,' said the gentleman, a large landed proprietor, who was with me; 'those men are following some bailiff up and down the town from house to house.' If it were not for the police, I was told on one occasion, the people would rise in some districts against the landlords, or rather their agents; for the bitter feeling is generally against some agent who is supposed to carry out his duties with little consideration for the tenant and much for the landlord. In

Mayo alone I was told there are 800 to 1,000 armed policemen, and as many more in the County of Galway, stationed there to protect the land, or rather the lives of the landowners.

It is very difficult for an Englishman to realise such a condition of affairs, or to conceive it possible in an English county. Take Norfolk, for instance, which has nearly the same area as Mayo – 1,356,000 acres in the former against 1,376,000 in the latter whilst the population of Norfolk, 438,000, is not far from double that of Mayo with its 246,000. Leaving Norwich, Yarmouth, Lowestoft, &c., out of consideration, let us imagine that in every small town or village of 300 to 5,000 people of that agricultural county companies of armed men were stationed in barracks, varying in number from five to fifty, whose duty it was, by day and by night, on foot and on horseback, to patrol the country; 800 to 1,000 men are thus employed in Mayo, while 236 rural police constables suffice for nearly double the population in Norfolk. What would dull Swaffham, Walsham, Fakenham, or peaceful breezy Cromer think of such semi-military occupation? Let us also imagine that, here and there, in some wild and out-of-the-way place, you find a 'hut' (temporary barracks) erected for a handful of men, marking, like the cross in the old highwaymen times, the scene of some recent outrage or attempted murder. Further, to complete the picture, let us remember that there are men, yes, and even a woman, it is said, who dare not cross the street of the town, or pay a visit, without the terrible penalty of an armed following.

Mayo was one of the proclaimed districts, and has been the centre of the great wave of anti-rent agitation which last autumn swept across the country and which has been productive of so much evil fruit. The districts around Claremorris and Swinford seem especially disturbed, and it may be noted that there is hardly a resident landlord in these districts, and that therefore the people are more left to themselves than is the case where a good resident landlord exists. Here, too, the misery of the population has been very marked, and the absence of men of independent position or judgment is most seriously felt in the administration of the Poor Law. The difference in the disaffected state of the people in North and South Mayo further illustrates this. In South Mayo, from Westport eastward, the chief landlords are nearly all non-residents – five or more – whose total rentals taken out of the county cannot be less than eighty thousand a year. Captain Knox, at Ballinrobe, is an honourable exception to this, and he, as Chairman of the Union, and also of the Relief Committees, is working hard in that district. It is in south Mayo that great seat of disturbance exists, and where, as I have noted, the largest body of police is quartered, and where there are many men who dare not stir out of their houses without their escort. In North Mayo a less hostile spirit as a rule exists. Many of the landlords are resident, and exercise a beneficial influence over their poorer neighbours and tenants. Sir C. K. Gore, Colonel Knox, and others, are instances of this. Nor must it be overlooked, in reference to the disaffected condition of Mayo, that it was in this county that the greatest number of evictions occurred in 1846–50; thousands were thus turned out of house and home, and the records of the Famine year have left a tale of suffering and sorrow which will not be soon forgotten.

The attempted process servings in this and the adjoining county have frequently been resisted by force. Fifty or sixty policemen have had to encounter large mobs of people, men and women, and have been compelled to retire from the scene. I have referred to one village which I visited, about three miles from Westport, which had been the scene of one of these encounters. In this instance, I believe, there had been little, if any, withholding of rent, it was absolute poverty which prevented payment, for many of the people had pawned their shawls and clothing, and were, so far as we could see, without other food than that supplied by the 'Committee'. So far as I know, none of these persons have been apprehended for interfering with the police in the execution of their duty; but in the neighbourhood of Castlebar, the 'Kilvine Rioters', both men and women, were convicted at the Castlebar Assizes, for violently resisting the police, whilst we were at Westport. The sentences were intentionally very heavy, viz., – three men were imprisoned for six months, with hard labour; one for nine, three for six months; two women were sentenced for six months, with hard labour, others three months, with hard labour, two little boys to two months; and others, men and women, to three, six and twelve months. And it is thought that these sentences have had a deterring effect in other cases, as we heard of processes being served on Lord Sligo's and other properties around West-port without difficulty. The families of the 'Kilvine Rioters' are now supported by the Land League.

Nor is the county of Galway less disaffected. I have heard from several residents statements of the alarm and agitation through which they passed last winter. Many were in fear of their lives, or of having their houses burned down; and as I have before said, it is thought by some that an agrarian revolution would have taken place had it not been for the constabulary. The Carraroe and Maam Riots, in which hundreds or thousands of people resisted the police who were protecting the process-servers, are too well known to need recounting. I met one of the inspectors of police who was present, who told me he thought if they had not charged at the moment they did that the people would have closed in upon the handful of police and by sheer force of numbers disarmed and trodden them down. As it was, thirty men and women were more or less injured by the bayonet, and several police, one of whom had hot coals thrown, not upon his head, but down his back. That this deep-seated disaffection is only partially quenched may be learned by the fact that within a few days a little yacht was burned down to the water's edge for some offence given by the owner, and today the Inspector of Police who had luncheon at the hotel, was engaged upon an inquiry into a case of reported shooting at a man last evening, within half a mile of this town (Oughterard). The Inspector himself took a loaded pistol out of his pocket before sitting down, which he said he always carried with him.

It cannot be doubted that this is sufficient evidence of a very serious state of society, which under the evil influence of certain men can at any moment be fanned into a flame. It is thought that many of the outrages are not committed by the poorest people, though the resistance to the police in process-serving is often undoubtedly so. The murderous attack upon the agent and his son, already referred to, which resulted in the death of one of the would-be murderers, arose in connection with a grazing farm of considerable size near Ballycroy, the lease of which fell in. The original rent of £10 was advanced to £32 and the owner of the lease declining to pay he was ejected. Such is the statement, and hence he induced persons to lie in wait for the agent with the deliberate intention of killing him. Such attacks, if they can be reached, ought to be punished most severely. A gentleman who visited the spot with the police the day after the affair, found the places where the men had spent the previous night in the heather, and two or three empty whisky bottles, cartridges, &c., &c.

Whilst condemning to the utmost such atrocious crimes, the question still remains to be solved: how can they be prevented? 'Put more police in the county,' is the answer of some, 'erect a hut for four or five policemen where an outrage occurs and charge them on the district itself, so that it may feel the inconvenience'; a useful reminder no doubt, but certainly not a remedy.

'It is very hard to have to pay the police tax. See, Sir, I have to pay 6s.,' said a woman to me one day, 'a man had better be quiet and pay his rent.' So far good, but the murderers are never found, and a reward of £500 for conviction of £200 and free pardon for information of accomplices have produced no result in the above case. Law is in fact set aside and agrarian crime respected and unpunished. The agrarian outrages in Connaught alone have increased four-fold in the past year, and are probably more numerous at this time in this province than in the whole of the three other provinces in Ireland together. And what is even more serious is the fact that not more than one in five of the offenders are discovered or punished. This applies solely to offences connected with the land, for as regards other crimes they are less frequent than in England, and as readily punished. And still the question remains, How can this almost universally disaffected tone be changed into one of content and loyalty?

39. Bernard H. Becker, *Disturbed Ireland: Being the Letters written during the Winter of 1880–81* (London: Macmillan, 1881, pp. 128–36)

Little information is available on Bernard H. Becker, other than he was born in 1833. An author and journalist, he worked mainly for the periodical *All the Year Round*, to which he also contributed a number of stories. A regular contributor to scientific journals of the period, Becker travelled Ireland as Special Commissioner of the *Daily News*, the same newspaper that had sent Harriet Martineau to the country thirty years earlier.

Ballinrobe, Co. Mayo, Friday night, November 12th. The march of the Ulster contingent last evening commenced smoothly enough at Claremorris. The dismal little country station was lined with troops, and perhaps made a more brilliant show than at any other period during its existence. After the manner of this part of the country the train due at 2.41 arrived at 3.30 p.m., and it was almost twilight before the well-guarded procession commenced. Perhaps two thousand persons assembled at dreary Claremorris, but the small representation of the countryside made up for the paucity of its numbers by the loudness of its voice. The groans which announced the arrival of the train were repeated again and again as the sixty-three officers and men of the Ulster contingent made their way towards the cars engaged for them. At the cars, however, some difficulty occurred; for the drivers absolutely refused to carry anybody but police. They were not bound, they said, to carry Orangemen, and would not carry them. This difficulty occasioned some little hustling, but the upshot was that the Ulster men, a well-grown, powerful set of fellows, were compelled to walk all the way from Claremorris to the infantry barracks at Ballinrobe.

The march was inexpressibly dreary. When any sound was heard it was a yell, and these expressions of disapprobation were repeated by Hollymount, and with increased vigour at Ballinrobe, where the streets were full of people. The Boycott Brigade was last night kept strictly within barracks, not a soul being allowed to venture out of the gate.

The general aspect of everybody and everything in Ballinrobe this morning expressed fatigue. The Ulster contingent, who call themselves 'workmen', were terribly knocked up by their walk of about thirteen miles from Claremorris, a fact which hardly speaks well for their thews and sinews, but in fairness it must be admitted that they were obliged to undertake their march after a long and fatiguing railway journey, at sundown, on a muddy road, and in alternate light and heavy rain. They were also poorly fed, for their carts and implements generally only came in here this afternoon, escorted by the Royal Dragoons, under Captain Tomkinson, during part of the distance, and for the remainder by a troop of the 19th Hussars; wherefore the Ulster 'workmen' hardly appeared to advantage this morning until breakfast had been supplied them in the infantry barracks. Then they straightened their backs and stood squarely enough to make a very old soldier exclaim with delight, 'Foine men, sorr, they'd be with me to dhrill 'um for a couple o' weeks'.

Poorly fed as the Orangemen were, their case was not nearly so hard as that of the military. It is all very well to send 'the fut and the dhragoons in squadhrons and plathoons' to the fore, but it is not clever to send them to Ballinrobe or elsewhere without tents, baggage or food. That furious Ulster Tories, 'spoiling for a fight,' should leave everything but repeating rifles and revolving pistols behind when rushing to possible fray is quite conceivable, but that the Control Department should always blunder when troops are moved rapidly is not quite so easy to understand.

By what appears almost persistent clumsiness the troops sent higher were allowed to arrive many hours before their tents, baggage, and provisions. Suddenly ordered to leave Dublin, two squadrons of the 19th Hussars, a not very huge or unmanageable army of a hundred and twenty men, came away without being allowed to bring rations with them. The effect of this blundering is that the Hussars have been pursued by their food and tents and on the night of their arrival were utterly without any accommodation whatever. The cooking pots have only just arrived here. Why it should take three days to convey a cooking pot over the distance a man travels in less than ten hours it is difficult to imagine; but the fact is absolutely true, nevertheless. The officer commanding the unlucky Hussars has more cause to complain than any of his men, for, owing to an accident to his own charger on the railway platform, he was obliged to ride a fresh horse, which, startled by the crowd, yesterday reared suddenly, and fell backwards upon Major Coghill, who is now confined to his room. It is hoped that no bones are broken, but this is not yet accurately ascertained, so great is the swelling and inflammation.

The hour of starting was late, by reason of everybody being tired with the hard, dull, wet work of yesterday, unrelieved by the slightest approach to a breach of the peace. Fatigue and disappointment had done their work, and only a few of the more ardent and sanguine spirits looked cheerfully forward to the march to Lough Mask House. The Orangemen, however, had not lost all hope, and one stalwart fellow, who told me he was a steward, and not an agricultural labourer, rejoiced in carrying a perfect arsenal, including a double-barrelled gun of his own, a 'repeater' of Mr. Maxwell's, and several full-sized revolvers. This honest fellow confessed that digging potatoes and pulling mangolds were not his regular occupations, but that he had come 'for the fun of the thing,' and to show them there were still 'loyal men left in Ireland'. This is hardly the place in which to discuss the loyalty which goes on an amateur potato-digging excursion armed with Remington rifles and navy revolvers and escorted by an army of horse, foot and police.

The quality of loyalty, like that of mercy, is not strained, but it has fallen upon Mayo unlike the 'gentle dew from heaven'. The people here are undoubtedly cowed by the overwhelming display of military force, but they vow revenge for the affront put upon the soil of the county by the Northern invaders. Against the soldiers no animosity is felt, but the hatred against the cause of their presence is bitter and profound. Mayo has its back up, and only waits for an opportunity of vengeance.

At eleven o'clock the march from the barracks to Lough Mask commenced. First came a strong detachment of constabulary, then a squadron of the 19th Hussars, commanded by Captain Webster, and next two hundred men of the 84th and 76th Regiments, who completely surrounded and enclosed the so-called 'workmen' and their leaders, Mr. Somerset Maxwell, who contested Cavan at the last election in the Conservative interest, and Mr. Goddard, a solicitor of Monaghan, who led the men of that county, with whom was the Mr. Manning to whose letters in the Daily Express, a Dublin newspaper, the Orange movement is attributed in this part of the country. In the rear came the men and wagons of the Army Service Corps.

To the astonishment of most of those who formed part of the procession the number of persons assembled to witness it was almost ridiculously small, and popular indignation roared as gently as a sucking dove. In their own opinion the most law abiding of Her Majesty's subjects, the Ballinrobe folk indulged but very slightly in goading or hissing, and when the little army got clear of the town its sole followers were a couple of cars, a market cart, and a private gig driven by a lady, the tag-rag and bobtail being made up of a dozen bare-legged girls, whose scoffs and jeers never went beyond the inquiry, 'Wad ye dig auld Boycott's praties, thin?' There was no wit or humour racy of the soil, no flashes of bitter sarcasm, no pungent observations: everybody felt that the thing was going off like a damp firework, and that, bating the 'Dead March' from Saul, it was very like a funeral. Still, those who ought to know declared that the absence of any demonstration was in itself a bad sign. Hardly any men were seen on the line of march, but it was said that scouts were on every hill, and that pains were being taken to identify the Orangemen. It was also heard on the best authority that Mr. Ruttledge's herds had been threatened and ordered to quit his service by the mysterious agency which rules the rural mind of Mayo.

Silently, except for an occasional laugh or two from a colleen standing by the wayside, we kept the line of march towards Lough Mask. At the village, standing on two townlands, a few more spectators hove in sight, but at no point could more than a dozen be counted. As the sun now shone through the western sky it revealed a picturesque as well as interesting scene.

Like a huge red serpent with black head and tail, the convoy wound gradually up a slight hill, the scarlet thrown into relief by the long line of grey walls on either side, beyond which lay green fields and clumps of trees dyed with the myriad hues of autumn, the distance being filled in by the purple mountains beyond Lough Mask. Presently came the angle which marks the extremity of Captain Boycott's land. Taking the road to the right, we approached the house under ban, and around which a crowd of peasants had been expected. The only human beings in sight were the police guarding the entrance by the lodge, and those stationed near the hut on a slight eminence to the right. Here the surrounding trees contrasted vividly with the animated and highly coloured scenes beneath. Completely enclosed by foliage was an encampment of the most picturesque kind.

On the greenest of all possible fields in front of the tents the officers commanding the escort, the leaders of the Ulster Brigade, and the resident magistrates were received by Mr. Boycott, who appeared in a dark shooting-dress and cap, and carried a double-barrelled gun in his hand. A little further on stood Mrs. Boycott and her nephew and niece, the house itself seeming almost deserted. The workmen, like the troopers, formed in line, and appeared to be equally well armed.

Presently the arduous task of stowing the uninvited Northern contingent was undertaken. The troops, who had remained on the ground all night, and had been reduced to straits by the failure of the commissariat, had, after some reflection and the exercise of considerable patience, taken care of themselves as best they might. Sheep had been slain, and chickens and geese had lent savoury aid to the banquet of the warriors, who also, in the absence of other fuel, were constrained to make short work of Lord Erne's trees. But they had done their work cheerfully in the cold and wet, and had pitched tents for the Ulster men. When the belligerent 'agriculturists' came to be told off into these tents an amusing difficulty, illustrative of the light handling necessary to the conduct of affairs in Ireland, interrupted the dullness which had hitherto oppressed all present.

Those 'agriculturists,' who hailed from Cavan insisted that they would foregather only with Cavan men, while the men of Monaghan were equally indisposed to give a Cavan man 'as much space as a lark could stand on' in their tents. Moreover some jealousy was exhibited as to the situation and furniture of the tents assigned to the two wings of the army of relief. At last harmony was restored, and the edifying spectacle of Cavan and Monaghan fighting it out then and there, while Mayo looked on, was averted, greatly to the sorrow of a Mayo friend of mine, whose eyes sparked and whose mouth watered at the delicious prospect.

It seems that Mr. Boycott, fully aware of the feelings of Mayo folk after having Orangemen set on them, is about to leave the country, at least for a while, after his crop has been got in – probably a rational decision on his part. Meanwhile he is having a hard time of it between friends and foes. His enemies have spoiled a great part of his crop, and what they have left his defenders threaten to devour.

40. William Sime, *To and Fro, or Views from Sea and Land*   (London: Stock, 1884, pp. 65–71)

William Sime was born in Wick, Scotland, in 1851. Author of *King Capital: a Tale of Provincial Ambition* (1883), and *Cradle and Spade* (1886), he worked as a journalist in Glasgow, and later for the *Weekly Despatch* and *St. James's Gazette* in London. He moved to join the staff of the *Calcutta Statesman* in 1893, where he died only eighteen months later, in 1895. *To and Fro* contains several Mediterranean narratives in addition to his 'Notes from Ireland', which are all dated November 1880.

Saturday is the day to come upon Athlone, for it is then you see the population which has swarmed in from the margin of Lough Ree and for several miles down the banks of the Shannon. As you pass onward from the station, you find the roadway between the Shannon and the high wall of the barracks lined with donkey-carts, from which the farmers, and their wives and daughters are dispensing peats, pigs, and cabbages. It is not easy to tell when you are inside Athlone. The impression it gives is that of a town shut out from itself; for, following the barrack-wall, you are brought face to face, on the Connaught side of the town bridge, with a high keep. The space between the keep and the barracks is the market place, from the dingy rear of which the streets burrow their way uphill, narrow and circuitous. On Saturday the market place is full, the long line of peat-carts gathered together there in a confusion of groups – farmers, tidily dressed in rimless hats of a chocolate hue, with faded coats and tight gaiters; farmers' wives hooded from head to heels in dark cloaks, and their daughters, brown-eyed, open mouthed, and rosy, showing green horticulture instead of plumage in their smart hats. The chaffering is done very quietly to day; for tomorrow there is a Land League meeting, and it may be conjectured, from the look of them, that politics are fully as much in their minds as merchandise. At any rate, there is a subdued air about the buying and selling, as if a general consciousness of something else were present. It can hardly be the score or two of red figures on the parapets of the castle, who are looking down into the market place, that gives so serious a turn to their business. They have been there from time immemorial, and between the market and the parapets much English and Irish mirth has been indulged. Only today it has been whispered the garrison is rather stronger than it has been for a year or two, and the red coats who look over have no local ties. And it is a certainty that the strength of the constabulary has been increased by a hundred and fifty. In speaking to one of the smart upright men in dark uniform and short sword, he will admit that he has been served with charges of buckshot, though he hopes not to have to use them.

On the whole, however, Athlone, to be the scene of a land meeting on the morrow, is as decorous as it can well be. What impresses one most about the people as they swarm off from the market place, and cross the great bridge to the Leinster side of the town and block up the doorways of the shops, is their well-to-do appearance. If they are possessed with a revolutionary idea about the land, it sits upon them in the most prosperous style. To have attired themselves, as they have done, in the sound and gaudy second-hand raiments they exhibit, shows that they are definitely out of reach of the starving point. To look at the general aspect of health and robustness, it is obvious that in and around Athlone, at least, the demand for the land is not based upon hunger. If they want it, they want it for some other reason than that, under the present system, it starves them. One has only to see the district round about Athlone in company with people who have known it for a general, to understand why it is that the market place can produce a population so little like the starved and ragged wretches that are so often presented to the imagination. There is the Connaught side and the Leinster side; and though there is but a river between them, there is much variety in the character of the farming. It is from the Leinster side that the market place takes its look of general prosperity. Lord Castlemaine's tenants are mostly on that side; and though some of them have holdings of no larger area than four acres, the majority of them farm to the extent of ten, fifteen, or twenty. A walk on the Leinster side, under proper guidance, opens up the landscape in a very instructive way. It is, no doubt, an exceptional portion of Ireland. Country houses are frequent, and they are occupied. The tenants have thus in their midst a spectacle of comfort and tidiness to which they even try to adapt themselves according to their powers. And they do it, too, as one plainly sees in the snug, tight thatching of the whitewashed houses, or the neatness of the cabbage plots. On the road towards Auburn it would be impossible to say one was not in a land of plenty. To the east of Athlone one winds up a slope where, now and then, there are avenues of trees not yet stripped, and with the light of the sun bringing out the burnished bronze of their leaves. Lough Ree spreads its waters, grey and shivering in the November light, round shores which are either lined with thickets or bare edges of ridge. If it were not for the rolling expanses of brown bog-land on the east, the scene might be English. Taking a farmer's home at random, however, and putting some questions to him, it comes out that the bog-lands in the neighbourhood of

Athlone can only be spoken of in terms of praise. This year the harvest of hard peat has been of the best, and the stacks at the houses show that there is abundance of fuel for the coming winter. So it has been, too, with the corn crops all over the district. But Athlone, they say, standing by itself, is no index to prosperity in any other part of Ireland. Prosperous as they are, however, they are Land Leaguers to a man: only, to their credit be it said, they have no record of assassinations against them. There have been no outrages, no mutilations; and though threatening letters have frequently been exhibited, an authority who passed some of them through his hands gives the opinion that they were written by the persons who professed to receive them, with the object of abating rent. As for the rents in the neighbourhood of Athlone, those of them which have been asked for have, it is said, generally been paid without difficulty. On the Connaught side of the river, where the holdings are smaller, tenants are offering at 'Griffith's valuation'; and if any difficulty should arise at all, it will be in that direction.

Athlone in the morning of the land meeting is unnaturally quiet. Before the farmers have come in from the outlying districts, and while the church bells are pealing, one compact body of constabulary patrols the street with a measured tread, just to remind people, as it were, that force can be met with force. During the night the narrow streets on both sides of the river have been festooned with devices. 'Welcome to T. P. O'Connor,' says one of them, in gilt letters, in a lane just behind the garrison; while others of them express various patriotic and agrarian aspirations. Looking up and down the river from the central bridge, there is an ominous absence of life. The soldiers are not allowed to show themselves, so that the parapets display not a single red coat. When the constabulary have patrolled once they do it no more, so that the town is left to gather its groups by slow degrees, as the hour advances for the meeting. Among the flats below the town, where the poplar trees are, there are wreaths of fog on the river. It is there the stream goes over its banks, giving Dutch work to the small cottiers. By-and-by one unknown face after another shows in the windows and at the doors. At the bridge end burly men in woollen coats, with a 'hold the harvest', in their hats, stand talking; little boys, with a sash and a medal of Mr. Parnell, come out to enjoy the excitement. A thousand Parnell medals, it is said, have been struck and sold in the town for the day's wear. The time passes with a trumpeting of brass bands, the performers striving to cleave their instruments with wind. When the music stops there is a noise of cheering, which increases in volume and frequency, until a waggonette passes through to the Green, where a platform has been raised, and to which amidst the rain, farmers have been coming in their hundreds. Some of them, they say, have made a forty miles' journey of it to hear the leader; but the forty thousand that were expected have not all come. Various estimates are made. A skilled eye at the barracks calculates the number at two thousand; a clergyman accustomed to open-air congregations says half that number, and so forth. There are, at all events, enough to send up a great roar of welcome as the speakers step forward. But it is not all dead earnest, even after the proceedings commence. The Irish farmers want to have their land to themselves, and even come long distances in the rain to hear Mr. Parnell tell them how it is to be got; only they must have their laugh when occasion offers. To start with, there is a certain comic effect in the sudden disappearance of the centre of the platform with its load of orators. Some of the farmers enjoy the joke amazingly, and they laugh again when they see how much of the agitation is done for them by pantomimic gesture. The outside edge of the farmers hear little that goes on; but they show their sympathy with, every now and then, 'To hell with the landlords!' The women who are there are most enthusiastic; and a striking thing is that whole families are together, old and young, standing in rapt expectation to learn how they are to be delivered from rent. The audience is very much the market of the previous day, though, in addition to farmers, there are hangers-on who can have but little interest in the meeting, because they are too poor to hold any land. And it is a remarkable fact that it is the stout, well-clad farmer, with a jovial countenance, who responds to the denunciation of the landlords with hostile cries. It occurs to one, consequently, in looking from the landless hangers-on to the mole-skinned and woollen-coated farmers, that the cheers of the latter for Mr. Parnell are much of the same stamp as a body of shareholders might give to a chairman of a company moving a successful dividend. They cheer him with their hands at their pockets, feeling apparently that he is doing a stroke of finance for them. And they are enthusiastic enough. Many of them in their enthusiasm do not hesitate to say that Parnell – or 'Parnle,' as they call him – is a greater leader than O'Connell.

41. Henry Spenser Wilkinson, *The Eve of Home Rule: Impressions of Ireland in 1886* (London: Kegan Paul, 1886, pp. 1–6)

Henry Spenser Wilkinson (1853–1937) was an author, journalist and drama critic. Born in Manchester, educated at Oxford where he studied law, Wilkinson practised briefly, before taking up a post on the staff of the *Manchester Guardian*. Employed as Drama Critic for *The Morning Post*, he was an authority on military and naval matters, and became Professor of Military History at All Souls College, Oxford. Wilkinson also published *Citizen Soldiers* (1884), *Essays on the War Game* (1887), and *The Nation's Awakening* (1896), amongst others.

Ballaghaderreen, County Mayo, February 8th, 1886. Castlereagh, on the railway from Athlone to Westport, affords a convenient starting-point for reaching the eastern corner of Mayo, and from Castlereagh I started yesterday morning at five to Ballaghaderreen – about ten miles. A degree of dampness varying between mist and rain seemed to furnish the landscape with a congenial climate, and the crab-like motion of an Irish car, on which the traveller progresses sideways, afforded a convenient panorama of the country. The first few miles offer no striking features; one might be driving along an English country lane.

After about three-quarters of an hour we pass a straggling village called Loughglinn, just as the first few groups of peasants coming to Mass are entering from the country. As we leave the village and turn northwards the road before us becomes visible for a couple of miles in advance. It is no longer a lonely road. As far as the eye can reach it is covered by groups of peasants – men, women and children – coming to Mass at Loughglinn. I had noticed before that most of the country was bog. It was like Chat Moss, irregularly spread over a broken stony tract, and interspersed with straggling lakelets and rivulets in flood. But here and there a clump of trees or a thickset hedge had given variety to the scene, and prevented one's realising by a sweep of the eye the character of the soil. Just at this turn, however, when a populace seemed to spring suddenly out of the earth, the earth manifestly declared itself as barren rock coated with bog or flooded with water.

'Where do all these people come from?' I asked myself, and scanned the landscape. These cottages by the roadside are but one in every three or four hundred yards, and there is neither town nor village for miles. A bend in the road and a dip in the lie of the ground explained it. The cottages were everywhere. In every direction were cottages. Scattered all over the ground at irregular intervals of two or three hundred yards one from another were low whitewashed thatched buildings. They were incredibly small – smaller even than the little cots in which just below the snow line the Alpine cowherds tend their cattle in the summer. But the toylike appearance of the Alpine chalets was wanting. Evidently it is a country of small-holdings.

But what do the people live on? I have seen but one ploughed field since starting; hardly a bit of healthy looking green, miles of peat cuttings, and here and there half an acre of young cabbages preparing for transplantation. The whole aspect of the country was strange. I felt myself entirely without data for comparison, and a multitude of questions were exciting my speculations when we drove into the 'town' of Ballaghaderreen, a village formed by two rows of houses, one on each side of the road, for a length of about half a mile.

At Ballaghaderreen a hospitable welcome awaited me, and early in the afternoon I was on the road again, this time under competent guidance, to look more closely at some of the small-holdings. The road led up into the hills, on to a tract of what would in any other country be bleak and desolate moorland. The top of Kinderscout or the moors on the hills that surround the Woodhead Valley are the comparisons suggested by the landscape, though the moors here are only five or six hundred feet above the sea level.

But these Irish wilds differ from the English ones. In England the moors are a vast solitude. Here they are covered with habitations, and are the home of a large population. As far as we can see, that during the whole length of our drive, we find the hillside sprinkled with cottages, and the ground divided by low stone and turf fences into innumerable fields. Each of these fields has been won from the bog by years of infinite labour. First the peat has been cut away; then the space thus obtained has been filled with gravel, and a mixture of soils made such as enables a scanty crop to be obtained. But wherever such a field is neglected for a while the bog reclaims its rights, and rushes, shooting up through the surface soil, to challenge the husbandman to resume his work or to abandon to its primitive barrenness his hard-won plot. Many a pile of stones, carefully built, stands as a monument to the industry which first separated the rocks from the soil, while deep cuttings traverse the bog in every direction and help to carry off the water, which in this moist climate oppresses by its superfluity.

After a drive of some five miles through this strange contrast between wild nature and struggling humanity, the car stopped where a miserable footpath left the road at right angles. 'Shall we go along the boreen?' said Father Dennis, the parish priest, whose car had brought us;

and along the boreen, or sidepath, we picked our way to the first of a group of cottages which here studded the hillside.

Father Dennis is spiritually, morally and intellectually the father of the whole parish. For miles around he knows every man, woman and child. For each he has a word of friendly greeting, and it is evident from the bright smile which his appearance brings into every face that he is beloved and trusted by all. With ready kindness he had offered to accompany me to any point in his district, and to throw over me in my visits to the people the aegis of his friendship, so that they might speak in my presence freely. Another friend was with us, my host, who, though not a minister of religion, is none the less 'beloved by all the countryside'. I was convinced beforehand that an Englishman, unless he goes under such assuring auspices, would entirely fail in any attempt to gain the confidence of the country people, and all that I have seen and hear confirms this conviction.

A hundred yards along the broken footpath brought us to the first cottage. The tenant, a healthy clear-eyed man of six and thirty, stood in front of the door and welcomed my friends. At once he began, unasked, to tell them the story of his rent. The tenants on the estate to which he belonged had, it appears, agreed to act together in refusing payment unless a reduction of half a year's rent were agreed to. The agent offered a reduction of 15 per cent, which they refused, and he began to 'process' them. At once the combination broke down; the weaker vessels paid at the first sight of a process, and then one by one the others followed suit, so that practically all the rents have been paid except in some fifty cases, where the money is beyond the tenants' power to raise. Our sturdy tenant appeared ashamed of himself. He evidently felt that he had done a mean thing as he said, 'I've paid the rint, sorr, £5–£4.10s., for the year's rint, and 10s. for costs.' He explained that the holding was of 14 acres, of which he had half and his brother half, the total rent being £9.

The borders of the plot were pointed out, and a more miserable piece of land eyes never saw. It had been an undrained mass of bog and rock; years of labour had given it the appearance of fields, and portions of it had borne potatoes and possibly oats. But a strong imagination would be needed to see value in it.

42. Paschal Grousset, *Ireland's Disease: the English in Ireland, 1887*

(first published 1887; 2nd edn, Belfast: Blackstaff 1986, pp. 215–18; translator P. Grousset)

Paschal Grousset (1844–1909) was born in Corsica, but educated in Paris, where he studied medicine. A journalist and communist, he was sent to Ireland as Special Correspondent by the French newspaper, *Le Temps*, making two trips, the first in the summer of 1886, and the second in the summer of 1887. The full text, which reproduces most of the original *Le Temps* articles, was a success in Britain and France, although some controversy was aroused. This extract dates from the summer of 1887.

From Kilrush, on the coast of Clare, an excellent service of steamers goes up the estuary of the Shannon to Foynes, where one takes the train to Limerick. It is a charming excursion, undertaken by all tourists. The Shannon here is of great breadth and majesty, flowing in an immense sheet of water, recalling the aspect of the great rivers of America. At the back you have the stormy ocean; in front, on the right, on the left, green hills dotted with snowy villas. Few trees or none, as is the rule in Ireland, but a light haze that softens all the outlines of the ground, magnifies the least shrubs, and lends to all the view a melting aspect of striking loveliness.

The boats are few in number, though the depth of the channel would allow ships of the heaviest tonnage to go up to within five miles of Limerick. I notice hardly two or three sailing boats at anchor on this four hours' journey. What an admirable harbour for an active commerce would be that broad estuary, opening directly opposite to America, on the extreme point of the European continent. It is the natural point of arrival and departure for the Transatlantic steamers, which would reach New York in five days from there. Engineers have dreamed of this possibility. But to justify a maritime movement, and legitimise such enterprise, a great commerce, an industry that Ireland lacks, would be wanted. Gentlemen of an engineering turn, come back again in a century or two.

At Tarbert, where we stop to take passengers, a fort opens its loopholes, armed with guns, on the river. Redcoats are encamping at the foot of the fortress, and the morning breeze carries to us the rough voice of a non-commissioned officer drilling his men. One might imagine him addressing the *Invincibles* across the ocean somewhat after this guise:

'Here we are, keeping watch: If ever this alluring bay tempt you to come over, you shall find us ready to receive you!' ....

The helm trembles; the boat goes on its course, and soon Tarbert melts behind us in the sunny haze.

On board, the travellers resemble those seen in summer on all great rivers – merchants bent on a pleasure trip; judges and barristers, having taken leave of briefs; professors enjoying their holidays, with wives, daughters, sons, goods, and chattels – all have the sun-burnt complexion and the satisfied look one brings back from the seaside. They have been staying on the beautiful shores of the County Clare, and are returning home with a provision of health for one year. La Fontaine has already noticed that, travelling, one is sure to see 'the monk poring over his breviary'. Here the proportion is far greater than in the ancient coach; it is not one priest we have on board, but a dozen, all sleek, fat, and prosperous, dressed in good stout broadcloth, as smooth as their rubicund faces, and provided with gold chains resting on comfortable abdomens.

One remark, by the way. When you meet an Irish peasant on the road, he stops, wishes you good-day, and adds, 'Please, sir, what is the time?' Not that he cares much to know. He is perfectly well able to read the time on the great clock of the heavens. But it is his own manner of saying, 'I can see, sir, that you are a man of substance – one of the great ones of this earth – *since you have a watch*. My sincere congratulations!'

Well, all those travelling priests possess chronometers – we are obliged to notice it, since it appears to be a sign of easy circumstances in Ireland – and the rest of their attire fully carries out that symptom. Under the undefinable cut that at once betrays a clerical garment, their black coat has all the softness of first quality cloth; their travelling bag is of good bright leather; their very umbrella has a look of smartness, and does not affect the lamentable droop that with us is always associated with the idea of a clerical umbrella. Some of them wear the Roman hat and collar, with a square-cut waistcoat and the ordinary trousers of the laity, and stockings of all the hues of the rainbow. A young curate sports violet-coloured ones, which he exhibits with some complacency. I ventured to ask him, in the course of conversation, whether he belonged to the Pope's household. He answered with a blush of modesty that he had not that honour, and wore violet hose because he was fond of that colour.

That is a matter of taste; but I have a right to suppose, young Levite, that the mitre and episcopal rochet – perhaps even the cardinal purple – hover at night over your ingenuous dreams.

43. William Henry Hurlbert, *Ireland under Coercion: the Diary of an American*

(2 vols, Edinburgh: Douglas, 1888, vol. II, pp. 203–08)

William Henry Hurlbert (1827-95) was born in Charleston, educated at Harvard, and became a journalist and writer. He worked as Drama Critic for *Albion Magazine* (1855–57), before moving for two years to work with the *New York Times*. In 1861 he was arrested in the South for his anti-slavery activities and imprisoned in Richmond, from where he escaped the following year. Author of one dramatic work – *Americans in Paris: or a Game of Dominoes* (1858) – Hurlbert died in Italy. This text is based on a series of visits Hurlbert made to Ireland between January and June of 1888.

Dublin, Thursday, March 8. At eight o'clock this morning I left the Harcourt Street station for Inch, to take a look at the scene of the Coolgreany evictions of last summer. These evictions came of the adoption of the Plan of Campaign, under the direction of Mr. Dillon, M.P., on the Wexford property of Mr. George Brooke of Dublin. The agent of Mr. Brooke's estate, Captain Hamilton, is the honorary director of the Property Defence Association, so that we have here obviously a grapple between the National League doing the work, consciously or unconsciously, of the agrarian revolutionists, and a combination of landed properties fighting for the rights of property as they understand them.

We ran through a beautiful country for the greater part of the way. At Bray, which is a favourite Irish watering-place, the sea broke upon us bright and full of life; and the station itself was more like a considerable English station than any I have seen. Thence we passed into a richly wooded region, with neat, well-kept hedges, as far as Rathdrum and the 'Sweet Vale of Avoca'. The hills about Shillelagh are particularly well forested, though, as the name suggests, they must have been cut for cudgels pretty extensively for now a great many years. We came again on the sea at the fishing port of Arklow, where the stone walls about the station were populous with small ragamuffins, and at the station of Inch I found a car waiting for me with Mr. Holmes, a young English Catholic officer, who had most obligingly offered to show me the place and the people. We had hardly got into the roadway when we overtook a most intelligent looking, energetic young priest, walking briskly on in the direction of our course. This was Dr. Dillon, the curate of Arklow. We pulled up at once, and Mr. Holmes, introducing me to him, we begged him to take a seat with us. He excused himself as having to join another priest with whom he was going to a function at Inch; but he was good enough to walk a little way with us, and gave me an appointment for

2 p.m., at his own town of Arklow, where I could catch the train back to Dublin. We drove on rapidly and called on Father O'Neill, the parish priest. We found him in full canonicals, as he was to officiate at the function this morning, and with him were Father Dunphy, the parish priest of Arklow, and two or three more robed priests.

Father O'Neill, whose face and manner are those of the higher order of the continental clergy, briefly set forth to me his view of the transactions at Coolgreany. He said that before the Plan of Campaign was adopted by the tenants, Mr. William O'Brien, M.P., had written to him explaining what the effect of the Plan would be, and urging him to take whatever steps he could to obviate the necessity of adopting it, as it might eventually result to the disadvantage of the tenants. 'To that end,' said Father O'Neill, 'I called upon Captain Hamilton, the agent, with Dr. Dillon of Arklow, but he positively refused to listen to us, and in fact ordered us, not very civilly, to leave his office.'

It was after this he said that he felt bound to let the tenants take their own way. Eighty of them joined in the 'Plan of Campaign' and paid the amount of the rent due, less a reduction of 30 per cent, which they demanded of the agent, into the hands of Sir Thomas Esmonde, M.P., Sir Thomas being a resident in the country, and Mr. Mayne, M.P. Writs of ejectment were obtained against them afterwards, and in July last sixty-seven of them were evicted, who are now living in 'Land League huts', put up on the holdings of three small tenants who were exempted from the Plan of Campaign, and allowed to pay their rents subject to a smaller reduction made by the agent, in order that they might retain their land as a refuge for the rest.

All this Father O'Neill told us very quietly, in a gentle, undemonstrative way, but he was much interested when I told him I had recently come from Rome, where these proceedings, I was sure, were exciting a good deal of serious attention. 'Yes,' he said, 'and Father Dunphy who is here in the other room, has just got back from Rome, where he had two audiences of the Holy Father.'

'Doubtless, then,' I said, 'he will have given His Holiness full particulars of all that took place here.'

'No doubt,' responded Father O'Neill, 'and he tells me the Holy Father listened with great attention to all he had to say – though of course, he expressed no opinion about it to Father Dunphy.'

As the time fixed for the function was at hand, we were obliged to leave without seeing Father Dunphy.

From the Presbytery we drove to the scene of the evictions. These evictions were in July. Mr. Holmes witnessed them, and gave me a lively account of the affair. The 'battle' was not a very tough one. Mr. Davitt, who was present, stood under a tree very quietly watching it all. 'He looked very picturesque,' said Mr. Holmes, 'in a light grey suit, with a broad white beaver shading his dark Spanish face; and smoked his cigar very composedly.' After it was over, Dr. Dillon brought up one of the tenants, and presented him to Mr. Davitt as 'the man who had resisted this unjust eviction'. Mr. Davitt took his cigar from his lips, and in the hearing of all who stood about sarcastically said, 'Well, if he couldn't make a better resistance than that he ought to go up for six months!' The first house we came upon was derelict – all battered and despoiled, the people in the neighbourhood here, as elsewhere, regarding such houses as free spoil, and carrying off from time to time whatever they happen to fancy. Near this house we met an emergency man, named Bolton, an alert, energetic-looking native of Wicklow. He has four brothers; and is now at work on one of the 'evicted' holdings.

I asked if he was 'boycotted,' and what his relations were with the people.

He laughed in a shrewd, good-natured way. 'Oh, I'm boycotted, of course,' he said; 'but I don't care a button for any of these people, and I'd rather they wouldn't speak to me. They know I can take care of myself, and they give me a good wide berth. All I have to object to is that they set fire to an outhouse of mine, and cut the ears of one of my heifers, and for that I want damages. Otherwise I'm getting on very well; and I think this will be a good year, if the law is enforced, and these fellows are made to behave themselves.'

44. Arthur Bennett, *John Bull And His Other Island*   (4 vols, London: Simpkin, 1890, vol. II, pp. 219–29)

Arthur Bennett (1862–1931) was born in Warrington, and although by profession a chartered accountant, was an antiquarian, fellow of the Royal Empire Society, and author of *Travels in Norway* (1877) and *The Dream of an Englishman* (1893). This extract, which conveys the sectarian nature of much of Belfast life, reveals a narrator at once both sensitive to Irish difficulties, and at the same time horrified by the long-term implications of religious conflict. In the accompanying prefatory note Bennett informs us that it was written in 1886.

At last, we crossed the Brickfields and reached Falls Road, their southern boundary. Here, quite recently, a combat terrific in its magnitude had raged. It had commenced with the gradual assembling of a crowd of roughs who apparently expected an attack from the Shankhill party. The roads were strewn with the relics of former struggles, and, singular as it may appear, only two policemen were on duty in the neighbourhood at the time, so that the circumstances were favourable for a gigantic riot. Presently a small party of men and boys were seen to be approaching from the direction of Shankhill, and at once they were wildly assailed. They stood their ground. Their allies thronged from every street to aid them, and their assailants multiplied as if by magic, and soon the whole strength of the two parties was engaged. The five streets abutting on the Brickfields were packed with mobs as fierce as tigers; the open space itself was one grim battleground; and it was said that never in the memory of the oldest inhabitant had such a spectacle been seen before. Backwards and forwards the rival forces swayed as now the one prevailed and now the other; the air was thick with flying stones and whistling bullets, and the night was riven with shouts of anger and with shrieks of pain. Soon a small body of police arrived, but they were quite powerless; and, though they were rapidly reinforced, the tumult still continued, and upon their heads the frenzy of the crowd was turned. They boldly fought their way between the conflicting mobs, and many of them were badly wounded. Anon they would succeed in driving the rioters back, but shots were fired from the surounding streets, and in almost every by-way minor feuds were raging; and again and again the struggle in the open would commence anew. The rain fell in torrents, but so strongly were the passions of the populace aroused that they forgot to heed it now, and seemed to lose all reason in the uncontrollable fury of the hour. At last a squadron of the Guards appeared, and they were promptly followed by 200 infantry; and, as they formed across the Brickfields, the rioters slowly retreated; but several charges had to be made before the side streets were cleared, and the shouts and cheers of the hostile factions gradually died away in the distance.

And now we noticed that, upon this very spot, another crowd was gathering, and had already attained proportions that were positively alarming. Were they about to fulfil their challenge and meet their enemies and fight it out? Were we going to witness another struggle as desperate as the last? No wonder that we watched the threatening multitude with keen anxiety; for every moment its numbers grew, and its demeanour was ominous to a degree. My guide declined to proceed any further, and well he might, for beyond the road lay the stronghold of the Catholics, and strange tales were told of the fate that had befallen those of either party who were rash enough to trespass on the enemy's domain. But here we lingered, watching every movement of the crowd, and momentarily expecting the discharge of a volley of paving stones, or the rattle of arms to resound upon the dull afternoon air. What might have been the issue of the incident, I cannot say, for at this juncture, and just as the crisis appeared to be approaching, we saw that, through the doors of an adjacent building, a body of soldiers were making; and, in a few seconds, with measured tread, a portion of the Black Watch strode down the steps and into the street, just opposite to the scene of the commotion; and, at the sight of them, the multitude began to dwindle with even greater rapidity than that with which it had assembled, and, as we turned abruptly to recross the Brickfields, and retrace our steps to Shankhill Road, had almost disappeared.

In the course of our ramble, my attention was particularly directed to the window of a spirit vaults, at which a girl was said to have been shot dead in sheer recklessness; and, close at hand, was a fruiterer's, the window panes of which were simply riddled with rifle shots, the police standing, so my informant declared, at the end of an adjoining street and firing blindly when the thoroughfare was quite clear, though luckily, in this instance, no one was injured, notwithstanding the fact that there were people in the shop at the time. He was terribly severe upon the police, who had enraged the inhabitants to such an extent that their reappearance in the district was expected to be the signal for a fearful outbreak. The Orangemen, he said, were not implicated in the outrages at all – only the scum of the town had, as yet, joined in the struggle, but so strong was the local feeling that he expected that they would turn out in all their strength if it continued much longer, and then the results would be appalling. Evidently they had his entire sympathy in this, and might have counted, if necessary, upon his active co-operation. He had himself, on several occasions, been in imminent danger; and once had been obliged to run for very life amid a shower of stones and bricks and bullets. In spite of his strong sympathy with the Orange cause, he appeared to be, by nature, a peaceable and respectable citizen; and he pointed out to me that the houses in his own quarter were of a thoroughly substantial character, and altogether superior to the generality of the residences of the Nationalist community. Among the latter, the police were comparatively safe; but the Protestant population absolutely hated them, and this, so they all averred, not because they were the representatives of the law, but because they had abused their powers and acted with partiality, as a result of which many a home was darkened by the shadow of bereavement. The soldiers, on the contrary, were prime favourites, and the inhabitants fraternised with them in the most hearty manner imaginable, and brought them food and tea, and did all they could to show that for them, at least, thus far, they had nothing but goodwill.

My own opinion was that, while the police might, in isolated instances, have acted indiscreetly, the sweeping charges which were brought against them were altogether unreasonable; and that, if the people desired the luxury of a periodical free fight, it was absurd of them to expect to escape scot-free. Party feeling, however, appeared to have completely blinded them. The Commissioners appointed to investigate the matter stated that 'the evidence leads us to believe that the riots, at a very early period, and certainly from and after the 8th June, assumed, to a great extent, the aspect of a determined attack by the Protestant mobs upon the police, and upon the places of business of Catholics residing in Protestant quarters of the town.' ... Of course, there were retaliation and faults on both sides; but, so far as we can judge from the evidence, twenty-eight public houses owned by Catholics were assailed and looted during the course of the riots, and only one or two public houses owned by Protestants. This state of affairs may, to a considerable extent, be accounted for by the fact that the vast majority of public houses in Belfast are owned by Catholics; and that, when rioting once begins, those engaged in the pursuit are but too prone to attack any house in which intoxicating drinks can be procured; but, at the same time, these incidents seemed to show, and we have arrived at the opinion, that, for a considerable period, at all events from the 8th of June to the 19th September, the principal actors in the rioting were what is known as the 'Protestant mob'. They ascribe their exceeding bitterness to the unfortunate suspicion to which I have already referred, and proceed to demonstrate its utter groundlessness, and to entirely exonerate the police from blame. 'We are of opinion,' they say, 'that they were subjected to almost unparalleled trials; that they passed well through the ordeal; that nothing occurred during the riots to impair the high reputation which the Royal Irish Constabulary has at all times borne for courage, discipline, and humanity; and that the charge made against the police of having acted with cruelty towards Protestants from sectarian motives was proved to be without a shadow of foundation. The police acted towards both sides with the strictest impartiality, and if crowds on one side suffered more severely than on the other, it was owing to the following of their own persistence in attacks upon the police.' They suggest a number of alterations in the local police arrangements, but significantly add 'that alterations in the law or in its administration cannot produce the complete good results we desire until a great change takes place in public opinion in Belfast. We earnestly hope and trust one beneficial effect of the recent riots and of our enquiry will be to render all classes of the population of Belfast thoroughly ashamed of the disgrace these disturbances have brought upon their great and prosperous town; and that they will combine by every conceivable exertion, public and private, to terminate the disastrous feuds and bitter animosities which now prevail in Belfast, and to avert the renewal of such calamitous and disgraceful transactions as it has been our duty to investigate.'

To all of which I heartily say ditto; but that these 'disastrous feuds and bitter animosities' do exist is only too evident, and less serious measures than the establishment of a Parliament in Dublin might fan them to a sevenfold flame. To regret the fact is the duty of every peaceful citizen. To ignore it is the function of the men who ask us to 'Remember Mitchelstown!'

Before I returned, my companion offered to conduct me through Old Lodge Road, and show me McKenna's public-house, about which the whole of England had been talking as we left. This road, like Falls Road, was nearly parallel with Shankhill Road, and, after recrossing the latter, and turning up a side street, we were almost immediately over-taken by a mounted soldier, who spurred his horse along at a rapid rate right in the direction in which we were going.

'There's something up, or he wouldn't be hurrying like that!' said my guide.

We walked on, and presently entered another long street, in many respects resembling Falls and Shankhill Roads – the same poor houses and shops and spirit stores, and, just before us, a large building the windows of which were broken and boarded up, and everything about the place in a state of complete dilapidation. This was the whisky-store of Stephen McKenna, in which, on the night of Saturday, the 7th of August, a number of policemen were quartered, and from which they had fired upon the crowd, who assailed them with the fury of madmen, and flung all manner of missiles against the doors and windows; while, on Shankhill Road, and in all the neighbouring streets, the mob united in attacking them and their allies, and a struggle, terrific in its magni-tude, raged for hours.

A similar scene occurred on the following day, when, once again, from the shelter of the store, the police discharged their rifles, with fatal effect. The firing on the two occasions resulted in the death of five persons and the wounding of some twenty-five besides. An apothecary's shop had been pointed out to me as having been crowded, on these memorable occasions, with the wounded and the dying.

We did not see any more of the mounted soldier, and could not hear of any disturbance; and so we sauntered on to the upper end of Peter's Hill. Parting from my guide, at this point, with many thanks for his kindness, I retraced my way up bustling North Street, with its multitude of small shops and eager housewives, laying in their stores for the weekend, and pictured to myself the spectacle which the street must have presented when, as the Islandmen returned from their work, in rough procession, they were assailed by the inhabitants with stones and bottles and brickbats, and, gaining with a rush the end of Peter's Hill, rallied, and retaliated with a double ferocity hurling iron bolts at their adversaries, the rival crowds approaching each other, with murder in their eyes, until, at last, the military appeared, and, with fixed bayonets, charged them, and, assisted by the constabulary, succeeded in reducing them to submission.

With these terrible scenes fresh in their memory, and liable, at any moment, to recur, it is not surprising that the people should wear a stern demeanour; that quiet folk should studiously avoid this quarter; and that the most active and enterprising town in Ireland had, for several weeks, experienced all the haunting uncertainty of a modern Reign of Terror.

45. Madame [Marie Anne] de Bovet, *Three Months' Tour in Ireland*

(first published 1891; first English translation, London: Chapman, 1891, pp. 109–13; translator A. Walter)

Marie Anne de Bovet was a successful biographer, novelist and travel writer who visited Ireland in 1888, and again in 1890, the latter trip resulting in *Trois Mois en Irlande*, which was first published in Paris by Hachette in 1891. This extract describes a meeting that took place in Waterford, with William O'Brien, editor of the Land League journal, *United Ireland*, speaking to a crowd estimated at 20,000. Hardly surprising that during the course of the day de Bovet 'never saw the helmet of a constable'.

Waterford is a charming halting-place for tourists. On the left bank of the Suir, covered with wooded hills and pleasant villas, are lovely shady walks. There are also plenty of excursions on the sea-coast. There is first the port of Dunmore, at the entrance to the bay, where a huge deserted jetty shelters empty docks. The cost was £100,000 sterling to protect a few pleasure boats and bathing machines. A large cromlech and Merlin's grotto constitute all the wealth of Dunmore. Opposite it, at the furthest point which shuts in the bay on the east, is the very ancient lighthouse of Hook, perched on a rock 150 feet above the sea. It is an old Danish tower whose venerable walls the Admiralty have disfigured by an abominable chess-board pattern in black and white. At the end of the little Bay of Tramore, to the south of Waterford, stretches a pretty beach, a small family Brighton, very unpretentious, where there are a few bathing machines for women, while the men simply undress in a cleft of the rock.

As in most Irish towns, the capital included, life for the inhabitants of Waterford is dull enough – no aristocracy, no upper middle class, little money, the horizon bounded by local politics. The county, of which it is the principal town, possesses no fewer than eleven newspapers.

I was lucky enough to be present at one of those grand popular out-of-door meetings which constantly keep alive the spirit of rebellion in Ireland. These 'monster meetings', as they are called here, are announced weeks beforehand in all the villages of the adjacent counties, by placards headed with the three cabalistic letters, I.N.L. – Irish National League, with the war-cry of the Nationalists at the foot, 'God save Ireland!' At two o'clock the ceremony began with a carnival procession. First a squadron of farmers on horseback with green scarves; then trade unions, football clubs in striped jerseys of many colours, temperance societies, rural branches of the League, with flying banners embroidered with sacred subjects on a green ground, preceded by trumpets blowing with more spirit than accuracy, and a big drum overpowered by sharp fifes whose grating sound is not really so very disagreeable; then came a car on which was enthroned a very pretty girl, dressed entirely in green, leaning on a harp, and personifying Erin; lastly, in several landaus, the Mayor and Corporation of Waterford accompanied the orators, of whom the principal were T.D. Sullivan, the poet member, and William O'Brien, a hero of the Nationalist party. This procession, accompanied by the noise of crackers and deafening hurrahs, made the circuit of the town, which was decorated with Irish, French and American flags – without an English one, of course – and with transparencies of Mr. Gladstone and Mr. Parnell swinging from the top of be-ribanded and garlanded poles.

On the hill of Ballybrocken was erected a rough wooded platform, decorated with evergreens and furnished with benches and chairs for the distinguished part of the audience – notables of the town with their wives, priests, journalists, a group of Liberal politicians of both sexes from England, come to see 'what sort of animals we look at close quarters', as an Irish member said to me, laughing. In the centre a massive table served as a rostrum. Half-a-dozen ragged men armed with long sticks prevented ordinary mortals from invading the reserved enclosure; proud of their office, they acquitted themselves bravely, and turned out intruders with rough blows and vehement oaths. Over this vast space, crowded together round the platform, were 20,000 eager listeners, mostly peasants, men, women and children.

By how many of those present could the orators hope to be heard? I have heard them put at one quarter, and I can easily believe it, at least as far as concerns Mr. O'Brien, one of the most singular speakers I have ever heard. But all paid the most profound attention. A responsive crowd, if ever there was one, easily moved, inflammable, quick-witted and keen, understanding every hint, warm in its demonstrations, and interrupting frequently with the savage vociferation which here takes the place of applause, or with furious groans for some detested name, that, for example, of Mr. Balfour, universally designated in the comic papers by the sobriquet of Clara. A mark of enthusiasm much in use here is a frantic twirling of handkerchiefs, generally dirty, held by one corner; when thousands of hands are simultaneously engaged in this manoeuvre the effect is most exhilarating. For three hours gushed the interminable Irish eloquence. William O'Brien first and foremost, with a vehemence of manner and a violence of expression contrasting curiously with the softness of his voice and the courtesy of his language off the platform. These passionate crowds require the eloquence of a tribune, and the Irish are past masters of the art. They smart for it sometimes. Absolute freedom of meeting is the corner-stone of British liberty, nevertheless the special repressive laws which the Government is obliged to enact in Ireland, allow it to prosecute the authors of speeches outrageously seditious. This time no consequence of the kind troubled the orators, but Mr. O'Brien was just released from a gaol in which he had been confined for four months, and was about to be imprisoned anew for a similar offence. Out of a hundred Irish Members of Parliament, there are generally half-a-dozen under lock and key. They find, it is true, some compensation in the intoxication of popularity and the sense of power. It is wonderful with what precision and dexterity they work the agitation, maintaining discipline among a people so excitable and so continually excited. In the course of this day, charged with the electricity of faction, I never saw the helmet of a constable; a reinforcement of 250 men arrived the previous evening, but at the insistence of the mayor, who undertook to preserve order if the police did not interfere, the sheriff kept them carefully concealed. In the evening, at a public dinner in the town-hall, two hundred persons assembled, and the speeches recommenced in the form of toasts, amid cheers and hurrahs without end, varied by national songs sung by some of the guests, – a sort of ballad more sentimental than heroic, the words trivial and the music worthless. At midnight they were still haranguing, but I had given it up, and long afterwards the noise of their acclamations kept me awake in my room at the Imperial Hotel. Waterford, however, does not often enjoy a fete like this. Ordinarily it shows deserted and silent streets, illuminated at nightfall by the electric lamps, provided by an enterprising municipality. There is no society, and amusements are scarce.

46. Mrs J.J. [Marietta] Lloyd, *A Trip to Ireland*
(Chicago: Donohue, 1893; pp. 91–94)

No biographical information could be found on Marietta Lloyd, who sailed from New York on 18 June 1885, and arrived at Queenstown harbour nine days later. This extract, which describes a visit to Castle Kiven, near Fermoy, County Cork, is notable less for the details of the castle's furnishings – which so impressed the narrator – than for the image of exuberant disrespect presented by the servant girls who worked there.

We were attracted out by the music of the little skylark, and soon made up our mind to take a ramble as far as we could walk; and so we started for Castle Kiven. We took the road east for a short distance, then north, viewing many fields of grain, potatoes, turnips, etc. We had traversed nearly a mile when we came to the lovely little 'Lodge' of Castle Kiven. As we approached, the lodge-keeper came out and asked us if we desired to visit the castle. We answered, it would be a pleasure to us; whereupon he unlocked the iron gate and admitted us. The gate was then swung to and fastened to its massive stone piers. We passed down the walk leading to the castle, which is a large and magnificently built mansion. We went up the granite steps, which are built in a half-circle, and rang the bell. It was answered by a woman who oversees the servants and attends to the reception of visitors. We were invited in and shown the different apartments, from the first floor to the top. The rooms were all artistically furnished and in a style differing greatly from our American.

We were first shown through the parlor, drawing room, dining room, ball room and silver closet, all on the first floor. In the ball room hung a crystal chandelier, of magnificent beauty, filled with wax tapers.

There was no furniture in this room but the stand for the musicians; it had a finely polished floor and snow-white walls.

In all the rest of the rooms were fire-places, and the mantel shelves contained many rich pieces of bric-a-brac; but what consisted of the most beauty were the curiously wrought candlesticks, which were conspicuous in every room, both above and below, and no two pair alike.

I did not see a lamp in any part of the castle. We followed our guide up the broad polished stairs to the second floor. Here we entered another parlor furnished in a different color from the one below, but just as elaborate. I will here make special mention of one room on this floor. As we entered it we were told it was the 'courting room'; we took a good survey of that room, wondering in our mind how many blissful courtships had been consummated in the midst of that elegance, and ended in a happy union. There were so many beautiful pieces of furniture in it, but one attracted our attention more than all the rest, not only for its elegance, but for its curious construction. It stood in the centre of the room, 'This is the courting chair,' said the old lady. It struck our admiration for we had seen no such special chair for that wonderful epoch in human events. We sat down in it for a while to see how it would seem to sit in a real courting chair. And I think who ever invented that chair knew what he was about.

There were four seats with cushioned arms between each seat, and it was so constructed that each two seats were in a half-circle, and the high backs were all brought together, making the chair round. It would be hard to excel either in beauty or elegance. We next visited the 'Bridal Chamber'; it was also furnished with elegance.

On one side was the master's dressing room, on the other side was the mistress' dressing room. The wardrobes belonging to these rooms were opened for our view, disclosing the richest wearing apparel and such a variety of toilets for the different occasions for which they were required. We were led from room to room, through little boudoirs all separated by rich portieres, and throughout the whole castle there was nothing but the air of extravagance, more noticeable on account of its being in the midst of those who had to toil to support it in such luxury. The last view of the interior was taken in passing out through the main hall. There hung all the equipments for the hunt and the chase, saddles, bridles, whips, horns, spurs, caps and coats. The boots we had noticed in the wardrobe; everything accorded with the rest of the castle in elegance.

Before leaving the castle, the servant girls gave us a slight exhibition of the chase; they were just brimful of mischief and while we were rambling through the castle they partially donned themselves for the chase by putting on coats, caps, riding whips and gloves, and taking the horns, they went through different rooms sounding the horns as in the chase, and when we came down to the first floor again, we were startled by the sound; then they started and ran through and through the halls blowing those old horns till there was a perfect confusion of noise. It created quite a merriment for a while, as the old lady was screeching for them to stop, but they never heeded her until they were ready to give up the chase, and then such laughing. We thanked them heartily for such an exhibition, if it was on foot and on a small scale too, as it gave us an opportunity of hearing the hunter's horn as used in the chase, and which we enjoyed very much.

47. Alfred Austin, *Spring and Autumn in Ireland*
(Edinburgh: Blackwood, 1900, pp. 51–60)

Alfred Austin (1835–1913), Poet Laureate, trained in law, before moving to journalism. Austin was a prodigious author of many works, including verse, dramatic poems, fiction, literary criticism and, finally, his autobiography, published in two volumes before his death. He also wrote *Hibernian Horrors: a Letter to Gladstone* (1880). In the accompanying prefatory note, Austin informs us that although the text is based on articles first published in *Blackwood's Magazine*, in 1894 and 1895, he feels them worthy of republication, 'expressive as they are of the love and admiration the author has long felt for Ireland'.

On any other steamboat service with which I am acquainted, should you wish to have a private cabin it is not always to be had; and, if you are allotted it, it is rarely very spacious, and you invariably pay for it. On the Irish steamers between Holyhead and Kingstown, if you take the ordinary precaution of writing to Dublin in good time, you are sure of a private cabin, both large and commodious, and no charge is made for it, though you will do well, of course, not to forget the steward. I look on the arrangement as a foretaste of that Irish hospitality that has passed into a proverb. By a blunder of my own, my heavier luggage had been labelled at Euston only as far as Westland Row, though I was going on to Kingsbridge, and indeed farther, without breaking my journey. But, on explaining my mistake to the luggage-porter on board the boat, describing the things, and telling him they all bore a label with name and address written on them, he begged me not to give them another thought, for he would find and re-label them in the course of the transit, and I might count on their being at Kingsbridge Station. The civility and attention shown to travellers by the servants of English railway companies could not be surpassed. But, while they seem to be performing a duty, though performing it most cheerfully, in Ireland a similar service appears as if it were an act of personal politeness. Fine manners are surely some test of civilisation; and, if that be so, Ireland is not altogether barbarous, while we ourselves as a community, cannot boast to be, in every respect, supremely civilised. At the Kingsbridge Station I breakfasted as well as I should have done in any railway refreshment room in England; and again I noticed a personal desire that I should have everything I wanted; being treated as a living creature with individual tastes and peculiarities, not merely as one of a number of insignificant travelling units. But then, in order to receive this agreeable deference and discrimination, I suppose you must yourself manifest something of it, and exhibit some interest in those who are good enough to find you interesting because you are a human being.

But the Irish are so casual and inaccurate. Perhaps they are. I wanted a ticket to Ballycumber. The ticket-clerk asked me if Ballyhooley would do for me. Naturally, I said it would not; which evoked the exclamation, 'It's Prospect you're going to.' Which it was, only the ticket was stamped to Prospect and the station itself is inscribed Ballycumber. I remember that, at Westport, on asking why the train did not start, seeing that it was a quarter of an hour after the time named for its doing so, the answer I received was, 'The engine's gone cold,' – doubtless during a warm conversation between the driver and some of his friends; and a lady who was in the same compartment with me, and overheard the remark, told me that on the previous day a station-master had said to the driver of a locomotive as he steamed in and drew up at the platform, 'Where's your train?' The man had come without it. I suppose these casualties cause inconvenience sometimes, but they contribute diversion to irresponsible travel. Moreover, one sometimes reaps advantage from a free-and-easy system of locomotion. When going from Galway to Recess by the new light railway, I wanted at Oughterard to look at the river, but feared I should not be able to do so in the time allowed for our halt. 'Sure, we'll wait for you,' said a porter; and they did. In Ireland people like waiting. What they do object to is being hurried. They dislike 'tedious haste'.

Perhaps the fact that this light railway from Galway to Clifden was then but newly made, and scarcely yet in working order, rendered this obliging act of civility more feasible. What constitutes a light railway I do not know, for the one I speak of, though consisting of only a single line of rails, apparently resembled all other railways, save in so far as its stations and the buildings connected with them are exceptionally good. The gratitude expressed by the inhabitants of the district for the boon secured to them by Mr. Balfour is very striking. They declare, and are never tired of declaring that 'he's the only man who ever did anything for this country'; and they wanted to know if there was any chance of his coming there again, for 'would he not have a fine reception?', and when it was explained to them that his brother was now Chief Secretary they hoped he was 'the same sort of gentleman'. During the next fortnight I had to hear the changes frequently rung on this theme; so that when I got farther into the land, I could not help thinking what is known as 'Joyce's Country' might not inappropriately henceforth be called 'Arthur's Country'.

The admiration of Ireland I had expressed when I first visited it had brought me characteristic offers of gratuitous hospitality from the landlords of certain inns in Connemara. But my steps were not quite in their direction, and my first halt in that part of the world was at Recess, a first-rate headquarter for any one who wants to combine fishing with beautiful scenery. The Irish Tourists' Association and the Irish railway companies, acting together, will in due course endow the most picturesque parts of Ireland with the conventional model hotel, and I have no doubt they are wise in their generation in doing so. I have observed that many people, in travelling, are anxious, above all things, to meet with a reproduction, as far as possible, for the circumstances and conditions they left at home. That seems odd, since I should have thought absolute novelty was the chief charm of travel. Moreover, the best hotel is necessarily but a bad imitation of domestic comfort; whereas a good or even an indifferent inn atones for inferiority of accommodation by freshness of sensation. There is no necessity for dogmatism in this matter; and I do not doubt that the hotels of Parknasilla, Kenmare, Waterville, Derrynane, &c., recently established, will both attract and satisfy numbers of visitors to the exquisite scenery of Kerry. In Galway, and in parts of Donegal, similar accommodation for tourists will be provided. Only I should like to say a word in favour of the Inn, as against the Hotel, at least in the more primitive localities. It has always seemed to me there is the same difference between an inn and a hotel that there is between hospitality and entertaining. One is at home in an inn; one is not at home, one is on sufferance, in a hotel. It may not be easy to hit the exact distinction between the two; but I should think the proprietor ought, like Phaethon, to take the middle course, and that most people would rather, when among the mountains or by the ocean-cliffs, stay or abide at a rather primitive inn than at a strictly modern hotel.

Yet perhaps it is dangerous to offer advice of this kind; for I perceive an indignant tourist writes to the 'Times' because the milk for his tea was brought to him in Ireland in a cup instead of in the orthodox ewer, and he accordingly counsels holiday-makers to avoid that country! Fancy missing magnificent scenery for such a reason! I do not think he can have travelled much in Italy, to say nothing of Greece.

The inn at Recess, which I believe has now been replaced by a more pretentious one, was then primitive in its service, but otherwise not open to criticism save of the fastidious and carping sort. You must not look for division of labour in Ireland. It is everybody's business to answer your bell, – supposing there to be one, – to clean your boots, or to bring your hot water, and therefore it will sometimes happen that it is nobody's business. But you will never be wrong in asking anybody to do anything for you, and in time it will be done; and I can never understand why people who seem, in the course of the day, to have so much time on their hands, should be in such a hurry to have their needs of the moment responded to. If honest joints properly cooked, plain puddings, stewed fruit, good bread, good butter, good bacon, eggs without stint, and tea made with boiling water, do not satisfy people's appetite, they had better not go for change of air and scene to the Twelve Pins. The water for their tub, of a morning, will be brought them in instalments; but it will be brought. If you desire anything more dainty than I have named, you need not fear to invade the kitchen and take counsel with Miss Mullarkey. For in Ireland, as in Italy, the kitchen seems open to anybody, and you meet people there who have nothing on earth to do with the establishment. I suppose they bring news or gossip, have a fowl or a fish to sell, are the sixteenth-cousin-removed of the great grandmother of the landlady, or perhaps they too want a little change of air and scene. The English idea expressed by the words, 'No entrance here except on business,' is unknown in Ireland. Everybody has business that has anything to say; and everybody has something to say. The English, being a self-satisfied, self-sufficient, and quietly contented race, and not in the least terrified by the Universe, whose laws they have bitted and bridled and made to drudge for them, are sufficiently happy in remaining silent. They do not require the society of their kind, save for the purpose of helping to lift a load or overcoming *vis inertia* somewhere. But the Celt, the Irish Celt at least, when left to himself and the resources of his own nature, is oppressed and appalled by the vast unsympathising silence of things, and falls into lethargic melancholy. He wants to talk, in order to break the dumb spell of the surrounding mystery, to forget that he is a lonely segregated unit in a world of infinite indifference, and to intoxicate himself for a time with the idea that he is part of a goodly company, a protected member of the great human tribe. Moreover, it is part of his politeness, of his urbanity, to talk; and the taciturnity of the Saxon seems to him inhuman.

48. Kate Douglas Wiggin, *Penelope's Irish Experiences*
(first published 1901; 2nd edn, London: Gay, 1901, pp. 189–92)

Kate Douglas Wiggin (1856–1923), was an educator and novelist. Born in Philadelphia, Wiggin was inspired by the educational philosophy of Friedrich Froebel, but is largely remembered as an author of children's fiction: *The Story of Patsy* (1883), *The Village Watch Tower* (1895), and especially *Rebecca of Sunnybrook Farm* (1903). An extremely popular speaker, Wiggin fell ill on a visit to England in 1922, and died there the following year in a nursing home in Harrow-on-the-Hill.

We did not stop long in Belfast; for if there is anything we detest, when on our journeys, it is to mix too much with people of industry, thrift, and business sagacity. Sturdy, prosperous, calculating, well-to-do Protestants are well enough, in their way, and undoubtedly they make a very good backbone for Ireland; but we crave something more romantic than the citizen virtues, or we should have remained in our own country, where they are tolerably common, although we have not as yet anything approaching over-production.

Belfast, it seems, is, and has always been, a centre of Presbyterianism. The members of the Presbytery protested against the execution of Charles I, and received an irate reply from Milton, who said that 'the blockish presbyters of Clandeboy' were 'egregious liars and imposters,' who meant to stir up rebellion 'from their unchristian synagogue at Belfast in a barbarous nook of Ireland'.

Dr. La Touche writes to Salemina that we need not try to understand all the religious and political complications which surround us. They are by no means as violent or as many of in Thackeray's day, when the great English author found nine shades of politico-religious differences in the Irish Liverpool. As the impartial observer must, in such a case, necessarily displease eight parties, and probably the whole nine, Thackeray advised a rigid abstinence from all intellectual curiosity. Dr. La Touche says, if we wish to know the north better, it will do us no harm to study the Plantation of Ulster, the United Irish movement, Orangeism, Irish Jacobitism, the effect of French and Swiss Republicanism in the evolution of public sentiment, and the close relation and affection that formerly existed between the north of Ireland and New England. (This last topic seems to appeal to Salemina particularly.) He also alludes to Tories and Rarrarees, Rousseau and Thomas Paine and Owen Roe O'Neill, but I have entirely forgotton their connection with the subject. Francesca and I are thoroughly enjoying ourselves, as only those people can who never take notes, and never try, when Pandora's box is opened in their neighbourhood, to seize the heterogeneous contents and put them back properly, with nice little labels on them.

Ireland is no longer a battlefield of English parties, neither is it wholly a laboratory for political experiment; but from having been both the one and the other, its features are a bit knocked out of shape and proportion, as it were. We have bought two hideous engravings of the Battle of the Boyne and the Secret of England's Greatness; and whenever we stay for a night in any inn where perchance these are not, we pin them on the wall, and are received into the landlady's heart at once. I don't know which is the finer study: the picture of his Majesty William III crossing the Boyne, or the plump little Queen presenting a huge family Bible to an apparently uninterested black youth. In the latter work of art the eye is confused at first as the three principal features approach each other very nearly in size, and Francesca asked innocently, 'Which *is* the secret of England's greatness – the Bible, the Queen, or the black man?'

49. Michael Myers Shoemaker, *Wanderings in Ireland*
(New York: Putnam, 1908, pp. 260–65)

Michael Shoemaker (1853–1924), an American educated at Cornell, was a professional travel writer who achieved much of his success in the late 1890s and early years of the twentieth century. His wide-ranging travels resulted in texts including *Sealed Provinces of the Tsar* (1895), *Heart of the Orient* (1904), and *Islam Lands* (1910). Shoemaker's preface is dated 1 January 1908, but since the text breaks about two-thirds of the way through ('A year has rolled away since I wrote my last line') it seems reasonable to assume that he describes events dating from sometime in 1906.

Ireland has seen strange wild times, and no section of it more than this remote County Wexford. As I have stated, this estate of Bannow is eigh-teen miles from a railroad station now, but in another month a new line three miles away opens for traffic, and though a good thing for the property of all in the county, it will sound the knell of probably all the quaint and curious customs still in vogue here. If that railway company is wise it will build a seaside hotel in this neighbourhood. The climate is for most of the year delightful and is rarely subject to the howling tempests which so constantly sweep the west coast for half the year. Wexford abounds in beautiful scenery and almost every valley holds a charming home while quaint towns crowd the river banks and ruined towers crown the hills on either side.

The maintenance of many of these Irish estates becomes each year more and more difficult unless the whole is strictly entailed. This is especially the case with places of small income, say two or three thousand pounds sterling. In the days when rents were good and five per cent. obtained it was well enough, but to-day when three per cent. is all that can be hoped for and yet the old charges for dowers and legacies must be paid, the owner is perforce a poor man. At present the landlord seems to have no rights. His tenants may and do absolutely refuse to pay him rent and he is reduced to poverty. There is a case I know of where the tenants are amply able to pay him, but they simply won't. His only resource is eviction, which is slow, expensive, and brings down wrath upon his head. So he is forced to give up his home and retire to a cottage, while his tenants laugh at him.

In the case of the peasants, eviction is not only expensive but useless. No man will rent the hut of those turned out, no matter how many years drift by, and some landlords are reinstating their evicted tenants. Better them than empty farms.

With the new Land Act the tenants dictate that they will buy or nothing. Of course there have arisen the usual number of scoundrels who get behind these peasants, buy out their rights and in the end get the land for a song. There are several instances where such men who at one time broke stones on the highway are now landowners of considerable extent. I heard of one the other day who was just adding a billiard-room to his 'mansion'.

There is much said over here about the corruption of our city governments especially those of Chicago and New York, but I also hear that that of the city of Dublin is to say the very least nothing to boast of, and that graft has even penetrated London itself.

Home rule for the peasants of Ireland, so it is stated here, would be about as sensible as a rule of the blacks in America. When the leaders in Parliament found they could make no more money by the disturbances, they called them off, and one of the members of that august body was kicked all the way down his peaceful avenue before me here and out yonder gate for abuse of the late Queen.

During the boycott, Bannow House was in a state of siege and its owner forced to start a store on the lawn for his own workmen, who could not purchase anywhere. These provisions were brought from London under guard.

After his death – in 1881 – his grave, guarded by policemen for twenty-four hours – until the concrete in which his coffin had been buried had set, – was surrounded all the time by a howling mob who would have promptly 'had him out' otherwise.

He hated the parson and so left the church's legacy of two thousand pounds to the 'next incumbent', or rather the interest thereof, but the parson was equal to the occasion, and, resigning, got himself re-elected, and so became the 'next incumbent' and secured the interest.

There was another instance here where the holy man, this time a priest, did not fare so well. He had attacked a member of his parish from the pulpit, and thereby aroused the ire of the wife. She was about six feet tall, and following the priest into the vestry-room flogged him soundly. It was a foolish thing to do, as it roused the whole country round about and she and her household almost starved from the boycott which promptly followed. On her death it was necessary to bury her also in cement, to prevent desecration, every man at the funeral carrying a gun.

Fortunately those days are gone by, let us hope for all time, but with a people so ignorant and superstitious anything may happen and if that cattle driving does not cease old times will come again.

It is quiet enough here this morning; the peace of the country is intense, yet to me it is never a solitude, never lonely, and it is delicious to awake in the early light and feel the cool, damp air blow in upon one through the open window, while even at this hour of dawn yonder old reprobate of a wood pigeon is earnestly entreating Paddy to follow the way of the transgressor, – 'two coos, Paddy, two coos'. One can almost hear the stealthy rustle of the departing beasts and the soft footfall of Paddy. Far beyond the trees where the pigeons hide, the fair blue of heaven has been rain-washed during the night, and white clouds drift lazily off towards the sea murmuring in the distance.

To-day brings my stay at Bannow House to a close, I trust not for all time. After luncheon, bidding our hostess farewell, we roll away through the avenue of rhododendrons, over the meadows, through the forest, where the insistent birds try for the last time to corrupt my honesty, and so out on the highway and off to the north.

Our route takes us past the site of Scullaboyne House, a spot sadly famous.

In the dark days of the rebellion of 1798, New Ross and this vicinity of Bannow suffered horribly. Indeed the battle at the former town was the most sanguinary of that period, and an event which following it here too horrible to be passed over without notice even at this late date. Scullaboyne House, but lately deserted by its owner, Capt. King, and seized by the rebels, was in use as a prison. In the house itself were confined some thirty-seven men and woman and in the adjoining barn were over one hundred men, women and children, chiefly, but not exclusively, Protestants. After their defeat at New Ross the rebels sent word to destroy these prisoners. Those in the house were called one by one to the door and shot down, but a worse fate awaited those in the barn, where firebrands thrown into and upon its roof soon turned the whole into a red hot furnace. Children were tossed out of the windows to save them, but only to be impaled upon the pikes of the outlaws. Some authorities claim that two hundred and thirty persons met their deaths in Scullaboyne. Certainly the French Revolution can show nothing more horrible.

There is little left here now to recall the event save a few blackened fragments, which the rich grass and creeping vines are daily covering more and more each passing year.

It is claimed by the insurgent party that they had nothing to do with the slaughter – that it was the act of outlaws, such as are always to be found dogging the footsteps of contending forces. However that may be, the result was absolute ruin to the cause of the rebels. Be it recorded to the credit of the intelligent priests of the day that they at all times did what they could to prevent like occurrences and save human life and that amongst the sixty-six persons executed in Wexford, after that period, for murder and rebellion, only one was a priest.

But let us hasten away from all this.

50. R.A. Scott-James, *An Englishman in Ireland*

(London: Dent, 1910, pp. 203–08)

Rolfe Arnold Scott-James (1878–1959) was a journalist, editor and literary critic who joined the staff of the *Daily News* in 1902. A close friend of Wyndham Lewis, he published *The Influence of the Press* (1913) before moving, the following year, to become editor of the *New Weekly*. His later journalistic work included stints with the *Daily Chronicle*, the *Spectator*, and the *London Mercury*, where he also worked as editor. Among his writings are *Modernism and Romance* (1908), *The Making of Literature* (1928), and *Fifty Years of English Literature, 1900–50* (1951). In this extract, dated August 1910, Scott-James – who travelled for the most part by canoe on the River Shannon – is approaching Cloondra, County Longford.

When I reached Cloondra and went under its many-arched bridge I observed that it was still not quite ten o'clock, and I had travelled nearer eight than seven miles. It seemed that I was in time; for Mr. L., had named 10.30 as the utmost limit he could give me. But on proceeding a few hundred yards I was disgusted at the sight of lock-gates and the Shannon sweeping away to the left over a great line of sluice-gates. When I shouted for the lock-keeper some one at length appeared and said the lock-keeper was away; he would go and fetch him. The precious moments flew. I considered whether I should land and haul canoe and luggage round the obstacle. But a glance at the bank showed that landing would be difficult if not impossible; anyway, it would take too long.

It was half an hour before the lock-keeper arrived. It was of no use to vent my indignation upon him, so I held my peace, merely urging him to haste. When I came out on the further side it lacked but a few minutes to half-past ten.

I had travelled more than eight miles when I heard before me a grim sound. It was the hooter of a steamer. I redoubled my efforts. Again I heard the hooter. Then a dull, thudding sound. Rapidly as I was now moving the thudding sound became dimmer and dimmer in the distance, and I realised that the yacht was leaving me behind.

For several miles I pressed on, still hoping against hope. From here to Lough Ree the river was broad and imposing. Not once did I meet a boat, and for the most part the low-lying land was hidden from me by the tall, deep barrier of rushes. Now and again coming near the bank I would hear a strange sound wafted from beyond the barrier; the voices of invisible men and women talking in ordinary tones as they made hay. Near as they were, they seemed infinitely distant. It was as if I had always belonged to a universe of wind and water and rushes, and that these men and women spoke with curiously familiar voices, insistently near as in a dream, yet from an impenetrable world. Water, sky, rushes and wind in them all – these had become the material of my universe.

It seems strange to me now, but I remember that I became suddenly tired of water. Water and wind – they would not leave me alone, not for a moment. I began to feel something like nausea at their continued presence, as one may sometimes feel nausea from the ceaseless presence of a friend however on most occasions congenial. 'Leave me for a little time,' I would have said to the Shannon; but there seemed to be no leaving – that tall, waving barrier continued to hide the shore and the earth.

It was a little past mid-day when I came to a place where a brook trickled into the river and made for itself a lane between the rushes. Into this narrow channel I turned eagerly, and by some manoeuvring got the canoe to the shore. I stepped on to terra firma. On one side of the stream was a field where the hay had been gathered into great cocks; on the other side the hay still lay on the ground. Two hundred yards off stood a pretty farmhouse with trees round it, and close by sat two men.

I walked towards these men, who gazed stonily before them. When I came nearer they still gazed, and looked through me as if I had been an apparition. 'Good evening,' I said; but they made no answer. At last, by direct questions, I elicited a surly reply to the effect that a big steamer had gone by an hour or two ago. As they still stared through me, I left them and returned to the shore.

The canoe lay clammily in its oozy harbour. I dragged out my provision box, enticed a rug out of my sack, and tried to escape the remorseless wind by crouching under a hay-cock. Though the rain had stopped two hours ago I found my shoes and socks still wet through; so I kicked them off, and wrapped my limbs in the rug. I devoured almost a whole tin of baked beans – the last of my provisions – and drank whisky diluted with Shannon water – a commodity with which I was plentifully supplied. Feebly the sun came out and instilled comfort into me, and though the gale blew round from each corner of the hay-cock and caught up the ends of the rug, I found myself just warm enough, and inclined to stay here for ever rather than return to the stormy river which swept along beneath me.

As I lay there watching all things under the sun – the boisterous river, the flat bogland of the opposite shore, the twin hills which rose up in the west – Slieve Bawn and Clooncah – suddenly a vast object obtruded itself upon my sight. Up the river it came, puffing, booming, thudding, a prodigious thing – the Portumna. Once every week this great tub of a boat, mighty in its prow, preposterous in its shape, goes up and down the river between Portumna and Carrick. Behind it, one after another, were four fat barges, lumps of wood and cargo straining at a tow-line. As it passed, the lumberous steamer for some unguessable reason – probably for fun – sounded its raucous siren with a hideous noise which drowned the noise of the wind. Somberly and without humour this bulky procession filed past me up the river, and as the last barge was passing a great wave struck on the bank below me – it was the wash of the steamer.

And then I took to watching three couples who were making hay in the field adjoining – three men, in different parts of the field, each accompanied and assisted by a bare-footed woman. My attention was fixed by the young man and young woman who were gradually working down the furrows, tossing the hay as they went, towards the river. With what wonderful grace and agility the woman kept pace with the man, the wind whirling her dress round at each stroke of the fork, and then catching the tossed hay and whirling that round in similar curvilinear confusion. Man and woman seemed to be working together in continuous rhythmical motion, while the elements – wind and hay and light – moved round them, and acted the chorus to their tragic endeavour. Now and again, at rare intervals, the woman would pause, and the man would pause too, and they would seem to survey their achievement, as if taking stock of the results of human effort. And then on again, the wind catching wildly at the skirts of the bare-footed woman, as she tossed and tossed the fantastic, writhing hay; till at last the whole field had been set awhirl, and they paused, close by the river, resting on their forks. Then the woman laid down her fork and began walking, still afloat in the wind, towards the farm. The man waited, standing; then picked up her fork, and walked after her, at a distance.

51. B.E. Stevenson, *The Charm of Ireland*

(London: Murray, 1915, pp. 510–16)

Burton Egbert Stevenson (1872–1962) was an American author and sometime newspaper editor and librarian who founded the American Library in Paris in 1918, of which he was Director until 1920. Author of some forty novels, mysteries, and children's stories, he was also a Member of the National Institute of Arts and Letters.

The News-Letter is the great Belfast daily, and while I was looking through it, Monday, for fear I had missed some of the pulpit and platform fulminations, I chanced upon another article which interested me deeply, as showing the Protestant attitude toward control of the schools. The article in question was a long account of the awarding of prizes at one of the big Belfast National schools, as a result of the religious education examination, and it was most illuminating.

The chairman began his remarks by saying that 'nothing is pleasanter than to hear a pupil repeat faultlessly the answers to the one hundred and seven questions in the Shorter Catechism, without a stumble, placing the emphasis where it is due, and attending to the stops,' and he went on to report that these one hundred and seven questions had been asked orally of each of 396 children, that there was not a single failure, and that practically all the children were in the first honour list – that is, had answered faultlessly the whole one hundred and seven.

And then another speaker, a clergyman, of course, like the first, told impressively of the meaning of education. It was, he said, the duty of every child to store his mind with all manner of knowledge and to seek diligently to gain information from day to day. But religion was the sum and complement of all education. Without it, all other acquirements would be little better than the beautiful flush upon the consumptive's cheek, the precursor of sure death and decay. He reminded them that even the very youngest there was guilty in the sight of God, for that awful word sinner described them all.

Then a third speaker remarked that while the staff of the school was doing a fine work in teaching the boys and girls to read and write and cast up accounts, that that wasn't nearly so fine as teaching them the Catechism and encouraging them to study their Bibles. And then a fourth speaker emphasised this; and then there was a vote of thanks to all the speakers, and the prize Bibles were distributed, and everybody went away happy – at least, the adults were all happy, and I can only hope the children were.

From all which it is evident that the Presbyterians will fight for their schools as hard, if not harder, than the Catholics will for theirs. But to me, the thought of those poor children being drilled and drilled in the proper answers to the 107 questions of the Catechism, until they could answer them all glibly and without stopping to think, is a painful and depressing one. I suppose that is the way good Orangemen are made; but the Catechism has always seemed to me a rickety ladder to climb to heaven by.

I was fortunate enough to witness another peculiar symptom of Belfast's temper, that afternoon, when I went down to the Custom House, which stands near the river. It is a large building occupying a full block, and there is a wide esplanade all around it; and this esplanade has, from time immemorial, been the platform which any speaker, who could find room upon it, was privileged to mount, and where he might promulgate any doctrine he could get the crowd to listen to.

There was a great throng of people about the place, that afternoon, and a liberal sprinkling of policemen scattered through it; and then I perceived that it wasn't one big crowd but a lot of smaller crowds, each listening to a different orator, whose voices met and clashed in the air in a most confusing manner. And I wish solemnly to assert that the list which follows is a true list in every detail.

At the corner of the building, a reformed drunkard, with one of those faces which are always in need of shaving, stood, Bible in hand, recounting his experiences. At least, he said he had reformed; but the pictures he painted of the awful depravity of his past had a lurid tinge which held his auditors spellbound, and it was evident from the way he smacked his lips over them that he was proud of having been such a devil of a fellow.

Next to him a smartly-dressed Negro was selling bottles of medicine, which, so far as I could judge from what I heard, was guaranteed to cure all the ills that flesh is heir to. The formula for this wonderful preparation, he asserted, had been handed down through his family from his great-great-grandmother, who had been a famous African voodoo doctor, and it could be procured nowhere else. The open-mouthed Belfasters listened to all this with a deference and patience which no American audience would have shown, and the fakir took in many shillings.

Next to him, a company of the Salvation Army was holding a meeting after the explosive fashion familiar all the world over; and at the farther corner, a white-bearded little fellow was describing the horrors of hell with an unction and exactitude far surpassing Dante. I don't know what his formula was for avoiding these horrors, for I didn't wait to hear his peroration.

Just around the corner, two blind men were singing dolefully, with a tin cup on the pavement before them, and straining their ears for the rattle of a copper that never came; and farther along, a sharp-faced Irishman was delivering a speech, which I judged to be political, but it was so interspersed with anecdote and invective and personal reminiscence, that, though I listened a long time, I couldn't make out who he was talking against, or which side he was on. His audience seemed to follow him without difficulty, however, and laughed and applauded; and then a little fellow with a black moustache advised the crowd, in a loud voice, not to listen to him, for he was a jail-bird. I saw the constables edge in a little closer; but the speaker took the taunt in good part, admitted that he had done twelve months for some offence, and thanked the crowd with tears in his voice because they had raised two pounds a week, during that time, for the support of his family. The crowd cheered, and the fellow who had tried to start trouble hastened to take himself off. Thinking over all which, now, it occurs to me that the speech may have been a labour speech, and not a political one at all.

I gave it up, at last, and moved on to where a man was making an impassioned plea for contributions for an orphan asylum. He had a number of sample orphans of both sexes ranged about him, and he painted a lively picture of the good his institution was doing; but how he hoped to extract donations from a crowd so evidently down at heel I don't see. Next to him, a frightful cripple, who could stand erect only by leaning heavily upon two canes, was telling the crowd how exceedingly difficult it was for a rich man to get into heaven. Next to him, a lot of women were holding some sort of missionary meeting; and just around the last corner, a roughly-dressed man, with coarse, red-bearded face, whose canvas placard described him as a 'Medical Herbalist', was selling medicines of his own concoction.

He had no panacea, but a separate remedy for every ill; and I listened to his patter for a long time, though obviously he didn't welcome my presence. He proved that slippery-elm was harmless by eating some of it, and argued that plantain, 'which ignorant people regarded as a weed, made the best medicine a man could put into his inside,' and he proved this proposition by saying that it must be so because plantain had no other known use, and it was inconceivable that the Lord would have taken the trouble to create it without some purpose. He also proved that he was a capable doctor because he was not a doctor at all, but a working-man and it was the working-man who made the world go round. Inconceivable as it may seem, this ignorant and maudlin talk was listened to seriously and even respectfully, and he sold a lot of his medicines. Medicine seems to be one of the dissipations of the Belfast folk.

The largest crowd of all was gathered before a man who held the centre of the fourth side of the esplanade, and who was talking, or rather shouting, against Home Rule. He was garbed as a clergyman, and he wore an Orange badge, and he was listened to with religious attention as he painted the iniquity of the Catholic church and the horrible dangers of Catholic domination. His references to King Billy and the Boyne and the walls of Derry were many and frequent, and he had all sorts of newspaper clippings in his pockets, from which he read freely, and though he was very hoarse and bathed in perspiration, he showed no sign of stopping. He intimated that, once Home Rule was established, the revival of the inquisition would be but a matter of a short time, that no Protestant would be allowed to own property, that no Protestant labourer could expect employment anywhere until he had abjured his religion, that their children would be taken away from them and reared in Catholic schools, and he called upon them to arm and stand firm, to offer their lives upon the altar of their country, and not retreat a step before the aggressions of the Scarlet Woman. I don't know how much of this farrago his audience believed, but their faces were intent and serious, and I fear they believed much more than was good for them. I happened upon a song of Chesterton's the other day which brought those strained and intent faces vividly before me:

> The folks that live in black Belfast, their heart is in their mouth;
> They see us making murders in the meadows of the South;
> They think a plow's a rack, they do, and cattle-calls are creeds;
> And they think we're burning' witches, when we're only burning' weeds.

Those lines are scarcely an exaggeration; and after I had stood there listening for half an hour, I began to feel uneasily that perhaps, after all, there is in Ulster a dour fanaticism which may lead to an ugly conflict. Those political adventurers who have preached armed resistance so savagely, without really meaning a word of it, may have raised a Frankenstein which they will find themselves unable to control.

52. Douglas Goldring, *A Stranger in Ireland*

(London: Unwin, 1918, pp. 30–37)

Douglas Goldring (1887–1960), born in London, educated at Oxford, was on the staff of a number of magazines, including *Country Life* and the *English Review*, before becoming a Lecturer in English at Gothenburg University, Sweden, in the mid-1920s. Author of novels, essays and verse, Goldring wrote a number of travel narratives (on Portugal, the French Riviera, Sardinia), but revisited the subject of Ireland in later years: *Three Romantic Countries: Reminiscences of Travel in Dalmatia, Ireland and Portugal* (1951). This extract finds him in Dublin, recounting the funeral of Thomas Ashe, an Irish republican who died while being force-fed in Mountjoy jail in September 1917.

The spirit of Ireland is a will o' the wisp spirit which, alas, is not to be caught by the Englishman, however earnest and intelligent he may be, at

the soirees of the Dublin intellectuals. Yet it can always be found somewhere or other in Dublin, smouldering like a fire in her ancient heart. In
Dublin you feel it and perceive it for a moment: then it is gone. But in
the countryside you are always aware of it – in the soft cottonwool mist
which overhangs the infinite expanses of bogland, in the damp fields
which stretch down to the silent swollen rivers, in the grey, weeping
skies. And always you get a glimpse of it at a funeral. In no country in
the world I suppose is the memory of the dead kept greener than in
Ireland; and even the poorest of her sons and daughters manage to make
their last journey as 'carriage folk', with pomp and circumstance. It is a
strange sight in the West to see a funeral procession – the coffin with
two ancient women sitting keening on its lid, borne along on a cart with
the long trail of mourners following behind it through the soft moist air;
the mountains on either side framing the picture, the vivid green of the
fields throwing it into sharp relief and ahead in the distance, the mysterious Western sea. As for Dublin funerals, they are famous; and well do I
remember one at which the spirit of the Irish people burst into a great
flame, whose light must have been visible all over the world. This was the
funeral of Thomas Ashe, on a Sunday afternoon in September, 1917. I
did not witness the Lying in State of Ashe's remains, first at the Mater
hospital and then at the City Hall, but I went with two or three friends
to see the funeral procession as it passed along O'Connell Street on its
way from Cork Hill to Glasnevin. The experience was unforgettable and
though I had witnessed some thrilling scenes in Dublin before, such as
the welcome to Madame Markievicz on her release from prison, I was
quite unprepared for such an outburst of popular emotion.

The crowd grew dense as we neared O'Connell Bridge and it was
only by the exercise of much skill and by continuous shouting that our
driver managed to manoeuvre the car into a position, midway between
O'Connell's statue and the Nelson Pillar, from which we should be able
to view the procession. Among the different kinds of people I noticed as
we made our way slowly through the closely-packed throng were an
English Staff officer with a friend in mufti, the wife of a tobacconist
with her three rather grubby little boys, a prosperous Dublin doctor, a
member of the Convention secretariat, Lord MacDonnell, a chemist's
assistant, a Gaelic Leaguer, and several intellectuals. The wide street was
densely filled with spectators. The ruinous walls of a house just opposite
me, which had been broken up by shell fire during the Rebellion of
1916, had been scaled by adventurous boys, who sat there perilously
dangling their legs. The cabby remarked that the crowd was greater than
at the funeral of the late Charles Stuart Parnell; and certainly it looked as

if the majority of the population of Dublin had turned out on this mild September afternoon to do honour to the dead. The Sinn Fein colours were everywhere in evidence, but anything less revolutionary in appearance than this sober and peaceable gathering of citizens it would be difficult to imagine.

It was not until nearly an hour after we had taken up our place that the leaders of the funeral cortege appeared round the corner of Bachelor's Walk. First of all came a small advance guard of Volunteers, followed by about two hundred Catholic clergymen, among whose glittering top hats could be seen here and there the bare head and brown habit of a Capuchin father. Immediately behind the clergymen came the hearse, with the coffin wrapped in a Republican flag and half buried in an avalanche of flowers. The hearse was flanked by a picked guard of Irish Volunteers in their dark green uniform, the men carrying their rifles reversed and their officer marching behind them with drawn sword.

'Ah, they always kill the ones we love best,' said a woman near me, who had known Pearse and MacDonagh and the O'Rahilly. Her face was contorted with sorrow. For her, as for so many others in the crowd, the death of Thomas Ashe was a bitter personal loss.

Following the hearse came a long stream of carriages and mourning coaches. The presence among them of Archbishop Walsh's motor and of the Lord Mayor's carriage lent an odd touch of official dignity to a spectacle which a foreigner might well have mistaken for the funeral of some famous soldier, rather than that of a man who had been condemned as a criminal by the government of his country.

When the last of the carriages had gone by, there began the great procession. As it passed I think to any impartial observer it must have been apparent that it was indeed the fine fleur of the youth of Ireland who were marching thus to the graveside of their dead comrade. There were contingents of volunteers from many different parts of the country as well as from Dublin, contingents from all the Dublin trade unions, boy scouts, girl scouts, undergraduates of the National University, Gaelic Leaguers in their beautiful national dress, members of the Gaelic Athletic Association clubs carrying their hurleys, a detachment of the National Volunteers under the command of Colonel Moore. Even the Dublin Fire Brigade went clanking by on their engines, the men in full uniform with shining brass helmets, and all of them wearing Sinn Féin armlets. When I made an involuntary exclamation of surprise at this, the cabby cut in with 'Sure, aren't they Irishmen too?' One had the impression that every popular organisation in Dublin for men, women or children had sent its representatives, and the number of people taking part in the procession could hardly have been less than twenty thousand. Each group carried its own standard with the Republican colours either draped in black or marked with a black cross. Some of the flags were large and imposing and no doubt expensive, others were most touchingly 'home-made'. Near the middle of the procession there came a little band of school children. They were so small that their heads were scarcely visible beyond the thick hedge of onlookers, but their leader carried a rough banner attached to a bamboo rod. Across it had been worked very carefully with a needle and black thread the legend: 'In memory of Thomas Ashe who died for Ireland.' The procession, except when one of the numerous bands happened to be playing, was curiously silent; and the spectators seldom made any kind of demonstration, though there was some smiling and hand-clapping when the Countess Markievicz went by in her officer's uniform. Rarely I suppose has a great outburst of national feeling expressed itself in a ceremony so dignified, so orderly and so impressive.

When the funeral cortege first appeared, and indeed for some time afterwards, I was quite unable to realise the full significance of the scene I was witnessing. It was not until one of the bands struck up the extraordinarily inspiring 'Soldier's Song' that it came over me in a flash that in the eyes of the Irish Government all these people must be 'criminals', just as the dead man was a 'criminal'! Technically the bands-men were breaking the law by playing 'rebel' melodies. Hundreds of people had been punished for doing nothing more than this. Then again I remembered that the bearing of rifles by civilians was expressly forbidden. I knew that a conviction on this charge brought a long term of imprisonment; and there just before my eyes was a firing party, fully armed, with a policeman gazing at them benevolently! Again, all drilling was illegal. Just as I recalled this fact a volunteer officer blew a whistle immediately in front of me and a thousand men stopped as one. Another short whistle, the words 'left, right, left' and the procession had started again. Then surely, the carrying of hurleys was prohibited? I noticed an entire contingent go by, armed with the forbidden weapon. As for the volunteer uniform, Dublin was plastered with proclamations threatening pains and penalties to those who might have the temerity to put it on. Yet during the ninety minutes which the procession took to pass, I expect I saw very nearly every volunteer uniform which exists in Ireland. What a situation! I suppose the futility of Castle government was never more pitilessly shown up than it was on that Sunday . . . . .

Near me in the crowd, while the volunteer contingents were marching by, I noticed several private soldiers in khaki watching the scene with a puzzled expression on their faces. They had no doubt joined the British army in order to defend two sacred principles. 'Freedom for small nationalities' and 'Government with the consent of the governed'. What did they make of all this business, I wonder? They had every reason to look puzzled, poor fellows. Indeed I doubt if this distracted, tortured world could show anywhere a situation more involved and illogical and at the same time more grimly humorous. It seemed somehow unreal, incredible. Yet Ashe's dead body was real enough, and I at least had no excuse for taking refuge in the Englishman's favourite mental dugout! 'It can't be true.'

After the last of the funeral procession had passed along its way to Glasnevin and our car was being backed clear of the crowd, I found myself again near the staff officer, and a precious and revealing fragment of conversation was wafted towards me:

'Oh, yes, we do just the same in India,' he observed to his companion. 'We always give the natives a free hand with their religious rites!'

53. G.K. Chesterton, *Irish Impressions*

(London: Collins, 1919, pp. 117–26)

Gilbert Keith Chesterton (1874–1936) was a poet, novelist and critic. Simultaneously educated at the University of London and the Slade School of Art, Chesterton worked as a journalist, eventually becoming a full-time writer in the early 1900s. Received into the Catholic Church in July 1922, Chesterton was an anti-Imperialist, and a liberal. Among his published works are his autobiography *Orthodoxy* (1908), *What's Wrong with the World* (1910), innumerable essays, detective stories, poems and, of course, books of travel. In his later years he made a series of radio broadcasts for the BBC.

I met one hearty Unionist, not to say Coercionist in Ireland, in such a manner as to talk to him at some length; one quite genial and genuine Irish gentleman, who was solidly on the side of the system of British government in Ireland. This gentleman had been shot through the body by the British troops in their efforts to suppress the Easter Rebellion. The matter just missed being tragic; but since it did, I cannot help feeling it as slightly comic. He assured me with great earnestness that the rebels had been guilty of the most calculated cruelties, and that they must have done their bloody deeds in the coldest blood. But since he is himself a solid and (I am happy to say) a living demonstration that the firing even on his own side must have been rather wild, I am inclined to give the benefit of the doubt also to the less elaborately educated marksmen. When disciplined troops destroy people so much at random, it would seem unreasonable to deny that rioters may possibly have been riotous. I hardly think he was, or even professed to be, a person of judicial impartiality; and it is entirely to his honour that he was, on principle, so much more indignant with the rioters who did not shoot him than with the other rioters who did. But I venture to introduce him here not so much as an individual as an allegory. The incident seems to me to set forth, in a pointed, lucid, and picturesque form, exactly what the British military government really succeeded in doing in Ireland. It succeeded in half-killing its friends, and affording an intelligent but somewhat inhuman amusement to all its enemies. The fire-eater held his fire-arm in so contorted a posture as to give the wondering spectator a simple impression of suicide.

Let it be understood that I speak here, not of tyranny thwarting Irish desires, but solely of our own stupidity in thwarting our own desires. I shall discuss elsewhere the alleged presence or absence of practical oppression in Ireland; here I am only continuing from the last chapter my experiences of the recruiting campaign. I am concerned now, as I was concerned then, with the simple business matter of getting a big levy of soldiers from Ireland. I think it was Sir Francis Vane, one of the few really valuable public servants in the matter (I need not say he was dismissed for having been proved right) who said that the mere sight of some representative Belgian priests and nuns might have produced something like a crusade. The matter seems to have been mostly left to elderly English landlords; and it would be cruel to record their adventures. It will be enough that I heard, on excellent testimony, that these unhappy gentlemen had displayed throughout Ireland a poster consisting only of the Union Jack and the appeal, 'Is not this your flag? Come and fight for it!' It faintly recalls something we all learnt in the Latin grammar about questions that expect the answer no. These remarkable recruiting-sergeants did not realise, I suppose, what an extraordinary thing this was, not merely in Irish opinion, but generally in international opinion. Over a great part of the globe, it would sound like a story that the Turks had placarded Armenia with the Crescent of Islam, and asked all the Christians who were not yet massacred whether they did not love the flag. I really do not believe that the Turks would be so stupid as to do it. Of course it may be said that such an impression or association is mere slander and sedition, that there is no reason to be tender to such treasonable emotions at all, that men ought to do their duty to that flag whatever is put upon that poster; in short, that it is the duty of an Irishman to be a patriotic Englishman, or whatever it is that he is expected to be. But this view, however logical and clear, can only be used logically and clearly as an argument for conscription. It is simply muddle-headed to apply it to any appeal for volunteers anywhere, in Ireland or England. The whole object of a recruiting poster, or any poster, is to be attractive; it is picked out in words or colours to be picturesquely and pointedly attractive. If it lowers you to make an attractive offer, do not make it; but do not deliberately make it, and deliberately make it repulsive. If a certain medicine is so mortally necessary and so mortally nasty, that it must be forced on everybody by the policeman, call the policeman. But do not call an advertisement agent to push it like a patent medicine, solely by means of 'publicity' and 'suggestion', and then confine him strictly to telling the public how nasty it is.

But the British blunder in Ireland was a much deeper and more destructive thing. It can be summed up in one sentence; that whether or no we were as black as we were painted, we actually painted ourselves much blacker than we were. Bad as we were, we managed to look much worse than we were. In a horrible unconsciousness we re-enacted history through sheer ignorance of history. We were foolish enough to dress up, and to play up, to the part of the villain in a very old tragedy. We clothed ourselves almost carelessly in fire and sword; and if the fire had been literally stage-fire or the sword a wooden sword, the merely artistic blunder would have been quite as bad. For instance, I soon came on the traces of a quarrel about some silly veto in the schools, against Irish children wearing green rosettes. Anybody with a streak of historical imagination would have avoided a quarrel in that particular case about that particular colour. It is touching the talisman, it is naming the name, it is striking the note of another relation in which we were in the wrong, to the confusion of a new relation in which we were in the right. Anybody of common sense, considering any other case, can see the almost magic force of these material coincidences. If the English armies in France in 1914 considered themselves justified for some reason in executing some Frenchwoman, they would perhaps be indiscreet if they killed her (however logically) tied to a stake in the market-place of Rouen. If the people of Paris rose in the most righteous revolt against the most corrupt conspiracy of some group of the wealthy French Protestants, I should strongly advise them not to fix the date for the vigil of St. Bartholomew, or to go to work with white scarfs tied round their arms. Many of us hope to see a Jewish commonwealth reconstituted in Palestine; and we could easily imagine some quarrel in which the government of Jerusalem was impelled to punish some Greek or Latin pilgrim or monk. The Jews might even be right in the quarrel and the Christian wrong. But it may be hinted that the Jews would be ill-advised if they actually crowned him with thorns, and killed him on a hill outside Jerusalem. Now we must know by this time, or the sooner we know it the better, that the whole mind of that European society which we have helped to save, and in which we have henceforth a part right of control, regards the Anglo-Irish story as one of those black and white stories in a history book. It sees the tragedy of Ireland as simply and clearly as the tragedy of Christ or Joan of Arc. There may have been more to be said on the coercive side than the culture of the Continent understands. So there was a great deal more than is usually admitted to be said on the side of the patriotic democracy which condemned Socrates; and a very great deal to be said on the side of the imperial aristocracy which would have crushed Washington. But these disputes will not take Socrates from his niche among the pagan saints, or Washington from his pedestal among the republican heroes. After a certain testing time substantial justice is always done to the men who stood in some unmistakable manner for liberty and light against contemporary caprice and fashionable force and brutality. In this intellectual sense, in the only competent intellectual courts, there is already justice to Ireland. In the wide daylight of this world-wide fact we or our representatives must get into a quarrel with children, of all people, and about the colour green, of all things in the world. It is an exact working model of the mistake I mean. It is the more brutal because it is not strictly cruel; and yet instantly revives the memories of cruelty. There need be nothing wrong with it in the abstract, or in a less tragic atmosphere where the symbols were not talismans. A schoolmaster in the prosperous and enlightened town of Eatanswill might not unpardonably protest against the school-children parading in class the Buff and Blue favours of Mr. Fizkin and Mr. Slumkey. But who but a madman would not see that to say that word, or make that sign, in Ireland, was like giving a signal for keening and the lament over lost justice that is lifted in the burden of the noblest of national songs; that to point to that rag of that colour was to bring back all the responsibilities and realities of that reign of terror when we were, quite literally, hanging men and women too for wearing of the green? We were not literally hanging these children. As a matter of mere utility, we should have been more sensible if we had been.

PART III
1921 – 2000

Introduction

The early 1920s were marked by political developments that would have striking repercussions for Anglo-Irish relations. The first Black and Tans were recruited in January 1920, in February a curfew was imposed on the Dublin Metropolitan Police district, while the Auxiliaries were recruited in July of that year. On 21st November 1920 – the 'first' Bloody Sunday – the IRA killed fourteen suspected secret agents, the Auxiliaries killed the commandant and vice-commandant of the Dublin IRA, while the Black and Tans opened fire on a Gaelic football match in Dublin, killing twelve. By the end of the year martial law was declared in Counties Cork, Tipperary, Limerick and Kerry, while damage worth two and a half million pounds was reputedly inflicted by the Black and Tans and Auxiliary police in their sacking of Cork city, on 11–12th December. While 1921 did not begin any more hopefully, with reprisals on both sides continuing unabated, a truce was eventually signed between representatives of the British army in Ireland and the IRA on 9th July 1921.

Not surprisingly, a drop in the number of travellers to Ireland, especially British travellers, is discernible throughout the 1920s, and it is not until the early 1930s that we begin to see an increase in their numbers. The first narrator in this section, Wilfrid Ewart, was travelling through Ireland at an especially dangerous time – April to May 1921 – and he becomes momentarily embroiled in the paranoia of those years. But by the time of John Gibbons's trip, at the end of the decade, an improvement in relations appears evident, even if the quaint moment related suggests a rather uneasy, stuttering advance. From 1922 until 1949, when Éire became the Republic of Ireland and left the Commonwealth, the two parts of Ireland were governed in ways that reflected their respective cultural and religious majorities. Not surprisingly, what both shared was a tendency to parochialism, and a generally conservative outlook. However, with the exception of a fall-off in numbers for the 1920s, this factor did not necessarily deter travellers, who continued to visit. Indeed, writers like Michael Floyd, Kees van Hoek, Stuart Mais and Lionel Rolt all journeyed throughout the country in the 1930s and 1940s, reporting and documenting for a wide readership. Texts such as Floyd's, and even those published after the war, such as Mais' and Manning's, depicted

Ireland as essentially charming: a restorative place of old values and certainties with which they could identify. And after 1945 especially, many writers enthused about Irish attractions, promoting the country as a pastoral idyll, a timeless space free of the uncertainties that afflicted much of war-torn Europe. Even the 1950s view of Ireland – of a cosy conformity that was more than a little unimaginative – did little to deter them, and women travel writers especially, such as Olivia Manning, Oriana Atkinson, and Clara Coltman Vyvyan, produced some fine travel accounts during this decade.

Despite the achievements of the 1950s, a noticeable drop in the number of published works for the 1960s occurred. One explanation for this fall-off is that since international travel was becoming available to many more people, writers were responding to these changing market demands and concentrating on different venues. Another possibility is that Ireland simply failed to interest, that at a time of increased liberality and generally fuller expectations abroad, Ireland seemed dreadfully unfashionable, a bitter irony given the modernizing influences, especially in the Republic. Another, more likely, reason is the re-emergence of violence, this time in Northern Ireland. We usually think of the outbreak of armed conflict in the North as beginning at the end of the 1960s, but unease and a level of disaffection was palpable from the middle of that decade. From 28 September to 3 October 1964, Belfast witnessed serious rioting over the removal of the Republic's tricolour flag from the headquarters of a Republican candidate in the forthcoming UK elections. On 8 March 1966, Nelson's Pillar in Dublin was blown up, and in June of that year a Catholic barman was shot dead in Belfast by the UVF. And of course, by 1968 politics in the North was in serious trouble, with marchers clashing with police in Derry, and student demonstrations taking place in Belfast. Another, perhaps surprising, element is how much violence took place south of the border. In June 1969 the IRA was involved in arson attacks on farms in Meath and Louth, in August the UVF was implicated in a bomb explosion at RTE headquarters in Dublin, and in October a UVF man was found dead at the foot of an electricity pylon in Donegal with 180 lbs of gelignite. It has become commonplace to remark on the sometimes simplistic views of travellers to Ireland, and on how many of them confused the North and the South. Perhaps given some of these earlier incidents the lines separating the two jurisdictions were less clear than we might imagine. Irish tourism may have boomed in the 1960s, but if travel writers visited the country few, it would appear, wished to make imaginative sense of it all. From 1930 to the present the Irish travel narrative has flourished, with this one exception: the years of the 1960s and 1970s.

Although the 1960s and 1970s saw a dramatic fall in interest, one notable text does exist: Richard Howard Brown's account, which was first published in 1974. Howard Brown is interesting not only because he faces the 'Troubles' head on, but because by doing so he sets a new trend, pulling the emphasis of Irish travel into a new direction. Moreover, by dealing with the Northern conflict, he showed that writing about Irish urban violence was not entirely unprofitable. Later writers, such as Paul Theroux and Bryce Webster, had more on their minds than documenting political strife on the streets of Belfast and Derry, but the fact that writers increasingly included the 'Troubles' as part of their itinerary, indeed regarded it as a necessary part of any Irish package, helped the revival of interest in the country generally. Howard Brown may not have been the only writer responsible for such a rehabilitation, but his text stands out as an example of risk-taking that paid off, a trend that has continued to this day. Indeed, not unlike travellers of the Famine era, today's writers almost feel it a duty to say something about the politics of Northern Ireland. This is not to say that the Northern conflict was solely responsible for the rekindled interest in Ireland, but now that the initial panic has died down, and some sense of what the conflict is (and was) about is understood, it may surely be claimed to have been a contributing factor. Some writers of course – like Pete McCarthy – avoid the North entirely, while others – like Paul Theroux – avoid the Republic. And then there are those who are endearingly unsure of what they intend, like Martin Fletcher, whose explicitly Northern Irish travels lead him into Donegal, past Moville, and Gleneely, and Culdaff, and on up until he reached Malin Head. The reason for such a detour by someone allegedly writing only about 'the good people of Northern Ireland'? Because once he looked at a map of Ireland, 'he knew [he] couldn't really end this journey in Derry'.

What is notable about this period is that although 'Britons' still visited in considerable numbers, there remains a fair representation of different nationalities, none of them more famous or more influential than Heinrich Böll. It took a full ten years before an English translation of Böll's text became available, but from its initial publication in German in 1957 it caught the imagination of many travellers, and encouraged a generation of German tourists to Ireland in particular. Before Böll there was Kees van Hoek, a Dutchman who worked for some time with the *Irish Independent* newspaper, and the American, Oriana Atkinson. But most of the writers, as has always been the case, came from Britain. The novelist, Olivia Manning, and the less well known Clara Coltman

Vyvyan, bring a quiet dignity to the lives of those with whom they came into contact, and also to their own writing. And then there is the remarkable Lionel Rolt, whose interests might have excluded him from this anthology were it not for the curious incident he relates: a moment of entomological wonder set against a gothic sense of place; a strange and apparently unselfconscious reflection afloat the loughs of County Leitrim.

54. Wilfrid Ewart, *A Journey in Ireland, 1921*

(London: Putnam, 1922, pp. 123–30)

Wilfrid Herbert Gore Ewart (1892–1922) had a varied career, as a captain in the Scots Guards, and as a novelist and journalist. He contributed to many periodicals and newspapers, including the *Nineteenth Century*, the *National Review*, and the *Fortnightly Review*, and published a highly successful novel, *Way of Revelation* (1921). Extracts from his Irish travelogue were first serialised in *The Times*, the *Westminster Gazette* and the *Sunday Times*, and are based on a visit he made from 18 April to 10 May 1921. Ewart was killed by a stray bullet in Mexico City, on New Years' Eve, 1922.

A May Day sun baked down upon the market square of Birr. It was early yet, and Sunday; the square was empty but for a few stray folk on their way to Mass. I hoped to walk the twenty-two miles to Tullamore by tea-time and, allowing for accidents, to cover at least half the distance in advance of the noonday heat.

The whitewashed and dun houses, the new-looking church on the first straight stretch out of the town were quickly left behind. There followed a bosky park-like country, uphill and down, the road ribboning ahead in long steady gradients. Green ridges rose on either hand, masses of yellow-prinked gorse filled the hollows, hawthorn in blossom and the whitish pink of crab-apple trees here and there sprinkled the green of hedgerows and fir-trees. Green was the prevailing tone of the countryside – a green so vivid and fresh and dew-sparkling as to suggest that a brand-new, super-beautiful world had been born in the night.

Mountains dreamed to the east. Slieve Bloom dreamed in the blue-grey majesty of mist, a hazy mirage lying upon the peaks, a bluish film of heat above the intervening country. After the first two or three miles wide, flat spaces of brackish brown bog opened up between the road and the mountains.

A few people passed at first – three men riding bicycles town-wards, a man and a boy driving a donkey-cart with a load of peat, a man herding cows from one field to another. All nodded or said 'Good morning'. Two wild-looking women came up behind in the donkey-cart, followed by some girls and men on bicycles, who turned down a side-road, being apparently on their way to Mass at a neighbouring village.

Three miles out a wide, deep trench had been dug across the road – a trench just wide enough and just deep enough to wreck any vehicle that should attempt to compass it. A long empty stretch between the bog and the hillside followed, at the end of which three holes, of the size and depth of shell-holes had been dug triangular-wise in the roadway, leaving a narrow pathway for the foot-passenger, but ensuring certain perdition to bicycle or car.

The chief characteristic of the remaining seven miles to Kilcormac was their extreme loneliness. Only at one place, some children were sprawling outside a broken-down farmstead which otherwise betrayed no semblance of life, although one suspected that its inhabitants were watching from the interior.

For miles at a stretch the only sign or sound was the hovering shadow and far-away whistle of a sparrow-hawk, the 'ting-ting' of green finches and chaffinches in the hedgerows, the melancholy piping of red shank from the bog, the cries of black-headed gulls which, doubtless nesting beside some nearby tarn, continually swept and swooped above the road. Yellowhammers vied in hue with the brilliant gorse, butterflies flickered along the grassy border. Goats, cows and donkeys completely independent of control made this their feeding ground, or lay asleep in the dust of the road.

A group of young men standing in the sunny Kilcormac village street eyed me suspiciously. I stopped at the inn, the landlord of which, to my surprise, served me with a will, pressed me to sit down and rest in his cool stone parlour, and finally refused my offer of payment.

I decided, after a quarter of an hour's rest to press on and break the backbone of the journey. After crossing a bridge that spanned a gurgling rocky stream, signs of Republican activity became more apparent. Trees recently felled lay by the roadside, some trenches that had been dug had evidently been filled in. I came suddenly up against a huge barrier.

This was at a point where the road curved round the flank of a hill and was shaded by trees. Four heavy beech-trunks interlaced with boughs had been thrown across it, forming a twelve-feet high obstacle not dissimilar to, though far more substantial than, a fence at Aintree. To circumvent this I climbed through a hedge, crossing the corner of a field, and joined the road through another hedge. The white walls of a farmhouse gleamed through foliage at a short distance, three hundred yards beyond the main obstacle a stiff fence of boughs had been erected, and fifty yards beyond this again was a newly dug trench. Of human or other being there was neither sight nor sound, the crow of a cock being the only sign that the farmhouse was inhabited.

But a mile further on a shifting patch of blue vividly contrasted with the hillside's emerald green. A dark-haired handsome girl accompanied by a child came down to the roadside.

'And where might you be making for?'

'Tullamore.'

'Have you your fiddle with you?'

The girl looked meaningly at my rucksack.

'Are you not the fiddler from Tullamore? Will you play us a tune?'

'I am travelling through Ireland. Perhaps I shall write in the newspapers.'

'Is that so? Will you give me one then?'

To be taken at one time for a local fiddler and a vendor of newspapers is not everybody's experience. Our colloquy continued for some minutes. When I continued my journey the girl and the child were laughing amazedly, still unable to make me out. . . . . .

After a while I sat down to rest near a cottage. An unkempt peasant woman brought me a glass of milk and, as the publican had done, refused payment. At the back of the dark cabin's interior I espied a young man lying on a bed. Half a mile farther on a figure stood on the skyline at some distance from the road, watching me intently. It continued to watch until I was out of sight.

My feet began to blister, thirst increased, and the heat raised a mirage over everything. Another four miles brought me to a public-house at crossroads. Half a dozen youths leaning against the wall of the inn cast anything but friendly glances at me and answered my question as to the distance to Tullamore gruffly. At this moment five young men on bicycles rode up from a side road and dismounting, joined in conversation with the original group. From the lowering glances directed at me, I realised that I was the object of their attention, but decided that there was no use in hanging about. After walking a few hundred yards, I had an instinctive intimation of someone following. Sure enough, as I looked over my shoulder, a man came into sight round a bend in the road. I waited for him to come up. A middle-aged peasant, he spoke with an air of surly suspicion and inquired sarcastically whether I had had much

difficulty in getting along the road. I replied that I had encountered
obstacles. We walked alongside for nearly half a mile, speaking laconically
of the crops and the weather. He then turned into a field and left me
with, as I thought, a rather sinister grin. Feeling certain now that something was 'in the wind', I plodded on apprehensively, not looking back.
Another half-mile brought me to a place where a large fir wood on one
side of the road faced a bog on the other. I suddenly heard the rustle of
bicycle wheels close behind and, looking round, was confronted by the
five young men.

'Stop! Hands up!'

They leapt off and laid their bicycles by the road. The leader of the
party, a dark, gipsy-faced fellow of about twenty-two, with a mop of
matted hair and a somewhat ferocious expression, seized my arms with a
policeman's grip, while another, who closely resembled him, dragged off
my rucksack with no light hand and passed it to his companions. All the
young men wore caps and dark suits of clothes. My pockets were turned
out, my purse, containing several £1 notes and other trifles, being taken.
I was then ordered to sit down by the roadside.

The half-hour that followed was much less than pleasant. Innocuous
tourist though I was, friend of Ireland though I believed myself to be,
the little slip of paper with which I had armed myself down-country
alone seemed to stand between me and a peremptory fate. For to the rest
of my identifications and references, which filled a large envelope, my
captors paid no attention whatsoever. My eyes wandered repeatedly to
the bog and my thoughts to the number of people who had lately been
found in bogs with brief notes attached to them. On a parallel road just
a week ago (I graphically recalled) a police inspector had been
kidnapped and had not been heard of since.

Meanwhile the five Republicans were busying themselves with my
mundane possessions. The contents of the rucksack lay in the road, my
papers (and incidentally my pyjamas) were being dismembered. I could
hear one of the party (who seemed to be a sort of Intelligence Officer)
reading aloud the wording of my precious slip of paper. Another seemed
profoundly interested in Justin McCarthy's 'Outline of Irish History'; a
third was perusing the hieroglyphics in my note book. A long muttered
conversation followed, during which the only words that caught my ear
were 'man' and 'road.'

At last the leader turned from the group. 'I think the man's all right.'

I was thereupon handed back the contents of my pockets and curtly
told to count my money, which out of politeness I omitted to do (but
which I afterwards did and found correct.) I now noticed that the three

subordinate members of the party were decent, respectable-looking youths of ages between eighteen and twenty-one. They helped me to put my things together and lifted my rucksack onto my shoulders.

We parted with mutual 'good afternoons'.

Two miles short of Tullamore, the bridge spanning a swift-flowing little river had been blown up – so thoroughly demolished at the centre, in fact, as to leave a chasm too wide to jump. The only alternative was to wade the stream – no unpleasant task for swollen feet – and to make a detour through some birch-woods to a point where it was possible to join the road again.

That was the last physical obstacle. But, walking into Tullamore rather conspicuously dusty and a traveller, battery after battery of coldly hostile glances were directed at me, by men who scowled as I passed, scowled after me, scowled up at the window of the inn where I sat at dinner. Everybody seemed to see in an English stranger a potential spy. At first I was inclined to put this feeling down to an undue sensitiveness induced by the events of the day; but the veracity of it was confirmed next morning when I was openly reviled by an apparently sober and respectable Irishwoman on the railway station platform who evidently took me for a plainclothes Black and Tan. The first remarks that caught my ear were: 'I said I will not be walked over. I can only die once, and I'll be happy to give my life for Ireland.' The lady's choicest sentiments then became unprintable; suffice it to say that everything not good enough for Irishmen was 'good enough for English dogs', and that the majority of her sentences ended with the exhortation, 'Shoot me if you like! Yes – trample on my dead body!'

55. John Gibbons, *Tramping through Ireland*

(London: Methuen, 1930, pp. 92–99)

Although the 1930s seem to have been a productive period for John Gibbons, with *Abroad in Ireland* and *My Own Queer Country* published in 1936 and 1937 respectively, little biographical information is available. Indeed, even Gibbons's itinerary can sometimes lack a certain clarity, with the reader barely conscious of movement (a statement about the travel-narrative form perhaps?). Nevertheless, this extract, with Gibbons slowly travelling from Sligo towards the Donegal coast, reveals a sharp intelligence, and an awareness of the subtleties of Irish and British political self-perceptions, despite the anecdotal touch and the apparent gullibility displayed.

Somewhere in quite a recent English guide-book to Ireland, I saw the statement that 'many of the hotels are not so bad as they look,' and having been in Ireland it struck me as funny. For you will often find electric light in hotels so tiny that their 'opposite numbers' at home would still be in the oil-lamp and tallow-candle stage (only Ireland seems somehow to have missed the Gas Age). And it has nothing at all to do with the Shannon scheme, the little local electric light concerns having been going for years. But I do not know what will happen to them when the national system gets into being.

You see its poles all over the country, very much as in France or Italy. Only the things being poles and not tripods are not so ugly. And Ireland is very proud indeed about it, and at every station you will see advertisements of cheap trains to Limerick just to let people have a look at the barrages and things. And then as far as I could make out, Ireland was extraordinarily sorry that England had not had the contract for the works. It went to the lowest tender and Germany got it. And, as I was told again and again, if England had got it there would have been more money for the country. 'For the Englishman,' they said, 'enjoys himself and spends. He brings his family and they all spend money. And Ireland might have had the bulk of their salaries.' Whereas when the thrifty German contractors and engineers came along the first thing they did was to erect a sort of fortress barricade, practically with sentries at its gates. And inside they put up a town of huts made of sections brought from Germany. And canteens, with every article sold of German origin. So that hardly a penny was spent in Ireland except on the barest wages of the cheap Irish labour taken on for the simple navvying work. Until in time the indignant locality rioted. So much so, in fact, that the Free State Army had to be called in to restore order. Lots of interesting odds-and-ends like that you pick up going through the country my way.

There are, however, other ways of travelling, as in one of my public-house evenings, I gathered. I was seeing nothing at all, a gentleman told me, missing Killarney and all the rest of the famous scenery bits. That was after we got friendly, for when we first met he hardly spoke at all, taking me, in fact, for a native. He himself was an English chauffeur, and generally of course he stopped in a proper hotel with His People; only this time there had not been room for him and they had sent him round to the public-house for a bed. It was his first time with the natives, and I think he was a little relieved to find us not at the moment drinking blood out of skulls. And then to an admiring audience he settled down to tell us all about it.

Every year, it seems, he and His People (who may or may not have belonged to the God of Abraham) did some country. Or was it that some country did them? The process consists in driving every day as far as possible without seeing anything at all, and to achieve this result one has of course to have a very powerful and costly machine. He told us all about it, and how it has valves and ball-bearings and things. I am almost certain it has ball-bearings. Certainly it has pneumatic tyres. It goes ever so fast, and it is called a Rolls-Royce. Some of the valves gave a bit of trouble explaining, but he was really very good and went over and over it again till at last we did begin to grasp the elements of the subject. 'Well well, sorr,' and 'Is that so, sorr?' the admiring chorus came again and again. I am proud to say that I got it out several times myself, and I flatter myself that I got the precise accent obviously demanded by the occasion. And it was hours before the unfortunate man discovered that nearly every soul in the circle of primitive tribesmen sitting round that public-house kitchen fire was a driver on one or other of the lines of motor-buses that linked up at the townlet. And nobody gave so much as a single snigger.

They made up for it upstairs, though, and it was hours before the other two in my room would let me go to sleep. I especially remember that particular room, because it had two perfectly extraordinary pictures in it, one of a soul being saved and the other of a man being damned and going straight from his bed into a truly realistic hell. It was the 'damned' one that was over my bed. The others particularly pointed it out to me. One of them, though, was only a conductor, so anyway one would not be likely to take his word on the subject of destinations. Travelling my way one did see life!

There was another public-house I remember where, after closing time had come and they had shut the bar up, only leaving two or three of the more favoured 'regulars' inside, they switched on a gramophone and one of the girls danced to it. A daughter I should think she would be, for they do not have barmaids in those sort of places. Anyway, there we were, and very nice it all was. And then about half-past eleven or so the very same girl suddenly snapped the gramophone to and announced decisively that it was bedtime. I, she supposed as she turned the towns-people out, would as an Englishman be of course a Protestant? Only I happened, I said, to be a Catholic. Then as that was so, she went on, I should probably wish to join her mother and the rest in the saying of the Rosary. Now that, I think, could never have happened in an English small-town inn.

There was another musical evening too, with another gramophone playing Irish reels and jigs, and men taking it in turn to dance to the thing. But not a bit like the things we see in Irish turns on the music-halls at home. Ever so decorous and almost prim. It is what they teach them now in the schools, on the same principle that they teach them their painstaking Gaelic. And then some one sang some of that too.

There was an old man sitting there, and he took strong exception to the Irish. It was not, he said, the true Gaelic at all, not the same stuff that as a lad he had learned from his father without any of your schooling at all. And to make his point he started singing himself, with no gramo-phone or anything else. An interminable song it was, but what it was all about I do not know. Because of course I could not understand a single word of it. So for my special benefit he started again with some of the old Irish songs in English, and this time I understood very well indeed. Some of them must have come down from the Rebellion times of 1798, and one of them was about the potato famine of the eighteen-forties and how we English starved the Irish. The odd thing was that the old man apologised to me before each song, and then went on to sing it. All about English soldiers being tyrants and despots and things, and once, I know, we were 'demons'. And to nearly all these things the people knew the chorus, and sang it. There was one bit about 'England quaking' that went with such a swing that only just in time did I pull myself up from joining in it. Real pep they put into the business, and to one bit about hating England I put it genially to the man next to me that he sang the verse as though he really meant it. 'But I do mean it,' he said, 'and so does every one else in this room.' It made me jump a bit, for, after all, though a joke is a joke there is a limit. I am English and I must not for very decency listen to everything. And yet if I walked out into that one-horse village ten miles from anywhere, where on earth was I to spend the night? I was fumbling uneasily for my hat when the atmosphere cleared again. 'But,' the man went on, 'my hating England does not mean that I hate the English.' I tell you it was all most peculiar.

Perhaps the most extraordinary bit of all came at the very end just before we went upstairs. First they sang the 'Soldiers' Song', the thing that has become the sort of national anthem for the modern Free State. Personally it did not impress me very much. Not the words at least. The only soldiers that I ever knew mostly only sang one song, and that was not about being soldiers at all. It was called 'I want to Go 'Ome,' and we sang it once coming down from Pilkem Ridge. Anyway, this blessed thing was their song, and it seemed only civil to stand up to it. So I did. Then as a sort of return compliment they said that they would wish to sing 'God Save the King,' only as nowadays the younger generation of Ireland generally does not know the words I should have to lead them.

And then standing bolt upright with all those kindly people waiting gravely and courteously for me to begin, the awful and almost inconceivable thing came to me. I am an Englishman; I believe with all my heart and soul in 'The King' and all that it stands for; and I would wish the thing to be played all round the world in salute to the Union Jack. But as I stood there the dreadful knowledge suddenly came to me that I do not know the words of it. Except just the opening lines that they play as you leave the theatre.

Most fortunately the old man who had sung the rebel-despot songs was able to help me out. But it was an awfully near thing.

56. Michael Floyd, *The Face of Ireland*
(first published 1937; 2nd edn, London: Batsford, 1947, pp. 92–95)

No biographical information could be found on Michael Floyd. His Irish travelogue, republished after ten years, with a few minor revisions, was originally published as part of a travel series entitled 'Face of Britain Series', which had a heavy emphasis on scenic attractions rather than on what Floyd disparagingly calls 'the human and historical factors'. Not surprisingly, a faint tension appears in the following description of Belfast with Floyd at times anxious but ultimately fascinated by the city's industrial power, and the fact that even in sleep it appears fully alert.

So to Belfast; and what a vast, noisy, invigorating place it is, in its cradle of green basalt hills at the head of the lough! I am not one of these who regard a great industrial town with shuddering distaste as so many square miles of concentrated aridity, punctuated by a few public buildings and churches. Belfast, of course, can show you squalor in plenty if you care to look for it; and I must admit that I cannot summon up much enthusiasm for some of its civic buildings, the Edwardian splendour of the huge City Hall in Donegall Square leaving me more than cold. But it is the vigour of the city that impresses you. In the last hundred years it has seen something like a twelvefold growth, and is still hard at it. You can almost feel it expanding around you, generating new aims, new industries, a new outlook. It was a great industrial heritage those Ulster city fathers brought to life some two centuries ago along the Lagan, and one that Belfast people will still fight tooth and nail to maintain, as their stern efforts to counteract world depression during the last decade have again shown.

Consider the part that Belfast products play in your daily life. There are, of course, the ships that carry you over the seas, including some of the greatest liners in the world; there are the tobacco you smoke, the linen sheets between which you sleep, the whisky you drink and the ginger-ale you add to it – that is if you have acquired a somewhat perverted transatlantic habit. Finally, there is the rope that may hang you one day. All these commodities the city produces in generous measure, and many more. No wonder it hums with life and energy – though 'hum' is perhaps hardly the word for it nowadays. The place literally roars, and the sound is punctuated by the sharp clang of steel, the rattle of looms and the wail of sirens.

Life in Belfast is a strenuous and exacting business, and I have sometimes amused myself by comparing conditions today with those obtaining about 150 years ago, as depicted in a delightful set of coloured engravings made by one Hincks to record the manufacturing processes of Irish linen. These delicately coloured ovals give an almost idyllic flavour to the processes of drying, rippling and boging; beetling, scutching and hackling; spinning, reeling and boiling – and one notices that the industry was to a large extent carried on by families in their own cottages, the fresh neatness of which is delightful. For certain processes, of course, large-scale wooden machinery was used which was housed in barn-like structures, and the beetling machine in particular, worked by water-power, was a triumph of cumbrous ingenuity. But the plates I like best are those that show the almost pastoral side of the manufacture: the ploughing and harrowing of the flax, for instance, in a rolling County Down landscape; the wet and dry bleaching, where the material is laid out in billowy strips on a green slope above the Lagan, and a couple recline in the foreground, clasping hands beneath a tree; and the 'viewing' at the Banbridge market, a scene of dignified activity against a sedate Georgian background. Most of this has naturally disappeared in the last hundred years; the flax is now largely imported from abroad, while the acres of whirring looms that nowadays fill the York Street district would certainly give the artist a shock. But I think he would have an eye for the population of fresh-faced girls who tend the machines and, when the sirens blow, stream home across the little bridges that span the river in a chattering crowd. They are splendid specimens, these Belfast mill-girls – tough, hard-working and proud, with a ready wit and a quick temper that can produce, I am told, some astonishing flowers of invective.

There is a fineness, too, about the big, tight-lipped Ulstermen who daily fill the shipyards of Harland & Wolff with a clangour that has now, I am glad to say, reverted to something of its old shattering tempo. You could fill volumes with the stories of the ships, great and small, that have emerged from under the raking gantries of these yards, which are such a grand sight at night, shot through by arc-lights that emphasise their tall spidery skeletons. A brass plate affixed to the wheelhouse of a ship engraved with this firm's name is a talisman of good design, sound construction and seaworthiness all the world over. For the Belfast ship-yards have a great tradition and a fine pride. Every man working in them knows that he is producing a commodity as durable and sterling as human hands and brains can make it, and that something of the spirit of Belfast goes out in every one of her ships.

Such is the civic pride of the place that it seems a pity that most of its important buildings – as is the case with almost every large British industrial town – came into being at such an awkward period for their architectural dignity – though I must qualify this statement with a good word for the new Parliament Buildings which we have already passed at Stormont. Otherwise, it must be confessed, one misses the gracious Georgian note of Dublin. Royal Avenue and the streets around Donegall Square, with their big shops and hotels and jostling traffic of trams, are cheerful and attractive thoroughfares, it is true, to which a sense of spaciousness is imparted by the appearance of green shoulders of hill filling their vistas in the distance. But they contain little of architectural interest, and do not entirely represent the Belfast that spreads hugely around them to the verges of the basalt ridges and the shores of the breezy lough, with its slow procession of shipping coming to unload against the quays that flank the Lagan right into the heart of the city.

For me, perhaps, the most typical Belfast picture is one of broad cobbled streets stretching far into the distance, flanked by low lines of houses, taverns and shops that are punctuated every now and then by rather arid churches of almost every known denomination. Down the centre grinds a creaking succession of trams and over the rooftops rise the outlines of gantries, factory chimneys and steamer funnels. Loaded lorries and drays edge their way among the tramcars, and occasionally the whole procession of traffic is suspended by the passing of a street demonstration, with waving banners and thumping drums, or a funeral. Children play at the street corners and shawled women go by on their shopping rounds with baskets. If some of these streets are rather grey, depressing places by day, at night for an hour or two they seem to come into their own. There is a clatter of voices from every bar-parlour, the cinemas flash forth their wares in coloured lights and the children swarm in shrill bands. Belfast is taking its pleasure after the labours of the day, and the roar of the city has subsided a little, so that you can detect individual voices and laughter. Soon, when the lights are lowered in the bars and fish-shops and the cinemas have disgorged their audiences, a great quiet will settle over the town, openly disturbed by the clank of a belated tram or the wail of a siren out on the river.

57. Kees van Hoek, *An Irish Panorama*

(first published 1945; 2nd edn, London: Longmans, 1947, pp. 136–39)

Kees van Hoek was born in Holland, where he trained as a journalist. A Catholic, he wrote for newspapers across Britain and Ireland – the *Daily Express*, the *Daily Telegraph*, the *Irish Times* and the *Irish Independent* – but worked as a newspaper correspondent all over Europe: in Berlin, Paris, Rome, Geneva and the Balkans. Well known for his interviewing skills, many of van Hoek's articles were syndicated across the world, and found their way into newspapers such as the *Chicago Tribune* and the *Sydney Morning Herald*. This extract briefly describes the midlands town of Portumna, County Offaly, before shifting to the monastic settlement – and scenic beauty – of Clonmacnoise during the summer of 1945.

Portumna is but a very small town, even as Irish towns go; and it looks as if it has been built up out of a toy box, and dusted but an hour ago. Nowhere are the streets so spotless, nowhere do all the windows glitter and sparkle like mirrors, and nowhere in Ireland have the choicest gifts of flowers and plants been so liberally strewn about. In St. Brendan's Street, wherever the eye roams, on either side and from one end to the other, stand neat and gay flowerpots, or painted square wooden boxes, a couple in front of every house, each holding shrubs or plants. From the spick and span facades of the two-storeyed houses, one decorated in yellow with red, another in bluish grey with green, flowers and creepers trail from window boxes; in fact, there is hardly a window without its sill-box of geraniums. Flowers are everywhere, colossal bouquets like waving forests of tall, white, gold-hearted marguerites between the tombstones of the old churchyard. Round the new Vocational School the young shrubberies and flower-borders have been designed by a Dublin expert.

On the site of the one-time stables alongside the Church, a wall-back rock garden has been conjured up, while beside the Presbytery at the end of the Market Square a beautiful floral garden has been draped round the base of the statue of Christ the King. Behind the plinth towers a cedar of Lebanon, and all around tall creamy rose bushes, clumps of velvet dahlias, snapdragons and hydrangeas in deep red patterns, create a joyful mosaic.

Even geographically the heart of Ireland is that hallowed spot of Irish history, Clonmacnoise. We went there by a beech and ash lined country road along the Suck, the pleasantly winding river which separates Galway from Roscommon. Flocks of sheep dotted the bronzy banks, frisky lambs alongside their gravely nibbling still winter-coated mothers. Pairs of sturdy horses were drawing ploughs, the ploughmen's eyes set on the smooth green pasture curling wide open into a dead straight, deep rich brown furrow. Curlews and plover had the sky to themselves.

Suddenly, without warning, we came to what seemed a chunk of the Great Wall of China magically transplanted to this peaceful landscape. A forbidding high wall astride a mighty mound, the square set fortress, still strong enough to withstand the assaults of time, the threatening rows of embrasures within its steep flanks now minus their guns and cannon once covering the Shannon. Nowadays there is a dance hall behind these twelve-foot-deep walls; two greyhounds and a cat dozed together in front of a turf fire, onions were drying on the flat roof where once the sentinel kept watch and ward. This indeed is the heart of Ireland, the strategic crossing between Leinster and Connacht, where foreign martial might once guarded the greatest river of Ireland at one of its widest sweeps.

I shall always remember my first view of Shannon-bridge with that great thrill − deep below us, from the roof of the fortress, its fifteen peerless arches spanning the lordly river. A poem in stone, hallowed by the centuries into a sparkling mosaic of moss green and rust colours, of infinite shades between silver and grey. Lined high by a many-recessed parapet, it shone like a straight silk ribbon held between two bracelets. A farm-hand standing in his turf cart appeared to be sailing along the narrow channel of the long, slender bridge, twenty feet above the dimpled water. Only one other bridge have I ever seen to compete with its setting, that at Avignon. And, like the Rhone there, the vista of the Shannon here is truly majestic and immense. The sky, that glorious spring day, was a vast canopy of powdered silver-blue, and all Ireland seemed arrayed around us in all her riches along the banks of her mightiest river.

Along the slight ridge of the gently swelling Offaly bank we reached Clonmacnoise. Atop a daintily ribboned, neatly stone-walled road past the whitest whitewashed cottages, rose suddenly the first Round Tower of Clonmacnoise. Fifteen hundred years of history have etched Clonmacnoise indelibly on the face of Ireland: the centuries have mellowed the gaping remains of old ruins with silver mosses, and corroded lime has turned powdered snow under the golden light of spring. The arches of its once seven churches are open to the sky, but its doorless porches still adorned by the craftsmanship of monks of before the year 1000 with petrified lace or stone chiselled into faultless rope. Here in the centre of hundreds of tombstones towers the Cross of Clonmacnoise, erected over the grave of King Flann, Anno Domini 914, and to this day it teaches the Passion of Our Lord and High Resurrection on its weather-beaten, wind-swept panels.

The nave of that gem of a cathedral sanctuary, where Roderic O'Conor, the last High King of Ireland, is buried, lies open to the sky. I looked out at the Shannon and pictured his body being carried solemnly from Cong. A road winds its way in unspoilt rural beauty from Clonmacnoise to Bunn Talmhan, the End of the Land, where St. Patrick himself once crossed the river on his way from Roscommon to Offaly. I waited in the shadow of St. Finian's Tower, still a perfect candle to the past, although already old when history was young – for the sun to set over the heart of Ireland. The wide bends of the river were transformed into bejeweled curves, even the bog glowed warm and golden; on the pastures the brown and black cattle became mere silhouettes. The ducks quacked in the tall, lightly swaying rushes, the silent swans glided along in aristocratic abandon; the only sounds in the air were those of the fleetly-winged wild geese winging in a great armada towards the distant spires of Athlone.

58. S.P.B. Mais, *I Return to Ireland*

(London: Johnson, 1948, pp. 64–68)

Stuart Petrie Brodie Mais (1885–1975) was a broadcaster, novelist, freelance journalist and sometime lecturer at the University of London. Appointed literary critic
to the *Evening News*, then book reviewer for the *Daily Telegraph*, Mais published
widely, but retained a particular preference for travel literature, of which he
published over twenty volumes. Although Mais had visited Ireland many years
earlier, as a student from Oxford, he describes Ireland as 'a mystery, an enigma',
and cites the Englishman's sentimentality for the place as his main reason for
returning. The extract chosen is headed 'Dublin, Thursday 31st July, 1947'.

I sat in the porch once more, watching the silk-stockinged girls going
off to work and the bare-legged girls and men in shorts carrying heavy
rucsacs, going off into the hills. The holiday season has begun. The ticket
offices have large queues. The trams and buses and trains are all over-
crowded. We spent a pleasant interlude arguing about the trees in
O'Connell Street. Donald Johnson said they were maple or sycamore. Jill
was certain that they were plane trees. Neither I nor Imogen nor Lalage
nor a priest sitting with us, nor Bestwick, a pleasant young reporter who
came to interview me, could make a guess. This was one of the days
when a sort of Ascot fashion-parade took place in the lounge of the
Gresham after morning mass. It was a special occasion, a young priest's
ordination, but it was an occasion also for a display of smart clothes, and
drinking in the Winter Garden. Because my raincoat was now unwear-
able owing to yesterday's cloud-burst, I went down to Mr. Figgis who
took me to a shop where I was fitted with a double-sided Burberry
which cost me eleven guineas and would have cost me twenty-two
coupons if I had had any.

Jill immediately decided that she, too, ought to have a similar one at
similar cost. It was, I may say, a very useful coat, quite impossible to get
in England despite the fact that they were made over there.

All my clothes were in need of fresh pockets, linings and patches,
and I was delighted in my innocence to find in Prescott's in D'Olier
Street, a shop where they seemed delighted at the prospect of mending
it, and promised to have it back within a few days. I was green to Irish
promises then, and delivered up my coat into their hands.

I was told that there were number 51 Parker pens on sale in some of
the shops. I spent many fruitless hours trying to track one down. There
was every other variety but not the Parker 51.

The problem of the trees in O'Connell Street was solved, as I saw a photograph of several hundreds of pied-wagtails assembled like starlings among the branches of what the caption described as the 'plane trees of O'Connell Street'. So Jill had been right. She is scarcely ever wrong about trees.

At 12.30 I was called for by a Derbyshire man called Bannister who took me off to the Hibernian Services Club where I had been invited to luncheon with another man from Matlock called Broughton who had now risen to the position of General Manager of the L.M.S. in Dublin, a man much sought after as in his hands rested the responsibility for the sailings and sailing-tickets across the Channel. I imagine his life to be no easy one, but he certainly did not give the impression of allowing his responsibilities to weigh heavily on his shoulders. He, the pure-bred Englishman, gave me the feeling that he was more easy-going and light-hearted than any of the Irish among whom his lot was cast. The Services Club looks out on the trees and lakes of the famous St. Stephen's Green, has a most imposing exterior with pillars, a great terrace of wide steps and huge porticos. Inside, it is as handsomely furnished as the Travellers' or the Atheneum, and on that sunny July morning was bustling with activity. I saw few members of the services. It seemed to be filled with affable and successful Dublin business men, several of whom I met in the bar where we spent a preliminary forty minutes drinking excellent sherry and listening to an exchange of witty and original stories. There was more spontaneous laughter than I had heard in England for months. I took the opportunity to look round the vast pictures of old British battles and trophies of lions, bears and tigers brought home by members of the Services.

One of the brightest spirits was a tall man called Hogg, who was a Scots sea-merchant from Galashiels. I was introduced to the President of the Club, a stately and imposing lawyer who also bore a Scots name.

The pick of the bunch was a real Irishman, a dapper little man with the build of a jockey. His name is Tyson. He is a tailor in Grafton Street, known intimately to all the leading race-horse owners and jockeys, as he makes the racing colours not only for the King, but for Lord Derby and all the other well known riders and owners. He himself is an enthusiastic rider to hounds, and waxed lyrical about the Meath and Kildare hunts. His own home, which he asked me to visit, is perched high on a rock above Killiney, with a view that, he claimed, excels any in Europe.

We all ate together at a large round polished table and we had lobster and carrageen, which is a variation of ground rice.

Ladies, I was surprised to see, were allowed to have luncheon in the same room, though they were not admitted to the club bar. It was a riotously hilarious meal, as different as possible from any that I can remember in any London club. The spirit was that of a picnic party. I went back with Mr. Tyson to his shop after luncheon to inspect the photographs of his own horses, and found it crowded with a very smart crowd of English men and women over for the Dublin Horse Show. They were buying such a prodigious number of clothes that it was obvious that no one was bothering about any forthcoming difficulty with the Customs. Silk shirts seemed to be the main object of the Englishmen's search. I was glad that Lalage was not present. One curious characteristic of the Irishman is his insistence on lurid, flamboyant, and to my mind incredibly vulgar, patterned ties which look as if they had come from Chicago. There is of course a close link between the United States and Ireland, but the link is closest in this craze for the tie that shrieks.

The colours of Trinity College, on the other hand, are as harmoniously blended and as dignified as those of any Oxford college tie.

While I was in the shop I saw Captain Nicolls, one of the four riders in the English team, whom I had seen ride a faultless round at the Royal Show at Lincoln earlier in the year. My need was a sports coat, but Mr. Tyson had no size that would fit me. After tea at Mitchell's, where I had the inevitable pancake, I met Johnson's representative, Mr. Thompson, who took me to Dan Byrne's bar, which is a popular rendezvous of the Grafton Street crowd. The chief characteristic of this bar is a succession of red and blue bottle-ends that light up the under-part of the counter. He then took me round to Waddington's Picture Gallery where I saw an exhibition of modern Czechoslovak paintings. They struck me as crude, meaningless and mad, yet some of them, by Geza Szobel, were priced at ninety guineas.

They were mainly cubist, surrealist, distortions of parts of the human body, inconceivably ugly and nightmarish. I found a strong and pleasant contrast in the pictures of Ireland, by Derek Clarke which reminded me of a picture depicting two Connemara peasant families, that I had very much liked, in the Academy. They were by the same artist. There was one of some grey walls and a donkey sidling up a street in a West country village that I wanted to buy to make a dust-jacket for this book, but Lalage overruled my desire to buy it for sixteen guineas, and it is certainly true that I have no wall-space on which to hang any further pictures.

We dined at the Gresham at 8s. 6d., each on grapefruit, salmon, roast duck and raspberry melba, and then went to join Inglis's 31st birthday party at the Gaiety Theatre to see Donagh McDonagh's play 'Happy as Larry', a queer, fantastic poetic melodrama about a wife who poisoned her husband in order to marry her husband's doctor. McDonagh's father was killed in the 1916 Rising. His play later came to London and had a huge success.

Lord Dunsany told me that McDonagh got the idea from a Chinese story and that there was a close aesthetic link between the Irish and the Chinese.

I sat next to a lovely black-haired young girl who turned out to be a granddaughter of Erskine Childers. Her comments on the play were witty and apt. I was carrying my pocket edition of Tristram Shandy and in view of the fact that she was obviously well read, I was surprised to find that she knew nothing of Sterne and told me that she thought Tristram Shandy was not the sort of book that women would ever care about. It had not occurred to me before, but now I come to think of it, there is a distinctly masculine appeal about Uncle Toby and Corporal Trim. A woman might find the diversions and digressions irritating.

There was a second play that night, a knockabout farce called 'The Beginning of the End' by Sean O'Casey, which delighted Lalage and Imogen.

Two clowns smashed crockery, and one clown was pulled up a chimney on a rope that broke. The children yelled with laughter. The only interesting thing about it was how O'Casey came to write it. First the nightmarish Czech surrealists, then the Chinese poetic melodrama, then the slapstick clowning. I was getting some curious side-lights on the Irish character.

59. L.T.C. Rolt, *Green and Silver*

(London: Allen, 1949, pp. 150–55)

Lionel Thomas Caswall Rolt (1910-74) was an author whose interests lay mainly in engineering history (he trained as a mechanical engineer) and inland navigation, and whose publications largely reflected that expertise: *Inland Waterways of England* (1950), *Navigable Waterways* (1969), and *Victorian Engineering* (1970). Although Rolt's preferred method of transport was by boat, he was fortunate in being able to travel along Ireland's Grand Canal and Royal Canal in the later 1940s, since fuel shortages were only then beginning to ease (the government had instructed that all propellers from pleasure craft be removed during the war). This extract finds him travelling towards Lough Key, County Leitrim.

We traversed the narrow and tortuous reach of the Boyle from Drumharlow, passed under the bridge at the village of Cootehall, and crossed Lough Oakport, a lovely little lake set in the wooded demesne of Oakport House. I have traversed few more beautiful stretches of inland waterway than the Boyle from Oakport to Lough Key. Trees grew thickly about the banks, their branches stooping to trail their leaves in the water. Between them flowed the clear still stream, darkly in their shadow or golden in the sunlight. I eased the boat till we were only just making headway against the gentle current, gliding with scarcely a ripple over the smooth surface, and in this way we passed beneath Knockvicar Bridge and so came to the lock and weir above.

Clarendon Lock, Knockvicar, looked very dilapidated. The locksides were overgrown. The gates on one side were chained up, being obviously rotten and unusable, while their opposite numbers looked little better. Because there is no longer any commercial traffic on the Boyle, the Board of Works apparently concern themselves very little with the state of the navigation. It is to be hoped that they will not allow this lock to become unworkable and so prevent boats from entering one of the most beautiful lakes in Ireland.

Mr. Conlon, the lock-keeper occupies a cottage by the bridge and out of sight of the lock. While Angela and Martin prepared lunch and Richard fished from the sill of the weir, I strolled down the path through the trees to advise him of our arrival and to suggest that he come up when his dinner hour was over. It was some time before he put in an appearance; but who cared? Here, certainly, it was a case of 'time enough', for the sun that warmed the beams and the weathered stones of the lock, the soft air and the murmur of the weir soon stilled activity to drowsy content so that I doubt whether we would have concerned ourselves overmuch if Mr. Conlon had not appeared at all that day.

Lough Key shares with Lough Gill, near Sligo, the title of 'The Killarney of the West'. Arthur Young, in his *Tour in Ireland* (1780) seems to have been much impressed by the beauty of the lake. 'It is one of the most delicious scenes I ever beheld,' he wrote, 'A lake of five miles by four miles, which fills the bottom of a gentle valley of circular form, bounded very boldly by the mountains. Those to the left rise in noble shape; they lower rather in front and let in a view of the Strand Mountain near Sligo, about twenty miles off. To the right you look over a small part of a bog to a large extent of cultivated hill, with the blue mountains beyond.'

As we sailed across the sparkling waters of the lake that afternoon, threading our way between the wooded islets with which it is dotted (an island for every county in Ireland, it is said), I thoroughly endorsed the description of this eighteenth-century traveller. Ahead of us to westward rose the moorland ridge of the Curlieu Mountains. Properly speaking they have not the stature of mountains because they do not reach the 1000 feet contour, but, rising steeply from the lake shore, they certainly have, as Arthur Young put it, a 'noble shape'. Historically, the Curlieus possessed a strategic value despite their modest height, and on August 15, 1599 there was fought a great battle on their slopes between an English army under Sir Conyers Clifford and the Irish under Red Hugh O'Donnell which resulted in a great victory for the latter.

The whole of the southern shore of Lough Key is occupied by the demesne of Rockingham, and as we moved out toward the centre of the lake the view between the islands opened out so that we could see the great grey block of Rockingham House with its terraces falling towards the lake shore. Before we left Knockvicar Lock I had been studying the map of the lake and had decided that the best anchorage would be a bay immediately to the west of the house which looked well sheltered from the south and west by a wooded headland and by Drummans Island which appeared to be linked to the headland by a bridge. Accordingly we left the marked channel across the lake, giving Swallow and Orchard Islands a wide berth to port and keeping a careful look out for rocks. Most of the submerged rocks in this lake are marked by iron rods which do not project very far above water level and which may be missed, especially if the lake is rough. Moreover the islands should not be approached too closely in anything larger than a rowing boat as their shores are shelving and rocky. We reached our objective without mishap, and finding that the margins of the bay were reed-fringed – a sure sign of a mud bottom – we ventured fairly close in shore before letting go our anchor. Feeling that we were trespassing, our first action was to row ashore and enquire at the house whether we might remain at our anchorage and land on the demesne. We were assured that we might do so.

How can I describe our surroundings? The formal artifice of those who, a century and more ago, had laid out the demesne of Rockingham lay buried amidst a growth of trees, shrubs and flowers of almost tropical luxuriance where native species and strange exotics mingled in equally prodigal growth. The wooded headland which sheltered our bay had been converted into two islets by the construction of canals and these were spanned by graceful stone bridges, one of 'rustic' work, the other more formal with a balustrade. Water lilies floated in the dark, reedy waters of these still canals, and in a clearing by the margin amid bracken, heather and fern there grew tall spires of scarlet-spotted tiger lilies. Farther within the shadow of the wood there was nothing but a brilliant emerald green carpet of moss softer and deeper beneath the tread than any carpet ever made by man. The scene, in its air of unreality resembled nothing so much as some romantic setting for the ballet 'Lac des Cygnes'.

To complete the magic of this fantastic prospect, opposite our mooring and across the bay there rose out of the water a castle, perched upon an islet no larger than the perimeter of its foundations. We rowed across to this castle that evening, and as we neared it, found that what we had taken for windows were merely their semblance painted upon wooden shutters, for the building was but a shell, having been gutted by a fire so fierce that only charred fragments of beams and joists remained. What a strange spectacle this fire must have made. Imagine the castle blazing like a gigantic torch in the midst of this enchanted lake which would mirror the lurid flare of the flames, the black silhouette of the walls and the showers of sparks which must have fallen upon its surface with a hiss of steam. The building that was thus destroyed was actually a 'whimsy', a place of summer residence built by the owners of Rockingham upon the foundations of the ancient fortress of the Macdermots who once held the estates of Rockingham. For their support of Tyrconnel's rebellion and for their victory in the battle of the Curlieus, the Macdermots paid heavily. Their lands were confiscated and awarded by Queen Elizabeth, in 1630, to Sir John King, Muster-Master-General of the Queen's forces, and ancestor of the present owner of Rockingham, Sir Cecil Stafford King-Harman.

On the mainland behind Castle Island we came upon the mouth of another canal and walking up the bank beside it, discovered the ruins of a lock. These canals, we found out later, were not merely ornamental. They once combined beauty with utility by enabling turf to be brought by boat from the neighbouring bogs to a quay on the lakeside immediately below the house. Thence the turf was conveyed to the domestic quarters by means of an inclined subterranean passage beneath the terraces. I have seen private estate railways such as that belonging to the Duke of Westminster at Eaton Hall, but this was the first time I had seen a private canal system constructed for anything other than a purely ornamental purpose.

Rockingham has other unusual features. On the south or landward side of the house there is a semi-circular range of domestic offices sunk below ground level in such a way that the lawn which slopes smoothly to the park is level with their roof ridge, and the view over the park from the ground floor windows is thus unobscured. In the days of its construction, the fact that the domestics were thus relegated to sunless semi-twilight was doubtless considered a negligible price to pay for this amenity. Moreover, in this case, the tradesman's entrance was also underground, access being via a subterranean passage beneath the garden on the east side. When Richard and I had first approached the house to ask permission to moor we had modestly sought this back entrance in vain, and having completed a discreet circuit, gave up the search and approached the imposing west portico.

Rockingham House was built for General Lord Lorton by John Nash in 1805, and subsequently altered by him in 1820. An engraving of Nash's original design shows a two-storeyed façade surmounted by a dome. But it is said that his patron complained that this design did not compete in grandiloquence with another house which the architect was at that time building in the County of Tipperary, and the result was the present three-storeyed structure. There can be little doubt that Nash's original longer and lower frontage was better proportioned and certainly better suited to its lake-side site. As constructed, the great grey block towers in a too austere and uncompromising fashion for its romantic situation. Rockingham is an urban mansion set in the wilds of Connaught; it has an arrogance which is incapable for any concession to its surroundings. But having said this, and having been privileged to see its interior, I would be prepared to endorse Sacheverell Sitwell's opinion, expressed in his *British Architects and Craftsmen*, that Rockingham is probably the best example of Nash's country houses.

We returned from our exploration of castle and canal to an excellent dinner consisting of Angela's gillaroo accompanied by a delicious potato dish exotically entitled 'Pomme Anna', and followed by rhubarb and cream. That evening, too, we observed a curious disturbance in the water near the boat, and on going out in the dinghy we found that it was caused by the death throes of an enormous drowning insect. Its body was striped like that of a wasp or hornet, but it was at least twice the size of the latter, in fact, it was the largest insect I have ever seen alive. I am no entomologist but I hazard the guess that it was a Great Pine Sawfly (*Sirex gigas*) which is certainly found in Ireland. Somehow the discovery of this strange monster seemed to contribute a final touch of the bizarre to our surroundings. I should not have been surprised to see vivid humming birds hovering over the tiger lilies or, as dusk fell, great vampire bats come swooping out of the wood.

60. Olivia Manning, *The Dreaming Shore*

(London: Evans, 1950, pp. 199–202)

Olivia Manning (1908-80) was born in Portsmouth, but spent much of her life in London. She published thirteen novels, including *The Balkan Trilogy*, for which she is best known, two volumes of short stories, and a biography of Stanley in Africa. In 1976 she became a Commander of the British Empire. At this part in her winter journey she is travelling from Donegal's Bloody Foreland towards Letterkenny, then onwards to Donegal town via Barnesmore Gap.

In the bright, cold morning, I took the 'bus round the Bloody Foreland so was able to see to the end of the far-stretching main street of the three villages. I passed the barn-like Co-operative building and the writing on the wall – 'Down with England', 'To hell with England', etc. – which it had been courteously suggested I should not bother to read.

Beyond the last of the village houses was an area so littered with stones it was like a giant sea-beach. Even out here there were little cottages with tiny patches cleared for cultivation. Many people immigrated from these parts but as many stayed and many have chosen to return. The contentment with so limited a life is not easy for an English town-dweller to understand. It must come from an unusual richness of the spirit not known to many of us. The average person here is of very high intelligence with great quickness of wit and invention. Indeed one wonders if any of the notable Irish wits had anything more than most of their obscure fellow countrymen, beyond the energy to take their gifts to market.

As we rounded the Foreland there appeared, ten miles out at sea, Tory Island – pronounced 'Torry' – which at this distance has an air of being composed of gigantic slabs of red granite, some upright, some lying down. Of the many towers which gave the island its name, one remains – a fine round tower of red granite, fifty-one feet high, built of dry-stones like a beehive hut. There are also two ruined churches and the fragments of an ancient abbey said to have been founded by St. Columba. Almost nothing grows on the island and the present inhabitants, almost two hundred and fifty in number, live precariously by lobster fishing and kelp-burning and are often destitute. They pay no rent, rates or taxes and, until recently, elected their own king whom they obeyed in all things. A ship of the Royal Navy, H.M.S. *Wasp*, set out in 1884 to attempt to collect dues (for what there is no knowing) but was wrecked with heavy losses, and no other attempt has ever been made.

Tory Island, though so northerly and lying off so barren a coast, has never lacked inhabitants. It was the battlefield of the Nemedians and Fomorians, pirates from Africa who, in prehistoric times, fought beside the Tower of Conning. The Gaels have always loved islands, however remote, however barren, and in the west there is scarcely a scrap of spray-washed rock that has not a history. During the days of Paul Jones and Fineen O'Driscoll the Rover, pirates and wreckers made their homes where even the Irish fishermen could not. But times are changing. Peaceful, modern Ireland has little excitement and no wealth to offer the young people of these parts and the islands are becoming de-populated.

I had always supposed as a child that the Bloody Foreland was given its dramatic name after some activity by Judge Jefferies. Later I learnt it was named for the red colour of its rock, but there is little of this red rock to be seen except at the very tip of the peninsula. The whole of the barren bear's head of land with its rocky bluff and vast boulders, has a grey look. The red sandstone at the point is found again in Tory Island. The streaks of red among the local granite have obviously caught the imagination of local people for a great stone so marked in the grounds of Ballyconnell House at Falcarragh has given its name – Cloghaneely – to the whole district. The story is that the red veins on Cloghaneely are the stains of the blood of a chieftain called MacKineely, beheaded by Balar, the famous one-eyed King of Tory Island.

The rock of the Bloody Foreland supports as great a population as does the Rosses. The small whitewashed cottages dot the whole land-scape and under the bluff there is a village street with a little shop crowded with goods, its window full of picture post cards. As the 'bus turns towards Gortahork, there can be seen the lovely sheltered bay of Ballyness with its smooth brilliant sands. From here we returned to Charlie Friel's.

My problem was whether to go to Dungloe and Portnoo, or not to go? That night the moon shone on the quartzite of Errigal so it looked like a silver mountain – a mountain of frost in the icy night. Next morning the gale whipped in with the force of midwinter and I decided that to see Dungloe I must wait for the spring.

Shivering in the bleak grey morning I went down the road to catch the 'bus to Letterkenny and saw a family of tinkers coming into the village. I thought of the eighteenth-century wit who said he never knew what the beggars of London did with their cast-off clothing till he found it was sold to the beggars of Dublin. Among these tinkers a small boy with a tall twig carried like a masher's cane, swaggered past in rags to which he had managed to give a fantastic elegance. With all the airs of a circus master he drove before him an ancient horse so thin, so hock stiff, so unsteady on its frail old bones, one felt it would fall to pieces at a touch. Everyone on the road paused to stare as the heart-rending creature went past.

At Letterkenny I had to go after my jacket again. I did so with dread – but the jacket was waiting for me and the girl kept out of sight while the proprietress explained in a confidential whisper how it had reappeared in the bedroom and no one had said a word. While I was hearing this, the girl passed in the background and glanced quickly at me. I wanted to say 'It doesn't matter, it doesn't matter at all – and when you come to London you'll have the time of your life.' But the matter could not be brought out into the open like that. Nothing had happened. Only an atmosphere of suppressed scandal hung in the air. The girl did not write to the address I gave her. She probably thought she had done for herself there.

As the 'bus drove southwards towards Stranorlar, the air turned to summer. First I took off my coat, then the jersey I had put over my blouse and still it was warm. As I waited for the Sligo 'bus in the shut deserted streets of Stranorlar (if ever one has to waste time in a strange town it is always early closing day), the sun shone brilliantly from a cloudless sky. At last the Sligo 'bus came in from Derry and we set out over the boglands to Donegal Town. The road runs through the Barnesmore Gap. I do not know why I had never heard of the Barnesmore Gap, but there it was rising and opening before us, the tall dark mountain sides rising sheer from the road to form a narrow U, for me the most startlingly impressive because unexpected. It was an almost deserted district. The bogland with its haze of purple-red colour ran to the mountain edge.

Whenever I could I had got the front seat of the 'bus but this time I had been unlucky. Two girls sat in the front seat and a third leant forward from the seat behind and kept her head between the other two. The three of them together blotted out the whole window. As the Gap rose up out of the distance one of them exclaimed:

'Will you look now what is before us! 'Tis the Gap of Dungloe.'

'Is that what it is!' said another in mild surprise.

The third as we advanced on the Gap, murmured to herself: 'The Gap of Dungloe! The Gap of Dungloe!' while the rest of the 'bus fidgeted but said nothing.

61. Oriana Atkinson, *The South and the West of It: Ireland and Me* (New York: Random, 1956, pp. 96–99)

Little biographical information could be found on Oriana Atkinson, save that she was the wife of the *New York Times* drama critic, Brooks Atkinson, whom she married in 1926. In 1945-46 Brooks Atkinson served as a *New York Times* correspondent in Moscow, and Oriana accompanied him. The result was a series of articles on Russia by Brooks Atkinson, which won him the Pulitzer Prize in journalism in 1947, and a bestselling memoir authored by Oriana, entitled *Over at Uncle Joe's: Moscow and Me*. Oriana Atkinson was a native New Yorker, and also wrote articles and short stories. This extract finds her in Galway city.

In olden times, the village well was the center of gossip and visiting. The pawnshop on High Street seemed to have taken the place of the well. The women talked gaily – and Gaelic, probably. They spoke so fast, and they spoke in such soft, delightful Irish voices that I couldn't make out a word they said. They were as merry as crickets, those women, and they had an air that was almost greedy. They seemed to be really hungry for this conversation and companionship in the brownish light of the murky pawnshop. They seemed like drug fiends craving their stimulant. They threw themsleves whole-heartedly into the conversation, and although they saw me and recognised me for a stranger, they paid no attention, but chattered away.

I was due for another surprise: the pawnbroker himself. He was not at all what I had thought a typical pawnbroker in a poor district of an Irish town would be like. I thought that of course he would be an oppressor of the poor, a grinder of faces in the dirt, a squeezer-out of hard-gotten pennies. This pawnbroker, who entered by a rear door, came into the store and was greeted like an old friend who had been delayed. He must be the handsomest pawnbroker in Ireland. He was tall, slim, and his white hair grew strong and bushy upon his noble head. His nose was strong and proud, classical, really, but he carried it mildly. He greeted his waiting public like a matinée idol. They looked at him with friendliness, almost with affection.

Nobody seemed to be putting anything *into* pawn. Everybody seemed to be giving the pawn man money and taking things *out*. This wasn't the way I had heard it, either. I thought poor women were always wringing their hands and begging the miserly money-lender for a penny or two more on their rags. Not these women. There seemed to be a kind of ritual dance going on, the figures of which were well known to all the dancers. The motions and gestures were almost automatic.

One young woman was getting back a man's suit. It was a thin, poor bit of cloth and seemed to have taken on permanently the shape of the hanger. It was a light-colored suit, and maybe had never been worn. She took it absently and slung it over her shoulder, holding the hanger by its hook. She never stopped talking, even when she handed some money to the lady at the cash register.

With the beelike hum of the women as obbligato, I moved around the shop to see what the stock was. There were many pairs of high rubber boots, some cracked and useless, some fairly new, but all smelling of fishermen and brine. There were piles of soiled and ragged clothing, also emitting odors. Proudly displayed on a hanger of its own and hanging free where its beauty could strike the eye, was a dusty sweater, its pink wool worn tissue-thin. That sweater was old in 1902 and had been worn by a succession of careless owners ever since.

There was also a well-worn copy of *The Road Round Ireland,* by Padraic Colum; several unattractive clocks, none in running order; a flimsy bedspread or so – and nowhere to be seen the pure-gold shawl pin of the ancient Irish king. I was disappointed. I just stood there for a minute watching the eager women, the handsome man, the serene woman at the money machine, and trying to understand the cheery nonchalance of these people who might all have been poverty-poor.

Then another woman entered. She was shawled, as all the others were, and she was young and very frail and worn. At her heels pattered two children, and when she took her place among the other women the children leaned against her, waiting patiently. I looked down at these children and they were so delicate and slight that I hardly dared to breathe.

The boy's age (his mother told me later) was one and a half. The little girl was three years old. And it became clear to me at once that these were not human children; they were mer-children and lived in Galway Bay. Even then, in the dun light of the pawn-shop, there was a pale blue aura around them. So tender-frail, there were, so desperately new, I dared not even nod, lest the breeze engendered by the movement of my head should blow them out the door.

The boy baby's head was foamed over with delicate silvery bubbles that were probably hair. The girl's hair, so fair it seemed to have no color, hung in lank, silken strands to her shoulders. Their eyes were a sapphire blue, but so quiet in the little pale faces. The little ones did not move away from their mother to investigate any of the marvels so close at hand. They stood; they waited. They did not even glance at me.

I wondered what the penalty for kidnapping in Ireland might be. I decided to sling one of these babies under each arm and leg it across the street to where Sean O'Brien sat waiting for me in the car. Sean, well accustomed by this time to American idiosyncrasies, would scarcely turn his head to see what I was up to this time. With one child under each arm I would leap into the car and somehow or other slam the door. 'Step on the gas!' I would cry, and Sean would say mildly, 'Very good, madam,' and off we'd go, leaving High Street high and dry.

Somehow or other I would get those tender tots to America. And I'd wash them and comb them and dress them in things from Pat-Rick on Madison Avenue. And I'd stuff them full of orange juice and scraped beef and desiccated liver. And the blue-white of their faces would change to rose-pink and dimples would come across the backs of their thin, cold little paws. And they would stomp on the floor and go roaring through the apartment, shaking the dish cabinets and smashing the hi-fi and making noises like machine guns. Their mother would never miss them — be glad to be rid of them, no doubt. And then that dreadful woman, by a mere gesture, shattered my dream and ruined her children's future in America.

Without turning around, she made a kind of searching movement with one hand, her fingers widespread, as if she were holding a bowl upside down. She bent her knees, still without turning, all in an accustomed and absent-minded way. And her hollowed hand came into contact with the little girl's head; came into contact with it and fitted over it, neatly. The mother was reassured and the little girl seemed comforted. The mother withdrew her hand and went on with her chitter-chatter, and in a moment her other hand came reaching, the knees bending, the open hand fitting over the moon-bright ringlets of the cherub boy. Maybe she'd miss the children after all. Maybe I'd better leave them.

Unnoticed when I came in, unnoticed while I had been there, I now turned to leave and nobody noticed my going. The mother turned instinctively when she heard a movement near the children and it was then I asked the ages of the little ones. She told me simply, and turned away again without curiosity or interest.

As I left the dark shop, the boy removed a damp thumb from the coral of his mouth and opened and closed his fist at me and whispered, 'Bye'. His sister, evidently alarmed that she had overlooked some amenity, raised her hand, too, and the last I saw of the changelings they were standing solemnly opening and shutting their hands at me, waving farewell. At least I suppose that's what they thought they were doing. They were looking at each other.

62. Heinrich Böll, *Irish Journal: A Traveller's Portrait of Ireland* (first published 1957; this edn, London: Vintage, 2000, pp. 13–19; translator L. Vennewitz)

Heinrich Böll (1917–85) was one of Germany's best-known post-war writers. Author of numerous short stories, radio plays and journalism, he published *The Clown* (1963), *Group Portrait with Lady* (1971), and many others, to critical acclaim. Winner of the Nobel Prize for Literature in 1972, he was also renowned for his translations of several of the works of Shaw and Behan. Böll sailed from Liverpool to Dublin sometime in 1954, and although *Irisches Tagebuch* was published in 1957, the first English translation, by L. Vennewitz, appeared only in 1967.

At Swift's tomb my heart had caught a chill, so clean was St. Patrick's Cathedral, so empty of people and so full of patriotic marble figures, so deep under the cold stone did the desperate Dean seem to lie, Stella beside him: two square brass plates, burnished as if by the hand of a German housewife: the larger one for Swift, the smaller for Stella; I wished I had some thistles, hard, big, long-stemmed, a few clover leaves, and some thornless, gentle blossoms, jasmine perhaps or honeysuckle; that would have been the right thing to offer these two, but my hands were as empty as the church, just as cold and just as clean. Regimental banners hung side by side, half-lowered: did they really smell of gunpowder? They looked as if they did, but the only smell was of mold, as in every church where for centuries no incense has been burned; I felt as though I were being bombarded with needles of ice; I fled, and it was only in the entrance that I saw there was someone in the church after all: the cleaning woman; she was washing down the porch with lye, cleaning what was already clean enough.

In front of the cathedral stood an Irish beggar, the first I had met: beggars like this one are only to be found otherwise in southern countries, but in the south the sun shines: here, north of the 53rd parallel, rags and tatters are something different from south of the 30th parallel; rain falls on poverty, and here even an incorrigible esthete could no longer regard dirt as picturesque; in the slums around St. Patrick's, squalor still huddles in many a corner, many a house exactly as Swift must have seen it in 1743.

Both the beggar's coat sleeves hung empty at his sides; these coverings for limbs he no longer possessed were dirty; epileptic twitching ran like lightning across his face, and yet his thin, dark face had a beauty that will be noted in a book other than mine. I had to light his cigarette for him and place it between his lips; I had to put money for him in his coat pocket: I almost felt as if I were furnishing a corpse with money. Darkness hung over Dublin: every shade of gray between black and white had found its own little cloud, the sky was covered with a plumage of innumerable grays: not a streak, not a scrap of Irish green; slowly, twitching, the beggar from St. Patrick's Park crossed over under this sky into the slums.

In the slums dirt sometimes lies in black flakes on the windowpanes, as if thrown there on purpose, fished up from fireplaces, from canals; but things don't happen here so easily on purpose, and not much happens by itself: drink happens here, love, prayer, and cursing. God is passionately loved and no doubt equally passionately hated.

In the dark back yards, the ones Swift's eyes saw, this dirt has been piled up in decades and centuries: the depressing sediment of time. In the windows of the secondhand shops lay a confused variety of junk, and at last I found one of the objects of my journey: the private drinking booth with the leather curtain; here the drinker locks himself in like a horse; to be alone with whisky and pain, with belief and unbelief, he lowers himself deep below the surface of time, into the caisson of passivity, as long as his money lasts; till he is compelled to float up again to the surface of time, to take part somehow in the weary paddling: meaningless, helpless movements, since every vessel is destined to drift toward the dark waters of the Styx. No wonder there is no room in these pubs for women, the busy ones of this earth: here the man is alone with his whisky, far removed from all the activities in which he has been forced to participate, activities known as family, occupation, honour, society; the whisky is bitter, comforting, and somewhere to the west, across three thousand miles of water, and somewhere to the east, two seas to cross to get there – are those who believe in activity and progress. Yes, they exist, such people; how bitter the whisky is, how comforting; the beefy innkeeper passes the next glass into the booth. His eyes are sober, blue: he believes in what those who make him rich do not believe in. In the woodwork of the pub, the panelled walls of the private drinking booth, lurk jokes and curses, hopes and prayers of other people; how many, I wonder?

Already the caisson – the booth – can be felt sinking deeper and deeper toward the dark bottom of time: past wrecks, past fish, but even down here there is no peace now that the deep-sea divers have invented their instruments. Float up again, then, take a deep breath and plunge once more into activities, the kind called honour, occupation, family, society, before the caisson is pried open by the deep-sea divers. 'How much?' Coins, many coins, thrown into the hard blue eyes of the inn-keeper.

The sky was still feathered with manifold grays, not a sign of the countless Irish greens, as I made my way to the other church. Not much time had passed: the beggar was standing in the church doorway, and the cigarette I had placed between his lips was just being taken out of his mouth by schoolboys, the end nipped off with care so as not to lose a single crumb of tobacco, the butt placed carefully in the beggar's coat pocket, his cap removed – who, even when he has lost both arms, would enter the house of God with his cap on his head? – the door was held open for him, the empty coat sleeves slapped against the door posts: they were wet and dirty, as if he had dragged them through the gutter, but inside no one is bothered by dirt.

St. Patrick's Cathedral had been so empty, so clean, and so beautiful; this church was full of people, full of cheap sentimental decoration, and although it wasn't exactly dirty it was messy: the way a living room looks in a family where there are a lot of children. Some people – I heard that one was a German who thus spreads the blessings of German culture throughout Ireland – must make a fortune in Ireland with plaster figures, but anger at the maker of this junk pales at the sight of those who pray in front of his products: the more highly coloured, the better; the more sentimental, the better: 'as lifelike as possible' (watch out, you who are praying, for life is not 'lifelike').

A dark-haired beauty, defiant-looking as an offended angel, prays before the statue of St. Magdalene; her face has a greenish pallor: her thoughts and prayers are written down in the book which I do not know. Schoolboys with hurling sticks under their arms pray at the Stations of the Cross; tiny oil lamps burn in dark corners in front of the Sacred Heart, the Little Flower, St. Anthony, St. Francis; here religion is savoured to the last drop; the beggar sits in the last row, his twitching face turned toward the space where incense clouds still hang.

New and remarkable achievements of the devotional industry are the neon halo around Mary's head and the phosphorescent cross in the stoup, glowing rosily in the twilight of the church. Will there be separate entries in the book for those who prayed in front of this trash and those who prayed in Italy in front of Fra Angelico's Frescoes?

The black-haired beauty with the greenish pallor is still staring at Magdalene, the beggar's face is still twitching; his whole body is convulsed, the convulsions make the coins in his pocket tinkle softly; the boys with the hurling sticks seem to know the beggar, they seem to understand the twitching of his face, the low babble: one of them puts his hand into the beggar's pocket, and on the boy's grubby palm lie four coins: two pennies, a sixpence, and a three penny bit. One penny and the three penny bit remain on the boy's palm, the rest tinkles into the offering box, here lie the frontiers of mathematics, psychology and political economy, the frontiers of all the more or less exact sciences crisscross each other in the twitching of the beggar's epileptic face: a foundation too narrow for me to trust myself to it. But the cold from Swift's tomb still clings to my heart: cleanliness, emptiness, marble figures, regimental banners and the woman who was cleaning what was clean enough; St. Patrick's Cathedral was beautiful, this church is ugly, but it is used, and I found on its benches something I found on many Irish church benches: little enamel plaques requesting a prayer: 'Pray for the soul of Michael O'Neill, who died 17.1.1933 at the age of sixty. Pray for the soul of Mary Keegan, who died on May 9, 1945, at the age of eighteen'; what a pious, cunning blackmail; the dead come alive again, their date of death is linked in the mind of the one reading the plaque with his own experience that day, that month, that year. With twitching face Hitler was waiting to seize power when sixty-year-old Michael O'Neill died here; when Germany capitulated, eighteen-year-old Mary Keegan was dying. 'Pray' – I read 'for Kevin Cassidy, who died 20.12.1930 at the age of thirteen,' and a shock went through me like an electric current, for in December 1930 I had been thirteen myself: in a great dark apartment in south Cologne – residential apartment house, is what it would have been called in 1908 – I sat clutching my Christmas report; vacation had begun, and through a worn place in the cinnamon-coloured drapes I looked down onto the wintry street.

I saw the street coloured reddish-brown, as if smeared with unreal, stage blood: the piles of snow were red, the sky over the city was red, and the screech of the street-car as it swerved into the loop of the terminus, even this screech I heard was red. But when I pushed my face through the slit between the drapes I saw it as it really was: the edges of the snow islands were brown, the asphalt was black, the streetcar was the colour of neglected teeth, but the grinding sound as the streetcar swerved into the loop, the grinding I heard as pale green – pale green as it shot piercingly up into the bare branches of the trees.

On that day Kevin Cassidy died in Dublin, thirteen years old, the same age as I was then: here the bier was set up, *Dies irae, dies illa* was sung from the organ loft. Kevin's frightened schoolmates filled the benches; incense, candle warmth, silver tassels on the black shroud, while I was folding up my report, getting my sled out from the closet to go tobogganing. I had a B in Latin, and Kevin's coffin was being lowered into the grave.

Later, when I had left the church and was walking along the streets, Kevin Cassidy was still beside me: I saw him alive, as old as I was, saw myself for a few moments as a thirty-seven-year-old Kevin: father of three children, living in the slums around St. Patrick's; the whisky was bitter, cool, and costly, from Swift's tomb ice needles came shooting out at him: his dark-haired wife's face had a greenish pallor, he had debts and a little house like countless others in London, thousands in Dublin, modest, two-storied, poor; petty bourgeois, stuffy, depressing, is what the incorrigible esthete would call it (but watch out, esthete: in one of these houses James Joyce was born, in another Sean O'Casey).

So close was Kevin's shadow that I ordered two whiskies when I returned to the private drinking booth, but the shadow did not raise the glass to its lips, and so I drank for Kevin Cassidy, who died 20.12.1930 at the age of thirteen – I drank for him too.

63. C.C. Vyvyan, *On Timeless Shores: Journeys in Ireland*   (London: Peter Owen, 1957, pp. 38–42)

Little biographical information is available on Clara Coltman Vyvyan, other than that she visited Ireland some twenty years prior to this tour, stayed at Kilkenny, and had lunch with Countess Markievicz in Dublin, who 'spent all the afternoon talking like a waterfall'. Vyvyan also published *Down the Rhone on Foot* (1955), *Temples and Flowers: a Journey to Greece* (1955), and *Random Journeys* (1960), among others. At this point in her narrative she has just arrived at Mullaganagh, County Kerry.

We came in this sleepy, hopeful dazed condition to the grey house beside the lake. When we drew near, the splendour of that mansion faded, as in a fairy-tale, and we found a sad, neglected building wrapped in silence. One smoking chimney was the only sign of life. We passed a window, blind with cobwebs, and went on to seek the front door. A rusty plough lay sideways in the mud, two forlorn black cows were stumbling over branches and scraps of galvanised iron that lay, without a purpose, here and there. An angry goose came hissing towards us and then turned back to assemble her goslings. Two sides of the house had now faced us with their silence and dilapidation; we turned the next corner and, crunching on rounded pebbles, came to a front door, that never could have been opened within human memory, judging by its appearance. Then we turned back again.

The silence hanging about that house was full, it seemed to us, of threats and malice. However, we found at last the back door which we had overlooked, so dingy and unwelcome it was, set there as if against its will in that sombre wall.

We knocked and listened in the stillness. We knocked again and we thought that we heard a human voice calling from upstairs. We waited in tense expectation. It was nearly nine o'clock, we were very hungry and the hotel in the Glen was fourteen miles away, fourteen long and lonely Irish miles. Breakfast was, in all our world, the only thing of real importance and then, after breakfast, sleep. Should we meet refusal? The house had not a giving look about it.

A step came heavily down the stairs and the door was shaken from within but even then it seemed reluctant to be opened and while it stuck we wondered what would be the face that, in another moment, would look out on us with enmity or welcome. We would almost have postponed the opening of the door, if only to indulge our hope.

It was a woman's face. She was a grey woman and her eyes were hard, unwelcoming, full of questions and hostility, but urgency rushed into our words and dammed up her refusal. We were very tired, both of us. And very sorry to disturb her. We had come from that little town on the other side of the mountain, hoping to find breakfast at the lodge. People had told us that she took in visitors. And what a beautiful spot it was, here beside the lake.

We did not mention our night beneath the moon for we felt sure that we should not meet with understanding.

'Very well,' she said at last, and it seemed as if we had dragged the words out of her and we began to feel a little ashamed of ourselves. 'But you won't see any breakfast for half an hour,' she added.

We followed at her heels, almost pushing her, so great was our longing for rest. The kitchen fire was burning. She led us over a stone floor to a front room full of furniture. There were many chairs of different shapes, two tables, a sideboard, a cupboard and a sofa. It was a spacious room with two great windows, both of them shut and both well and truly sealed with cobwebs. She left us and we dropped our packs; the Wanderer fell on to the sofa and I dragged three chairs together to make a bed. Only one thing mattered and that was the finding of a place to lie down flat on our backs, for a day and a night if possible but whatever might betide for a few blessed minutes.

We slept until she brought boiled eggs and tea and bread and butter, searching us, as she moved about, with her gimlet eyes that held curiosity but no spark of friendliness and when she left us we discussed the situation.

The house was like a vault, unloved, forlorn; it exhaled a breath that made us shiver. Had it been for many years the abode of toads and spiders or strange unhappy creatures that shun the light? 'The smell of frogs, the smell of frogs,' I had murmured as I fell asleep. A sense of loneliness and creeping sorrow had reached me from the spirit of the old dwelling-house, expressing itself in that haunting amphibian smell. But the Wanderer was like a startled deer. 'It is a cruel, haunted place,' she said, 'we must get away at once.' Her eyes were full of fear.

'Fourteen miles of mountain road between us and the Glen,' I reminded her.

Then the woman came in with a jug of hot water and I put our fate to the touch. Could she give us beds for the night?

No. She was not prepared for visitors.

We really would not give her any trouble and we really would put up with any sort of bed she cared to give us. I did the special pleading while the Wanderer looked on.

No. The house was not fitted up for visitors.

It would certainly be good enough for us and both of us were very tired; could she not let me have one look at her spare rooms?

This last question wrung a reluctant 'Very well' from her and I felt that the battle has half won. Once or twice during our talk a light had flickered across that grey face from which the piercing eyes looked out with an expression that I have never seen before nor since. Now, looking back on the experience, I believe that those eyes were saying: 'Shall I find the world without as terrifying as the world within?'

She showed me the dilapidated upper rooms where brown stains patterned every wall and plaster had fallen from every ceiling, leaving the laths exposed; there were holes in all the floors and the paint had flaked off the window sashes. There were three spare rooms; the middle one had a skylight in the roof but no window and I looked at it in silent horror. Then we entered the third and largest room and I said with enthusiasm: 'Oh, I'd much rather sleep here than in the dark one.' We were standing under bare laths like the bones of a skeleton, beside a fire-place with ironwork brown as rust, and the masonry of three walls was exposed where great patches of plaster had fallen away. Her face relaxed a little as I spoke and there was something like the shadow of a smile in her eyes, or perhaps it was no more than the shadow of a memory, for indeed that face must long ago have lost the habit of smiling.

'So would I,' she said.

Was she suffering from claustrophobia? Had the old house cast a spell upon her and had all this damp and decay and the windows sealed with cobwebs made a kind of prison for her spirit? Her eyes had answered me and a gleam of understanding had passed between us. She looked round the room that I had chosen, with a puzzled air, as if the idea had just occurred to her that she might do something to arrest the decay and hide the shabbiness that had gained upon her like an inexorable tide.

'I could push the bed out in the middle, where the ceiling is not falling,' she said at last. 'And the first room, where your friend will sleep, is not so far gone.'

Little by little we learned something of her history. Nearly twenty years ago her husband had died, leaving her with four children. The landlord of the lodge would do nothing and she had only one pair of hands.

'Nothing,' she repeated passionately, and her eyes had an almost evil look in them. The children were all out in the world. Night after night she would go to bed and be unable to sleep for the loneliness; she would think and think, lying there in the dark. Now and then her expression relaxed a little and some gleam of memory or hope seemed to light up that imprisoned mind. Yes, she was imprisoned, not hostile; this woman was the captive of things whose mastery she resented without hope – the solitude and decay of the house had her in thrall and the loneliness of many years had set its seal upon her face and now was looking out from those haunted eyes. It was something that was almost a living creature that lurked about the house and manifested itself in a smell of shadow-loving frogs and spiders. It was the woman's tortured loneliness and want of hope.

The rooms were spacious and, so far as the tenant's care was concerned, they were clean and orderly; the meals she brought us were well served and set out on a clean tablecloth. But we noticed that she brought things in from the kitchen one by one, with a rather puzzled air, as if she always knew that there was something she ought to have remembered.

And that, so far as we shall ever know it, is the story of the grey house at Mullaganagh; a neglectful landlord and a lonely woman, with things falling, year after year, into decrepitude, and everywhere a sense of decay, and the slow disintegration of bricks and wood and mortar re-echoing in her own solitude.

But of course, I have only touched the outer margin of the woman's loneliness, in these words, for who shall ever look into the spirit of another?

In the early morning when we first came near the lake, the water was dim, like a breath rising from the earth, too impalpable to bear reflection, too colourless to betray its presence there, a mere wraith in the heart of the mountains; but all through that day, while we sauntered along the shore or lay half asleep in the heather, the Lake of Mulla-ganagh was blue instead of grey, as it lay there unperturbed, still as ice.

64. Richard Howard Brown, *I am of Ireland: an American's Journey of Discovery in a Troubled Land* (first published 1974; 3rd edn, Colorado: Roberts Rinehart, 1995, pp. 124–28)

Richard Howard Brown was born (and still lives) in New York, and works as a freelance writer and marketing executive in publishing-related fields. Brown's text draws memory, history and place together to provide a powerful, though never less than balanced, portrait of Ireland in the early 1970s. At this point Brown is in the city of Derry, in March 1973, where one year on from Bloody Sunday, 30 January 1972, violence continues to escalate.

Gerry Fallon, Kathleen's husband, the welder who had not worked in three years, a big-faced man with tight curly hair that was more gray than brown, told me I was so dark around my eyes that I looked like a racoon.

'You need some kip time,' he said. 'If you're off to Donegal tonight, you'd better grab some kip time in the kid's room.'

I was tired from the late nights and from not being able to sleep on the couch in the morning with Mrs. Maguire up and around her small apartment by seven-thirty, and that night we were to drive over to Donegal to see Peter's retired bartender friend from Boston.

Kathleen took me into the children's room and it was like a small barracks with twin beds and two cribs. The linoleum on the floor was buckled and broken away. There was a white painted bureau with a statue of the Blessed Mother on it squeezed into the corner and a tinted print of the thorn-encircled Sacred Heart of Jesus over one of the beds. I lay in my clothes on top of the bed next to the window and Kathleen said to pull the comforter over me and she'd wake me at seven.

I was wearing a woolen shirt and a fleece-lined leather jacket and still I could feel the damp chill from the walls, and even the comforter seemed damp and cold on top of me. I lay quiet and tried to let my mind go free so I could sleep but instead I thought how remarkable it was that I was there. At home I had a wife and three teen-aged children and two cars and a cat. The apple tree next to the kitchen was probably going to fall down on my house if something wasn't done about it soon.

What time was it there? My watch said five-sixteen. That meant it was just past noon at home. My sons and daughter were at school and my wife was probably cleaning up the house or out shopping or on the phone to her sister.

We had lived in that house for a dozen years and it was part of me all right, but they were doing what they were doing and it had nothing to do with me now or with where I was.

There weren't any apple trees where I was and the only car was Peter's, and that was rented from the South. That had nothing to do with the way these people lived. These were the poor of Derry in Northern Ireland. I was insurance- and mortgage-poor from living in the suburbs of New York, which was nowhere near the same thing.

Well, there were plenty of poor at home if that's what I wanted. I didn't have to travel to Northern Ireland to find the poor. But if it was the Bronx or Brooklyn and there was no Ireland to talk about and no discrimination against Catholics to resent, what would I know of people like these? What would we have in common with no history and no heroes and no idea of the eight centuries of resistance to define them for me?

Forget home. I hadn't come to Derry to think of home. I was lying on a strange child's bed, cold in all my clothes, smelling the damp brackish smell of the room, three thousand miles away from that.

Outside the window was the open walk area of St. Joseph's Place and beyond it, the waste ground where the Saracens loaded with para-troopers had come roaring and weaving through the crowds on Bloody Sunday the winter before, so I thought about that.

When Bloody Sunday happened, it was eleven in the morning at home and I was probably drinking coffee in the dinette and reading the book section or the entertainment section of *The New York Times*. And right outside that window and all around the building and across the street, hundreds of people like Kathleen and Gerry Fallon and Kevin Maguire and others whom I had met in the bars, had been running, terrified, trying to find a place to hide, because it wasn't just gas or rubber bullets, it was live rounds; and the paratroopers weren't just firing over their heads to scare them and restore order, they were killing people.

It had been a sunny, mild day for mid-winter and the afternoon had started with a march organized by the Northern Ireland Civil Rights Association to protest internment of suspected IRA men without trial or even formal charges. It was a large-scale demonstration in civil disobedience and more than fifteen thousand Catholics from all over Northern Ireland took part. The march stretched out for over six hundred yards and it took an hour to reach the Army's barbed-wire barricade at William Street, a quarter of a mile from the centre of the the city, where the stone throwing began.

Stone throwing was the standard expression of the people's anger against authority in Derry and a predictable response that day to the Army's presence at the barricade. It was a form of hooligan war that the soldiers knew how to contain and there were usually limits to the hurt that could be inflicted by either side. Sometimes the hurt was severe because when the Army retaliated with rubber bullets at short range, they could break a leg or shatter a jaw. A hit with a broken piece of pavement could be just as damaging, but the soldiers were protected by Plexiglas face masks that turned down off their helmets and big Plexiglass shields and flak jackets and knee and shin guards. The people had no protection against the six-inch rubber bullets or the water cannon or the CS gas other than the fact that they could usually run away from a confrontation more easily than the soldiers could.

There were thousands of soldiers on duty all over Derry, but the ones who came down into the Bogside and did the killing that day were paratroopers. Everyone knew that the paratroopers, with their red berets and their nine-year enlistments, were the cream of the British Army. They were the real professionals, the elite fighting men, the really mean bastards that you sent in to take the hard terrain in a war, not to control a crowd of angry stone throwers in a civil disturbance. You didn't need paratroopers for a street mob.

The march was supposed to end with speeches at the Guildhall on the other side of the wall in the business centre of the city, but it never got there. Only a few hundred marchers had reached William Street when the officer's voice came over the loudspeaker: 'You may not come through this barricade.' That's when the stone throwing started, and the Army retaliated with purple-dyed water from the water cannon and CS gas. The crowd was sullen and confused and some were afraid as word spread that an old man and a boy had been shot. Then there was the roaring sound of the Saracen armoured personnel carriers weaving in through the people milling around the Rossville Flats.

The paratroopers weren't wearing their distinctive red berets when they emptied out of the carriers, their faces blackened with pigment. They had steel helmets on with the Plexiglass masks turned back on top to give them a clear view for shooting. The stone throwing was over. The paratroopers hadn't been brought in for that. They were there to take on the IRA. It didn't matter that neither the Officials nor the Provisionals were around to fight. They expected to have it out with the IRA, and in the tough euphemism of the military, they were going to bloody its nose.

Kathleen Fallon saw a balding, middle-aged man in a dark blue quilted car jacket run across Rossville Street toward the crowded semi-open stairwell we had just climbed with the children and where, that day, she was flattened out on the stairs with scores of other people who were crawling over one another trying to get to the upper floors. Just as the man reached the building, his face disintegrated from a high-velocity bullet that a paratrooper fired into the back of his head.

Each time a bullet rang off the metal bars that crossed over the open areas of the stairwell there would be muffled curses and cries of fright and Kathleen prayed she wouldn't be killed and that her children were safe inside the apartment and that her husband was not among those who had been shot. But even with her eyes closed tight and the noise of the gunfire and the screaming, there was the image of what had happened to the man's face inside her head.

All that time Gerry Fallon was crouched by one of the low apartment houses across Rossville Street. He watched an armoured car track a girl in a maroon coat, the armoured car like a big steel slug, except that it could move much faster than the girl realized and it ran her down, knocking her into the air with her coat and dress flying up and her legs kicking and Fallon saw a flash of white underwear and then she was a crumpled pile of maroon cloth in the street.

He saw a priest crawl out to give the last rites to a man while bullets ricocheted off the pavement around him and then a boy waved his arms and screamed, 'Shoot me. Shoot me. Don't shoot the priest,' and the soldiers shot him and the boy fell and someone grabbed at his legs and dragged him away.

There was a teen-aged boy with Fallon, and another man who had been wounded in the thigh sat on the ground with his belt tied tightly as a tourniquet around his upper leg. A spinster who lived with her married sister on the ground floor above the Fallons was huddled down beside them crying hysterically, 'They're going to kill us all. They're going to kill us all.'

A paratrooper backed around the corner of the building, firing across the street as he came. He turned his head and saw them and spun around with his rifle on them and shouted, 'Move and you're dead.' It was possible, with the noise of the shooting and the screaming of the people all around them, that he had said, 'Move *or* you're dead,' and that what he meant was for them to get out into the street, and Fallon almost cried out to him to please say it again so that he would know what to do, when the paratrooper ordered them up against the wall of the apartment building with their hands on top of their heads. The boy beside Fallon grabbed at the barrel of the paratrooper's rifle, trying to turn it away and run, but the paratrooper was a grown man and stronger and he jammed the rifle into the boy's stomach and fired it and part of the boy's back came away with the blast.

Fallon and the woman stood with their faces pressed against the brick wall and the man with the tourniquet around his thigh sat with his back against the wall and his hands clasped on top of his head, mumbling prayers in Latin. The woman was sobbing with her mouth open and her face puffed and wet from crying, the saliva and mucus hanging down in thick strings from her nose and chin, and Fallon was certain, with the boy lying dead behind him, that he would never live to see his family again.

65. Paul Theroux, *The Kingdom by the Sea: a Journey around the coast of Great Britain*

(London: Hamish Hamilton, 1983, pp. 188–91)

Paul Theroux, born in the United States in 1941, has written novels, literary criticism, and travelogues, as well as children's fiction and journalism. He also lectured in English at Universities in Malawi, Uganda and Singapore, from the mid-1960s to the early 1970s. Theroux's work includes *Sailing through China* (1983), *The White Man's Burden* (1987), *Happy Isles of Oceania* (1992), and *Collected Stories* (1997).

I knew at once that Belfast was an awful city. It had a bad face – mouldering buildings, tough-looking people, a visible smell, too many fences. Every building that was worth blowing up was guarded by a man with a metal detector, who frisked people entering and checked their bags. It happened everywhere, even at dingy entrances, at buildings that were not worth blowing up, and again and again, at the bus station, the railway station. Like the bombs themselves, the routine was frightening, then fascinating, then maddening, and then a bore – but it went on and became a part of the great waste-motion of Ulster life. And security looked like parody, because the whole place was already scorched and broken with bomb blasts.

It was so awful I wanted to stay. It was one of those cities which was so demented and sick some aliens mistook its desperate frenzy for a sign of health, never knowing it was a death agony. It had always been a hated city. 'There is no aristocracy – no culture – no grace – no leisure worthy of the name,' Sean O'Faolain wrote in his *Irish Journey*. 'It all boils down to mixed grills, double whiskeys, dividends, movies, and these strolling, homeless, hate-driven poor.' But if what people said was true, that it really was one of the nastiest cities in the world, surely then it was worth spending some time in, for horror-interest?

I lingered a few days marvelling at its decrepitude and then vowed to come back the following week. I had never seen anything like it. There was a high steel fence around the city centre, and that part of Belfast was intact because, to enter it, one had to pass through a check-point – a turnstile for people, a barrier for cars and buses. More metal detectors, bag searches and questions: lines of people waited to be examined, so that they could shop, play bingo, or go to a movie.

There were still bombs. Just that week a new type of bomb had started to appear, a fire-bomb made of explosive fluid and a small deto-nator; it exploded and the fiery fluid spread. And it was very easily disguised. These bombs had turned up in boxes of soap flakes and break-fast cereal and pounds of chocolates. One in a tiny bag had been left on a bus, and ten passengers had been burned and the bus destroyed. That was my first day in Belfast – *Driver Steers Through Blaze Hell to Save Lives* displaced the Falklands news.

Threats, was headline in every newspaper, with this message: *If you know anything about terrorist activities – threats, murders or explosions – please speak now to the Confidential Telephone – Belfast 652155.*

I called the number, just to inquire how busy they were. But it was an answering machine, asking me for information about bombs and murder. I said, 'Have a nice day,' and hung up. On the way to Coleraine and the coast I was in a train with about ten other people, two in each car – and some got out at Botanic Station, a mile from Central. I had never imagined Europe could look so threadbare – such empty trains, such blackened buildings, such recent ruins: and poverty, and narrow-mindedness, and sneaky defiance, trickery and murder, and little brick terraces, and drink shops, and empty stores, and barricades, and boarded windows, and starved dogs, and dirty-faced children — it looked like the past in an old picture. And a crucifix like a dagger in one brute's lapel, and an *Orange Lodge Widows' Fund* badge in another's. They said that Ulster people were reticent. It seemed to me they did nothing but advertise. *God Save the Pope* painted on one ruin, and on another, *God Save the Queen.* And at Lisburn a large sign by the tracks said *Welcome to Provoland.* Everyone advertised, even urban guerillas.

Fifteen minutes outside Belfast we were in open country: pleasant pastures, narrow lanes, cracked farm houses. But in such a place as Ulster the countryside could seem sinister and more dangerous than a crowded city, since every person on the move was exposed in a meadow or a road. The old houses all stuck up like targets, and it was hard to see a tree or a stone wall and not think of an ambush.

No Surrender, it said on the bridge at Crumlin. That town was a low wet rabbit-warren set amid cow parsley and wet fields. And then Lough Neagh, one of Ulster's great lakes, and the town of Antrim. Now the train had a few more sullen skinny faces on board. The towns were no more than labour depots, factory sites surrounded by the small houses of workers. But the factories were shut, the markets were empty, and the farmland looked flooded and useless. We came to Ballymena. I asked a man in the car if it was true that in Slemish near here ('where St. Patrick herded his sheep') children used to be kept in barrels to prevent them fighting.

He said he did not know about that. His name was Desmond Corkery and he guessed I was from the United States. He wished he were there himself, he did. He was after coming from Belfast, he was, and was there a more bloody miserable place in the whole of creation? And dangerous? Policemen and soldiers everywhere — and they talked about Lebanon and the flaming Falklands!

I guessed that Corkery was a Catholic. I asked him my usual question: how do you tell a Protestant from a Catholic? He said it was easy — it was the way a Protestant talked, he was better educated. 'If he's using fancy words you can be sure -.'

And then Corkery became reflective and said, 'Ah, but you're never really safe. You go into a bar, and you don't know whether it's a Protestant or Catholic bar. It can be frightening, it can, sure. You don't say anything. You call for your beer and you keep your mouth shut, and then you go.'

But I began to think it was an advantage here, not English, not Irish; and it was a great advantage to be an American. I never felt the Ulster people to be reticent or suspicious – on the contrary, it was hard to shut them up.

'And it was around here,' Desmond Corkery was saying – we were past Ballymoney and headed into Coleraine; I had been encouraging him to tell me a story of religious persecution – 'just about here, that a bloody great team of footballers started to walk up and down the train. They were drinking beer and shouting. "Bloody Fenian bastards!" Up and down the train. "Bloody Fenian bastards!" Looking for Catholics, they were. One comes up to me and says straight out, "You're a bloody Fenian bastard!"'

I shook my head. I said it was terrible. I asked him what he did then.

'I said no,' Corkery looked grim.

'You told him you weren't a Catholic?'

'Sure I had to.'

'Did he believe you?'

'I suppose he did,' Corkery said. 'He slammed the door and went roaring off.'

We travelled in silence along the River Bann, and I thought how that denial must have hurt his pride, and it seemed to me that it was this sort of humiliation that made the troubles in Ulster a routine of bullying cowardice. It was all the old grievances, and vengeance in the dark. That was why the ambush was popular, and the car bomb, and the exploding soap box, and the letter bomb. The idea was to deny what you stood for and then wait until dark to get even with the bugger who made you deny it.

66. Bryce Webster, *In Search of Modern Ireland: an American Traveler's Odyssey*

(New York: Dodd, 1986, pp. 174–76)

No available information exists on Bryce Webster (even Dodd, her publisher, is no longer listed in the New York telephone directory), although her playful allusion to H.V. Morton's *In Search of Ireland* (1930) shows her aware of the tradition of travel writing on Ireland. Like Theroux's, Webster's impression of Northern Ireland during the 1980s is of a hardened, politically stagnating culture, unable to extricate itself from conflict, while being cynically manipulated from without.

Once in Derry, I knew what Dresden must have looked like after the war. Whole streets contained nothing but blackened hulls of houses and shops. Other streets had gaping black holes betweeen still-used houses, like ugly cavities in a row of teeth. Few people walked about, although I passed a priest walking his dog. I was on the route through the city, though, not into it, so I didn't expect to see the main shopping thoroughfare or the nicer neighbourhoods.

My map directed me up one street I couldn't use. There was a policeman inexplicably guiding people away from entering it. 'I don't know my way around,' I shouted to him. 'How can I get back on the route to Rathmullan?'

'I don't know,' he snapped. 'But you can't drive through here.'

Great. Lost in an erupting metropolis. I would have to find my own way, and it was getting dark. Logically, I should be able to drive parallel to the way I wanted to go, and eventually cross the road I wanted to turn onto anyway. But this was – sort of – Ireland, where little is as it seems and there's no such thing as a straight line, let alone a parallel street. Ah, but this was Ulster. And there *was* a parallel street.

I crossed over the River Foyle at a very famous site. There, the Irish Catholics, fighting to restore James to the throne of England, laid siege to the Derry Protestants (who still label Derry as *Londonderry* on their maps), and stretched enormous chains and booms across the river to prevent a relief fleet from sailing up the river and rescuing the beleaguered walled city.

The Siege of Derry in early 1690 was a terrible experience for the Ulster Protestants. They had offered resistance to James's armies in the north, and the Irish army had encircled Derry, cutting off all food and supplies. At the time, most of the city was on an island in the river. The siege dragged on for three months. The food supplies were quickly exhausted and the inhabitants ate anything they could find – domestic pets, rats, birds, and so forth. And the besieging army kept up a steady barrage of cannons against the walls, killing and wounding many, and starting fires around the city. But the Ulster Protestants held on, and an English fleet relieved them, finally, driving away the Irish army.

The Ulstermen soon thereafter also defeated the Irish army at the Battle of Enniskillen, once and for all destroying the Catholic domination of the province of Ulster. Of course, in battles at Aughrim and at the Protestant siege of Limerick, William and Mary's armies defeated James again, destroying the freedom of the Catholic Irish until the emanicipation laws of the mid-nineteenth century and, more basically, until the founding of the Irish Free State in 1922.

I tell the story of the Siege of Derry not for its importance as a battle but for its importance as a modern symbol. The 'Orangemen' of

Derry still celebrate – seriously, not exuberantly as we celebrate St. Patrick's Day – their victory at Derry, and the victory of William and Mary over James. This is hard for Americans to understand – the incredibly long and often bitter memories carried in the Irish bosom, both North and South. It's far different from our feelings about Yankees and Rebels of the Civil War.

Derry is also where the most recent Troubles began in 1972. According to the Catholic viewpoint, the trouble was caused because of a Protestant refusal to enfranchise the Catholics in Derry. It appears that since William's victory, the Protestants had gerrymandered voting privileges in Derry to favor themselves and disenfranchise Catholics. Or, at least, they had so weighted the Catholics' voting power that they could never gain even proportional representation on the Derry Town Council. During the late 1960s and early 1970s, a Catholic drive to gain full voting rights and rescind the seventeenth-century voting method was undercut. After this, violence broke out, and the situation has worsened continually to this day.

Truly, in Ireland's case, the sins of the fathers are visited upon their sons and their sons' sons many generations later. Nor are the sons themselves blameless.

Today these events seem to me to be modern excuses to overturn a separation between North and South that not many people, except the Catholics in Northern Ireland, really want to end. I told a prominent and well-informed person in the Republic that I thought no political leader in the South could possibly want to reunify the North and the South. Consider the situation: the Republic's population of 3.5 million people, almost 99 percent of whom are Catholic, is a homogeneous group hard for an American, used to the melting pot, to imagine. Why, I pondered, would political leaders in the South want to disturb this status quo by mixing more than 1.1 million Protestants into the situation? Even today, more than sixty years after the establishment of the Irish Free State, the few Protestants in the South still tend to hold the best jobs, control most businesses, graduate from the best schools, etc. Yet they have little political power. But, adding a million Protestants to the population of the Republic would give the Protestants at least one-quarter representation in the Irish Dail (or parliament) and dramatically increase their influence on national social, economic, and political policy – beyond the influence they have now as well-heeled and industrious inheritors of the Ascendency, the Anglo-Irish aristocracy. These influences are exactly what the leaders in the South have been trying to reduce or avoid since Irish independence. It would seem to me the

Republic's leadership has a strong vested interest in maintaining the division between the two. It is a division of religious and economic interests that have had ample time and space to solidify since they emerged clearly in 1690.

The authority with whom I spoke at first disagreed with me, but ended our conversation by saying, in different terms, what I had maintained all along: there is little for the Republic to gain by an actual, political reunification, but much to be gained by *seeming* to want it.

67. Eric Newby, *Round Ireland in Low Gear*
(London: Collins, 1987, pp. 54–58)

Eric Newby, born in 1919, is a professional travel writer. Author of many novellas and short stories, he is Travel Editor for the *Observer*, but is perhaps best known for his numerous publications: *Slowly Down the Ganges* (1966), *Wonders of Ireland* (1969), *A Traveller's Life* (1982) and many others. For this Irish travelogue Newby made several trips to Ireland over the course of a year, travelling through parts of the West, and visiting the Aran Islands, Cork and Dublin. In this extract he is travelling around the Burren, County Galway, in December 1985.

Beyond the bog was Coolbaun, a hamlet in which most of the houses were in ruins. In it the minute Coolbaun National School, built in 1895 and abandoned probably some time in the 1950s, still had a roof, and its front door was ajar. Inside there was a bedstead, a table with two unopened tins of soup on it, a raincoat hanging on a nail and a pair of rubber boots. It was like finding a footprint on a desert island. Hastily, we beat a retreat.

The first real village we came to was Tubber, a place a mile long with a pub at either end (neither of which had any food on offer), in fact so long that on my already battered half-inch map one part of it appeared to be in Clare, the other in Galway. The pub nearest to Galway was terribly dark, as if the proprietor catered only for spiritualists; the other had three customers all glued to the telly watching a steeplechase, none of whom spoke to us even between races. Meanwhile we drank, and ate soda bread and butter and spam bought in the village shop. 'Is this what they call "Ireland of the Welcomes"?' Wanda asked with her mouth full. Another coffin nail.

The nicest looking places in Tubber were the post office and Derryvowen Cottage, which was painted pink and which we passed on the way to look for something marked on the map as O'Donohue's Chair. What is or was O'Donohue's Chair? No guide book that I have ever subsequently been able to lay my hands on refers to it. Is it, or was it, some kind of mediaeval hot seat stoked with peat? Or a throne over an oubliette that precipitates anyone who sits on it into the botttomless rivers of the limestone karst? Whatever it is, if it isn't the product of some Irish Ordnance Surveyor's imagination, further inflamed by a spam lunch in Tubber, it is situated in a thicket impenetrable to persons wearing Gore-Tex suits, and hemmed in by an equally impenetrable hedge reinforced with old cast iron bedsteads, worth a bomb to any tinker with a pair of hedging gloves.

After this, misled by two of the innocent-looking children in which Ireland abounds – leprechauns in disguise – we made an equally futile attempt to see at close quarters Fiddaun Castle, another spectacular tower house more or less in the same class as the unfindable Danganbrack. 'Sure and you can't miss it. It's up there and away down,' one of these little dumplings said, while the other sucked her thumb, directing us along a track that eventually became so deep in mire that it almost engulfed us. From the top of the hill they indicated, however, we did have a momentary view of the Castle and of Lough Fiddaun to the north, with three swans floating on it, before the whole scene was obliterated by a hellish hailstorm.

The next part of our tour was supposed to take in the monastic ruins of Kilmacdaugh, over the frontier from Clare in Galway. However, one more December day was beginning to show signs of drawing to a close, and so we set off back in the direction of Crusheen. It really had been a no-day. Not only had we not seen the Kilmacdaugh Monastery, but we had not seen, as we had planned to do, the early nineteenth-century castle built by John Nash for the first Viscount Gort on the shores of Lough Cutra, similar to the one he built at East Cowes on the Isle of Wight, now scandalously demolished; or the Punchbowl, a series of green cup-shaped depressions in a wood of chestnut and beech trees where the River Beagh runs through a gorge 80 feet deep and disappears underground, perhaps to flow beneath O'Donohue's Chair; or Coole Park, the site of the great house which was the home of Augusta, Lady Gregory, whose distinguished guests, among them Shaw, O'Casey, W.B. and J.B. Yeats, A.E. (George) Russell and Katherine Tynan – a bit much to have all of them together, one would have thought, used a giant copper beech in the grounds as a visitors' book. To see all these would have taken days at the speed we were travelling. Well, we would never see them now.

So home to dinner, after which Tom took us to Saturday evening Mass in Crusheen. His mother was going the following morning, but if you attended Mass on Saturday evening you didn't have to do so again on Sunday. If asked, he said, we were to say that he too had been present. Meanwhile, he headed for Clark's to which most of my own impulses were, I admit, to accompany him.

The church was almost full; and the subject of the sermon was Temperance, an obligatory one in Ireland for the First Sunday in Advent. He certainly had a large enough audience for it. He was a formidable figure, this priest. Was he, I wondered, the same one we encountered in O'Hagerty's taking a dim view of the contents of a collection box? To me priests in mufti look entirely different when robed. Ireland, he said, was as boozy as Russia – a bit much, I thought, to accuse any country of being, with the possible exception of Finland. He then went on to castigate the licensed trade as spreaders of evil, something I have always fervently believed myself. If any Guinnesses had been present they would have been writhing with embarrassment. 'Just too awful,' I could imagine them saying, but then one imagines that any Catholic Guinnesses, if such there be, give the First Sunday in Advent and the Saturday preceding it a miss. And there were prayers for the wives of drunks, but none for the drunks themselves, or the husbands of drunks, all of whom I would have thought were equally in need of them.

We were in bed by nine-thirty, slept nine hours and woke to another brilliant day, this time completely cloudless. After another good break-fast, we set off on what, for Wanda, proved to be a really awful four-mile uphill climb to Ballinruan, a lonely hamlet high on the slopes of the Slieve Aughty Mountains, where a Sunday meet of the county Clare Foxhounds was to take place. Its cottages were rendered in bright, primary colours, or finished in grey pebbledash – one house was the ghostly silver-grey of an old photographic plate. The church sparkled like icing sugar in the sunshine, and across the road from it, in Walsh's Lounge Bar and Food Store, four old men, all wearing caps, were drinking whiskey and stout and sharing a newspaper between them.

The view from the village was an amazing one. Behind it gentle slopes led up to a long, treeless ridge; immediately below it, and on either side, the ground was rougher, with outcrops of rock – a wilderness of gorse and heather interspersed with stunted, windswept trees. Out beyond this a vast landscape opened up; the level plain, part of which we had travelled through with so many setbacks the previous day. Its innu-merable loughs, now a brilliant Mediterranean blue, blazed among green fields of irregular shape, bogs, woodlands and tracts of limestone, with here and there a white cottage or the tower of a castle rising among them.

And beyond all this, the far more immense bare limestone expanses of the Burren rose golden in the morning sunlight; Galway Bay could just be seen to the north-west; while to the south, beyond the Shannon, were the hills and mountains of County Limerick, their feet shrouded in a mist which gave an impression of almost tropical heat.

At twelve-thirty the hounds arrived in a big van, very well behaved, and soon more vans and horse boxes trundled up the hill, some drawn by Mercedes. Here, the hunt was more or less on the extreme limits of its territory. It normally hunted over stone walls on the west side of the County, and over banks and fly fences on the east and south. The rough country round us, on the other hand, might give shelter to hordes of hill foxes. Anyway, they were safe today. This was a drag hunt in which the hounds would follow an artificial scent.

By one o'clock those horses still in their boxes were becoming impatient, kicking the sides of them, and catching the air of excitement that was gradually gathering in the street outside. People were beginning to saddle up and mount now, especially the children, of whom there were quite a number. A big van with four horses in it arrived and one of their owners said to the driver, 'It's a lovely day! Let's go and have a jar now in Walsh's.' By now the bar was splitting at the seams.

This was not a smart hunt such as the County Galway, otherwise known as the Blazers, the County Limerick, the Kildare, or the Scarteen, otherwise the Black and Tans. It was not the sort of hunt that Empress Elizabeth of Austria, who loved hunting in Ireland more than anything else on earth and was so proud of her figure that she had herself sewn into her habit every hunting day, would have patronised. Most were in black jackets and velvet caps, some were in tweeds, others wore crash helmets, and one man with a craggy, early nineteenth-century face wore a bowler. One man in a tweed coat sounded suspiciously like a Frenchman, there was an elegant American girl in a tweed coat, and what looked like several members of the scrap metal business. A cosmopolitan lot.

The hounds were released; there were eight and half couple of them, which is a hunter's way of saying seventeen. After a brief period in which they were allowed to savour delicious smells, one of the Joint Masters, who was wearing a green coat with red facings and black boots with brown tops, took them up the road to cries of what sounded like, 'Ged in! Ged in! and 'Ollin! Ollin!' Then they were suddenly turned, and ran back down the street through a press of people and out through the village, down and over the flanks of Derryvoagh Hill and into the eye of the now declining sun. Soon they were lost to view to us and other followers, watching their progress from one of the rocks below the village.

'By God,' someone said, 'the next thing we'll be hearing of them they'll be in America.'

68. Thomas Keneally, *Now and in Time to Be: Ireland and the Irish*

(first published 1991; 2nd edn, London: Flamingo, 1992, pp. 123–26)

A native of Australia, Thomas Keneally was born in 1935. A sometime journalist, Keneally is better known for his novels, children's fiction, travel narratives, and screenplays. Trained as a high-school teacher, he has taught largely in the United States since the late 1960s, at the University of New England, and later at New York University and the University of California. Author of many works, such as *The Cut-rate Kingdom* (1985), *Towards Asmara* (1990), and *By the Line* (1992), he is probably best known for his *Schindler's Ark* (*Schindler's List* in the USA, 1982). Keneally now lives in Sydney.

At the major checkpoints into and out of Ulster, you enter a straitened world of speed bumps, high steel screens either side of the road, tall sandbag blockhouses and young British and Irish soldiers wearing camouflage gear and helmets and carrying M-16s. At the Derry/Donegal border some weeks ago, my vehicle was inspected by a little jockey of a soldier, a native of Liverpool. This was the enemy, I thought, as depicted in all those Irish songs, and in the long, slow-burning and wildly flaring history of Irish nationalism. But of course he was probably Scouse, Liverpool Irish, anyhow.

While he asked me questions and chatted, comrades of his in the blockhouse, behind tinted windows, might have been entering our vehicle number into their computer to see what they came up with. If they did, they would have seen it was a rented car, provided by Bord Failte, the Irish Tourist Board. At least I was hoping that was what they saw. At every crossing, however casually the Irish took all this unnatural activity, I was never fully at ease.

I was travelling at that stage with my daughter, and the soldier from Liverpool pretended to think she was a bimbo until she put him right. The note of his apology was very much like the ironic apologies any working-class lad in Britain or Ireland makes. Previous to questioning us, he had spent ten minutes searching through a snack foods truck – its interior, its suspension, under its bonnet. So he was probably ready for a bit of whimsical cheek.

Out of all the crossings I made in and out of Ulster I remember him particularly, because he was the British soldier I had the longest conversation with. For example, we had a bit of a chat about Tranmere Rovers, a third division team from the north of England which a businessman I know, the hamper king of England, Peter Johnston, bought and revived. It shares the same turf as Everton and Liverpool and yet has managed to survive and prosper.

About five days later, in the small hours, operatives of the Provisional IRA took hostage a family called the Gillespies in their house at Carriagh, on the Ulster side of the border near this Buncrana-Derry checkpoint. They had threatened the husband and father Patsy Gillespie in the past, because he worked in the kitchen at Fort George Army Base. Now they wanted him to drive a van containing a thousand-pound bomb into the checkpoint. They told him that if he didn't his wife and children would be shot dead. They told him that having driven the van into the checkpoint, he was then to leave it. There would be time for him to get away before they detonated the bomb. In reality, they detonated it by remote control as soon as he drew to a stop inside the metal walls of the checkpoint.

Five soldiers died immediately – they were all from the north of England – Blackpool, Warrington, Runcorn, Liverpool, Whitney. The youngest was nineteen and by an irony was Scouse – his name David Sweeney. They found pieces of Patsy Gillespie, Catholic father, over a hundred yards radius. 'No piece bigger than a man's fist,' a member of the bomb squad said.

If you had asked the Provos about this, they would have said, 'Well, he shouldn't be working for the enemy.' If you asked Patsy, he would have said, 'Well, I've got a family to support.'

This action against the Derry-Buncrana checkpoint was matched by a similar hostage-taking and proxy-bomb-dropping exercise against the Newry checkpoint, beneath the Mountains of Mourne on the main road to Dublin. The sixty-nine-year-old who was forced to drive that bomb was tethered to his seat, but managed to wrestle free before the detonation. A twenty-year-old private soldier from the Royal Irish Rangers was killed, and the structures of the checkpoint – metal sheeting, steel uprights – were blown all over the countryside.

By an irony, reality imitating art, Brian Moore, the Belfast-born novelist, had a month or so before published a novel in which proxy-bombing was the basis of the plot. Not that the bombers had read it. If they had, they wouldn't have done what they did.

With sad predictability, the Unionist parliamentarian Ken Maginnis, spokesman for generations of stultified Loyalist thinking, rushed the television cameras in the wake of these deadly demonstrations to demand that the British government introduce selective internment, the sort of policy which had served the IRA well as a recruiting catalyst in the 1970s. *And so it is and ever will be.*

The two explosions had occurred simultaneously about 4 a.m. But an attempt at a British Army regiment, the Sherwood Foresters, at Omagh in County Tyrone did no damage, as only the detonator went off.

Again, the banality of vengeance: the attacks were acts of revenge for the killing in late September, 1990, of two IRA men, Dessie Grewe and Martin McCaughey, by the trigger-mad SAS (Special Air Service, an elite squad of the British Army). You need a passionate tribal mind to keep track of the sequence of pay-back grievances.

Martin McCaughey's funeral was significant for me, because it was the first funeral of an IRA Volunteer I had ever taken particular note of. It was the normal, highly-charged, tragic, grievous, tribal, arresting affair. McCaughey's coffin was carried by his sisters, beautiful, raw-boned Irish girls. It is not fanciful at all to say that in their faces an ancient, unuttered sorrow and an ancient stamped-down resistance were legible. Men in balaclavas fired a salute over the grave, while the leader of Sinn Féin, Gerry Adams, spoke of 'unfinished business'. Armed security forces watched in a sullen phalanx from within the cemetery's perimeter.

It was in fact very likely that amongst the balaclava-wearers that day were members of the teams who some weeks later would blow the Newry and Derry checkpoints to pieces.

And at least, they would have said, we hit the right people this time.

The militant IRA always considered it to be its work to kill British soldiers. But the use of Patsy Gillespie to deliver a bomb is characteristic of another side of their existence: the control the IRA tries to exercise, and largely succeeds in doing, over its own. Like its opponent, the Ulster Defence Association, in its zone of control, it extracts protection money from all businesses in the Catholic sections of Belfast and Derry, and no doubt in other towns as well. Both organisations, IRA and UDA, exercise a rough, often morally hidebound justice of their own.

At the beginning of my time in Ireland, a boy and a girl who were shot dead by the hair-trigger Paratroop Regiment when they tried to run a road block in West Belfast, were in fact running away because they didn't want the IRA to find out they were joy-riding again. They had already had their two warnings. The punishment for habitual joy-riding is knee-capping. The miscreant is given a time and place at which the punishment is to be performed. He – or she – is also given money to buy liqour. Then they turn up at the appointed place, and are shot through the back of each knee, below the joint – the IRA members who fulfil this ritual punishment have a crude knowledge of anatomy and don't want to blow out the femur. It is curious that most people keep their knee-capping appointments with the IRA. But the alternative is a death swift as the one poor Patsy Gillespie suffered.

69. Rebecca Solnit, *A Book of Migrations: Some Passages in Ireland*   (London: Verso, 1997, pp. 119–21)

Rebecca Solnit grew up in California, trained as a journalist, was for several years an art critic, and is now primarily an essayist, critic and activist whose work focuses on issues of environment, landscape and place. Her books include *Secret Exhibition: Six California Artists of the Cold War Era* (1991), *Savage Dreams: a Journey into the Landscape Wars of the American West* (1999), *Hollow City: Gentrification and the Eviction of Urban Culture* (2001), and *As Eve said to the Serpent: on Landscape, Gender and Art* (2001). She is a contributor to a number of magazines, including *Los Angeles Art*, *Creative Camera* and *Sierra*. In this extract Solnit explores the Burren, County Galway, in 1994.

I was on vacation. Everybody else was on holiday. I left my knapsack in the hotel-cum-hostel with pub in the center of Lisdoonvarna and walked to Ailwee Caverns. I went less for the sake of the caves than for the route, through the barren windswept expanse of limestone on the southwestern lip of Galway Bay called the Burren, from an Irish word for a rocky place. It was a long walk, and it was raining. Up a crest, past one of the horrible tree plantations, which had picnic benches scattered around its impenetrable mass, on the apparent assumption that a forest is a scenic recreation site no matter what. Over a slope where stone was breaking through everywhere and some of the fields were not really fields but pavements of warped, riddled, hollowed-out pale limestone, in which little pools of water gathered, sweeping toward the misty distance.

Past the place the map said had a side road going to the Blessed Bush, where the imprint of St. Brigid's knees can be seen, in stone that must be less complicated than the terrain I was wandering through, for such a slight impression to be noticeable.

Down Corkscrew Hill, apparently named for the zigzag road down its steep side, into a more inviting landscape, with trees along the stone walls and soil rather than stone as its primary surface. Past a field, where a primeval white horse, with thick legs and Roman nose and stiff short mane, came up to greet me, to a country hotel. Inelegant rain garb shed, into the hotel, a sort of poor man's stately home, with its tattered prints and old volumes from scattered sets. Tea on a sort of settee in the room with the bar, a table away from the only other guests there, a well-dressed English family, three generations of women who looked like unhappy dolls and men who looked as immobile as the furniture beneath them. Outside again, the hills looked like topographical maps, because they had eroded into ledges or sills as regular as elevation lines, but beyond them was the sea. The cave was like many caves – long sinuous corridors resembling bodily passages, the literal bowels of the earth – and the tour guide was a young man with a good memory but no flair for reciting from memory, like most cave guides, but it was pleasant to be out of the rain. Then I ran into the Giantess on the road. She was better at vacation than I was: she had stayed in a town much closer to the caves and walked much less and met a man in a pub in Doolin who looked like Mel Gibson, but virtuously declined him. I thought we might keep running into each other, bound up on some parallel track of chimera chasing, but I never saw her again.

The next day it was raining harder. I walked to Kilfenora and bought a packet of chips and a chocolate bar in a dusty store where strangers or women must have been infrequent sights, because the man who sold them stuck his head right up against the dusty window and goggled after me, his tongue balled up between his teeth in concentration or wonder. The church in Kilfenora – technically a cathedral whose bishop is the pope – was half in ruins, full of graves, and had on one wall a carved fourteenth-century Bishop making a sign of benediction with the same two-fingered gesture drivers now salute each other with as they pass. No one passed me, however; the Burren on this stormy day seemed like an abandoned landscape, like the surface of a planet whose inhabitants had all vanished an indeterminate time ago. No cars, almost no birds, and signs of cattle in the fields but no cows, just a flat rocky expanse to the horizon, scoured and gnawed by wind and rain – nothing but botany, geology, meterology, and ruins. The wind was making the rain so horizontal it tickled my inner ear. There were pockets of water in the hollows of the limestone, and the slabs all fit together like pieces of an eroded puzzle, with long fracture lines making rows of rock. Even the whitethorn trees seemed lonely, each set at a distance from the next along the walls.

I had the dead for company at the eleventh-century church in the crossroads called Noughaval, another roofless stone structure being strangled by ivy, like a nervous system choking its bones. The surrounding cemetery's headstones amid the wet grass and nettles ranged from a past weathered into illegibility, tombstones become plain rock again, to the near present, with plastic flowers for remembrance, all ringed round by more stone walls. I had been walking a long time in the rain when I finally arrived at the great portal tomb of Poulnabrone. There were a few cars parked on the roadside and, despite the No Entry sign, figures wandering the stony field on which it reared up, a vast slab of stone held up high by a few uprights on a low mound of unshaped stones. The uprights had kept the slab balanced as a roof for four and a half thousand years, in defiance of gravity or celebration of balance. The roof hovered at a slight angle, so that it didn't echo the horizon but pointed beyond it, soaring. As I stepped across the treacherous footing of hollows, ridges, rows, and dips, I saw a figure in ink-blue clothes approaching from another angle. He reached the tomb at the same time I did, and because the rain was coming down harder, he invited me inside with a hospitable gesture. These are always where there is much wind and water, he said as we stood on the low mound under the slab, and added, I come from Brittany, where there are many such things.

He was at his ease and set me at ease too by immediately assuming affinity, as though since we were sheltered by the same megalith we must care about the same things and could skip the preliminaries. The Bretons, he declared in his French-accented English, are blue-eyed Celts, though he was dark-eyed and blackhaired himself, and he asserted that Breton was the most widely spoken of the surviving Celtic languages, spoken by far more people than speak Scottish, or Welsh, or Irish – he spoke it himself. I tried out a passage of Rimbaud of him: 'I have my ancestor's pale blue eyes ... only I don't butter my hair,' but he didn't recognise it, at least not in English. We wandered together over the rocky ground to the next field, talking of stones, Celts, fairies, pilgrimages, and old places. We had both been down the old pilgrimage trail of Santiago de Compostela, which begins in Paris, but he had gone the whole way, and on foot. He was more beautiful than Mel Gibson, but this is not a novel: his mother was waiting for him in the car, a cranky Colette in leather pants unimpressed by the wet pre-Celtic monuments he had brought her to see.

There were places in the Burren that had never been inhabited and hardly disturbed, and when the Office of Public Works tried to build an interpretive center for tourists in one of them a few years ago, it prompted one of the most heated environmental campaigns in Ireland, a campaign to leave the place undeveloped that was at least temporarily won. In the daytime it seemed possible to believe that human beings were rare, solitary creatures who existed largely to rearrange the stone according to slow passing fashions into tombs, stone forts, churches, walls, and that there was no other scale of time but the eons of geological formation and erosion, the millenia of architectural styles, the decades of building, and the hourly shifts of clouds and wind and rain. Every place exists in two versions, as an exotic and a local. The exotic is a casual acquaintance who must win hearts through charm and beauty and sites of historical interest, but the local is made up of the accretion of individual memory and sustenance, the maternal landscape of uneventful routine. The Burren seemed to be an old local place that was becoming almost exclusively exotic (which is not to argue against the pleasures of promiscuity or for never leaving mother). The decline in population since the Famine has nowhere been more precipitous than in the west, and of all the places I visited, the Burren felt loneliest for its abandonment.

70. Mark McCrum, *The Craic: a Journey through Ireland* (London: Gollancz, 1998, pp. 327–30)

Mark McCrum was born in Cambridge in 1958, and is the author of two previous travel books, *Happy Sad Land* (1995), about South Africa, and *No Worries* (1997), about Australia. He works principally as a journalist, and has written for the *Evening Standard*, the *Independent*, *Vogue* and *Punch*. In this extract McCrum's use of interview is shown to be a useful technique for dealing with difficult political issues: dignifying the speaker, while distancing the interviewer from the story narrated. McCrum's journey throughout Ireland took place in 1997.

Just over three months after Bloody Sunday, on the 4th May 1972, a little boy of ten had been taking his usual walk home from school in the Creggan. It was through a field and the playground of St. Joseph's secondary school, then up past the army look-out post, which, he remembered, was corrugated iron with sandbags behind, 'and there was like the porthole of the soldiers' look-out in the middle, and barbed wire in front'.

He ran past it, as he always did, and when he was 'about ten feet away, for some inexplicable reason a soldier decided to fire a rubber bullet at me. And it struck me on the bridge of the nose from about eight feet.'

The sandbags were the last thing Richard Moore saw. For when he woke up on the school canteen table he couldn't see. 'I kept saying, "I didn't do anything." So I was obviously aware of what had happened to me.'

He was taken to hospital in an ambulance. 'And I can remember the ambulance man saying to my daddy "There's a woman out here looking to get into the ambulance, will I let her in, who is she?" And I heard my daddy say, "It's his mother, don't let her in."'

'I spent two weeks in hospital and during those two weeks I thought I just couldn't see because of the bandages on my eyes. And I'm sure it must have been very difficult for my father and them because, you know, I kept talking about, when I get the bandages off my eyes, as if I was going to be able to see, and they knew that that wasn't going to be the case.

'After I got out of hospital my brother Noel took me for a walk in the back garden. "D'you know what has happened to ye?" he asked. And I says, "All I know is I was shot and all that." And he says, "But do you know what damage has been caused?" And I said, "No." And at that point he told me I had lost one eye and I wouldn't be able to see with the other one.'

Now, twenty-five years later, I sat over the desk from those useless eyes. The right one just a wide open socket of pale pink skin; the left had a fractional circle of redundant iris visible in the tiny triangle between the eyelids. They were shaded from too close a view by tinted glasses.

'I'm not bitter,' Richard told me repeatedly, as he took me through the stages of his later, blind life. 'Even when my children were born, I have never felt bitter about what's happened, I've just felt a sense of loss.'

'My daughter Niamh made her first communion last year, and she was wearing her wee dress and everybody was telling me how beautiful she looked and she was sitting on my knee and I was walking with her and all that sort of stuff. I realized that there is something about being able to see that situation, and I haven't got it.'

'I suppose I was philosophical in the sense that I would think about the soldier and think, "Does he realize?" There's two people, me and him. I've thought about meeting him, I've thought about how he's feeling. I mean, there was a day in his life, in the space of a minute – dramatically – I wonder, has it changed his life, because he's no different from you or me, and if I'd done something like that twenty-five years ago, and I was aware I'd blinded a young boy, then I don't think I could ever run away from that memory.'

Now Richard worked for a charity called Children of Crossfire, which helped, as the name suggested, children who were victims of war worldwide. Not that he'd gone straight into it. As a young man he'd run a bar for a while, but now he felt more content helping others. He laughed, self-deprecatingly. 'I don't mean that in a charity kind of way, the selfish thing is I just get more pleasure out of doing that than I did running my own business.'

Micky English was less forgiving. He had lost two sons of his four sons in the Troubles, and although he seemed to have accepted the loss of the second he hadn't at all accepted the loss of the first. He sat in the front room of his little house in the Bogside, chain-smoking and visibly trembling as we leafed through the papers and photographs that documented *his* fatal day, which was Easter Sunday 1981.

After the annual march to commemorate the 1916 Rising his eldest son Gary had gone off before the orations to play in a football match. The pitch was right beside the Catholic cathedral up on the edge of the Bogside.

And on that day there'd been a bit of sporadic rioting on the junction that had become known, after the Battle of the Bogside, as Aggro Corner. The joint RUC and army forces on the ground had shifted the riot up to a quieter junction by the football pitch, where they would try, Micky explained, and get a pincer action going so they could grab and arrest the rioters in between.

The football match was over and Gary and his friends had been having a kickaround. When the riot had appeared they had, out of curiosity, joined the large crowd that had gathered to watch. Micky had never, incidentally, had any trouble with Gary, in regard of rioting. 'He was a responsible young man, a worker, meticulous about his appearance, never went out without polishing his shoes, no matter where he was going.'

Now while they'd been standing watching, two army Land Rovers had sped down into the crowd, 'on a gradient that's something like 1 in 6, travelling at about 70 miles an hour.'

People were running away from them but one had struck his son, knocking him to the ground. It had then stopped and, in the eyewitness accounts of 90 per cent of the people who were there, reversed back over his son's body, killing him.

This was the point at issue, for the soldier in charge of the Land Rover had denied this second manoeuvre.

The case had gone to court in Belfast, it having been decided by the powers that be that the soldiers wouldn't get a fair trial in Derry, and there, their evidence backed by the trial pathologist, the soldiers had been acquitted of reckless driving and causing two deaths.

But Micky English was certain of his facts. He still had Gary's shirt with the W-markings on the fabric (the car's tyres had been W-tread Goodyears). He had the photograph of his son's body, with that wheel-thick band clearly marked, a diagonal right across his back. The soldiers' evidence was that the first impact of the Land Rover had knocked the son under the front axle, he had been pushed along with the vehicle. But if that was the case, asked Micky, why were there no abrasions on his front? Why were the knees of his trousers unmarked or in any way torn? Why were there no dragging marks?

Micky English had gone on a speaking tour throughout mainland Britain. He had fought for and eventually been granted an inquest, engaging an independent pathologist who had totally disputed the trial pathologist's findings; an opinion that was backed up by another British pathologist, who, according to Micky, couldn't believe that anybody could have come to the conclusions arrived at during the trial.

Helena Kennedy and Michael Mansfield had agreed to act, for free, on the English family's behalf, but the Northern Ireland Bar Association (whose chairman was, coincidentally, the barrister employed by the Ministry of Defence in this case) ruled that because these two distinguished champions of human rights had not taken the Northern Irish bar exams, they could not appear. 'I mean,' said Micky, 'we're supposed to be British, part of the British legal system, and they were told they couldn't do that case.'

Nonetheless, and despite facing a jury from North Tyrone, 'with not one Catholic on it', English's family had won two out of his three points. But Gary was still dead, the soldiers were still acquitted and Micky was left with a burning sense of injustice.

71. Martin Fletcher, *Silver Linings: Travels around Northern Ireland*   (London: Little, Brown, 2000, pp. 115–18)

Martin Fletcher was educated at the University of Edinburgh before joining *The Times* in 1983, and becoming Washington correspondent in 1989, a position he held until 1997 when he was posted to Belfast as European correspondent. In 1999 he published *Almost Heaven: Travels through the Backwoods of America*, which was shortlisted for the Thomas Cook Travel Book Award. This extract sees him in one of the most fortified areas of Northern Ireland: South Armagh.

In Northern Ireland I frequently felt that it was impossible for an outsider like myself to understand the hatreds and the passions of either side, but Willie took me on a 12-mile dolorosa across South Armagh that went some way towards enlightening me.

Every mile we passed the scene of some atrocity. At the brow of a hill beyond Bessbrook a wreath and some faded poppies were tied to a gatepost; this marked the site of the 1976 Kingsmills massacre, where the IRA ambushed a minibus one January evening and slaughtered 10 Protestant workmen with machine guns after letting the Catholic driver go. 'They cut them down like dogs,' said Willie as we surveyed the green and tranquil countryside. 'It's lovely terrain, but so deadly.'

We passed the Kingsmills Presbyterian Church where in 1980 the 'provies' shot Willie's uncle, Clifford Lundy, a former UDR member, as he was returning from his work as a lorry driver.

We drove through the village of Whitecross where Willie was raised until local republicans drove out his family with stones and petrol bombs when he was 12.

Just north of the village a black marble monument lists the three UDR soldiers who died in 1991 when the IRA rolled a 2,000-lb lorry bomb down a hill into the Glenanne UDR barracks that used to stand there.

Just west is the farm where the IRA ambushed Willie's father one August afternoon in 1975. A small brick memorial marks the spot where he was 'murdered by the enemies of Ulster'. Willie, 14 at the time, knows exactly who did it. 'There were ten involved, from the scout car to the man who pulled the trigger,' he said. Most were local, most he knew, and a few days later he faxed me all their names.

Another mile along the lane Johnny Bell, another of Willie's uncles, was gunned down ten weeks after his father's murder. Three IRA gunmen ambushed him as he arrived home.

Beyond that is the tranquil country churchyard where Willie's father and uncle are buried. 'My father knew he was going to die. He told me so,' said Willie as he showed me their graves. 'But he wouldn't move. These UDR men were all the same. They believed they had to stand their ground to give the government time to get its act together. They thought if they moved out the IRA were winning, and that they were the only protection the Protestant people had.'

A hundred yards beyond the church was another roadside memorial – this one to a 12-year-old Catholic girl named Majella O'Hare who was caught in the crossfire of a gunfight between soldiers and the IRA as she was on her way to confession.

In Newtownhamilton the once-pretty town square was still being rebuilt following a car-bomb attack on the security base a year earlier. The base itself was virtually unscratched.

Beyond Newtownhamilton we came to a low grey building with steel mesh windows at a quiet country cross-roads where the air reeked of slurry. This was the Tullyvallan Orange Hall. In 1975 two gunmen burst in and opened fire, killing four men including one aged 80. 'It was ethnic cleansing that went on here in the 1970s,' said Willie.

We had traversed the northern part of South Armagh, where there was still a significant Protestant population, but as we headed south towards the border the towns and villages became almost entirely Catholic and republican.

Here the Irish tricolour, not the Union Jack, flies from every flag-pole. Here signs are written in Irish as well as English, and the roadside memorials are to 'volunteers' killed by the security forces. Here the Queen's writ seems scarcely to apply, and you stand about as much chance of seeing a bobby on the street as you would of seeing Gerry Adams at Buckingham Palace. The few remaining Protestants are toler-ated provided they don't inform, and the security forces really do seem like an army of occupation.

What was also striking was the number of palatial new homes tucked away down the back roads. Republicans may consider themselves oppressed, but there is no shortage of money in South Armagh and little doubt where much of it comes from.

One traditional source was the Army. In 1994–5, to pick a year at random, farmers lodged 38,634 complaints of livestock being killed or injured as a result of helicopters flying overhead or other military activity, and £6.2 million was paid out in compensation. The compensa-tion process has since been greatly tightened up after it was discovered that three or four claims were being made for the same cow, that 'dead' sheep were turning up at auctions in the south, and that the hapless civil servants dispatched to investigate claims were being intimidated into reporting that whole flocks of chickens had died of heart attacks.

The even bigger source of money is smuggling. The border here is criss-crossed by tiny lanes and as porous as a sieve. You hear endless variations of stories of farmers with barns that straddle the border who put the cattle one end and the feed the other so that the animals smuggle themselves across. This is the United Kingdom's only land frontier. Drugs, alcohol and tobacco all come across in large quantities. Any number of commodities are smuggled north or south depending on the prevailing duties and exchange rates.

Diesel and petrol were the hot commodities while I was in Northern Ireland. The duty was at least 20 pence per litre less in the Republic, and a veritable tidal wave of the fuel flowed northwards. Customs officers in Belfast showed me a yard full of confiscated vehicles ranging from 18,000-litre tankers to elderly grocery vans with tanks inside, to a battered old trailer with a layer of turf covering one small metal fuel container. As many as half the petrol stations in Northern Ireland were believed to be selling at least some smuggled fuel. 'Huckster' stations consisting of a single pump in the back of a cargo container sprang up in back streets. By the most conservative estimates, the scam was costing the taxman £100 million a year in lost duty.

Willie grew noticeably tenser as we drove into the border town of Crossmaglen where, as an old song goes, there are 'more rogues than honest men'. Crossmaglen is a town that belongs in the north in no sense except the geographical. The place is such an uncompromising republican stronghold that even mail and newspapers have to be delivered to the Army base by helicopter, and rubbish leaves the same way. In fact a helicopter clattered in as we arrived, a machine gunner clearly visible by its open door.

Willie had more or less completed his tour by now, which was just as well as Crossmaglen made him distinctly nervous. In fact he wouldn't leave the car. South Armagh is a small place and someone could well recognise him. He wasn't afraid, he insisted. 'It's the fact that no one would come to your aid.'

This angry young Protestant dropped me in Crossmaglen with a parting shot. 'As far as I'm concerned this is our home,' he said. 'Ulster belongs to us. No IRA man or anyone else will push me out of it. They may carry me out, but they'll never push me out.'

72. Pete McCarthy, *McCarthy's Bar: a Journey of Discovery in Ireland*   (London: Hodder, 2000, pp. 67–70)

Pete McCarthy is a writer and presenter on TV and radio. Best known as the face of Channel 4's *Travelog*, for which he made over forty films around the world, McCarthy has also written and presented a number of environmental and arts programmes for BBC television and Radio 4. The following extract finds him in Dunmanway, County Cork, in the company of those he calls 'the new English'.

I suppose I was expecting some sort of commune, but what they've built is a village: different families, and couples, and singles, living on their own plots of land, sharing similar aspirations, but living their own lives. And, like a village, everyone knows everyone else's business.

'That's no bad thing. It's the way village life used to be, back home, but isn't any more.'

Davie is a broad-shouldered man in his thirties, originally from Devon. We're sitting on the grass outside his battered mobile home. Next to it is the house he's building. Below us, he's planted an orchard. Ponies are grazing off to our left.

'It all changed in England some time in the seventies. Everything modernised, and became homogeneous. You all had to live the same way, and local differences started to disappear. Townies moved in, and wouldn't speak to you if you were local. It's all burglar alarms now, and four-wheel drives to take the kids to school. I hate the way England is now. I could never go back.'

We go inside to make tea. On the wall is a poster of an alien smoking a spliff, captioned 'Take Me To Your Dealer'. I ask about the gardai.

'Ah, they know what we're about. It's a small place, and news travels. Y'know, if we started a cocaine factory up here or something, that'd be different, but that's not us and they know that. We look a bit rough, and we like a party, but we have to work hard just to survive, and we love our kids. I think people round here can relate to that.'

Further up the hill is the community centre Dominic helped build. There's a stone floor they cut from the mountain and laid themselves. There's a coffee bar, and toys for the creche, and a big Bob Marley quote on the wall: 'One world, one love, let's get together, it'll be all right.'

We pass cabins, roundhouses, a yurt-like affair, and dome. I can't help wondering about planners, and whether they're likely to move in with the bulldozers.

'I don't think anyone's going to evict us. They'd have thirty families, more than a hundred people to rehouse, for a start.'

Laurence is a mild-mannered, dreadlocked father of five. He lives in the most spectacular house I've seen – a thatched Hansel and Gretel fantasy. Inside the huge living-room, a tree trunk, still rooted into the ground, serves as a chair among more conventional furniture. He's recently added a conservatory on the front. Again, the floors are native stone, except for just below the conservatory window, where flowers are growing through bare soil. We're high up the hill. In England, you couldn't buy this view for a million.

'Anyway, if a building's been up five years and there've been no objections, you can get retrospective planning permission.'

He works as a thatcher all round Cork. There aren't many people left who can still do it. People come and watch, he says, and want to talk about it, and about the past that's disappearing. His kids are in the village school – one of the women from the mountain is a teacher there – and this is home now, for good.

'But do you feel you belong?'

He pauses and smiles. 'Well, I've no family links so I'll always be an outsider. We're a community within a community, I suppose, but I can live with that. They're good people, the Irish.'

The kids are reading, or watching cricket on the TV. I ask their dad if he's going to Danny's party at all.

'I'm getting a bit old for that sort of thing. Think I'll stay in and watch a video tonight. Would you like more tea?'

I drop Dominic at the foot of the lane leading up to Danny's at around nine thirty, and head back to Dunmanway. I'm starving. But by the time I park in the square, it's well after ten, and my best bet might be to hit the hostel and devour whatever the paedophile and the cyclist have been naive enough to leave in the fridge. Mind you, the Shamrock Bar, facing the square, looks inviting. I've a vague notion that I might have been in there with Uncle Jack on market days. A board in the window says, 'Lunches served, 12–2.' I'm eight hours and twenty-five minutes late.

Inside, the lights are dim and mercifully there's no TV, no juke-box, no Van Morrison or Shane McGowan or Saw Doctors, just the gentle hum of about twenty people talking to each other. As the landlord lets my pint settle, I say I realise there's probably no chance of food at this time on a Saturday night.

'I could do you soup and a sandwich, if you like.'

'That'd be great.'

'Hang on, I might do better than that.'

A quarter of an hour later he arrives at my table with a huge plate of hot chicken and ham and cabbage and potatoes. It's the Auntie Annie memorial dinner, on Saturday night, at twenty to eleven, in a pub that isn't serving food. I go back to my caravan a happy man.

The wind builds up and rattles the shutters, and the rain starts to come down, but I feel secure inside the caravan. It's a bit like going camping for the first time as a kid, and enjoying the sound of rain on canvas, knowing it can't reach you. I sit up and try to read a history of Dunmanway I've found on a shelf in the hostel, but find myself preoccupied by the present.

I'm struck by the strong sense of empowerment of the people I've met, by the control they've taken over their lives. It seems to me that if they're rebuilding ruins, and repopulating an area devastated by emigration, there's a good case for saying they should be subsidised rather than persecuted. And – if you leave Catholicism out of the equation – you can see them reverting to the values that much of Ireland has hurried to leave behind in the last thirty years. It's a basic, hands-on way of life, where crops are planted and dug, old machinery is repaired or cannibalised for parts, wells must be dug, roofs somehow kept on.

I'm sure that, for some older Irish people, this dirty-finger-nailed, electricity-free existence is an unwelcome reminder of a past they've left behind. Yet most people seem happy to accept them. No one points in the street any more. Scruffy? Noisy music? Parties? A weekend on the drink? It's not exactly unknown round here.

I find myself reading and rereading a page about Dunmanway's origins as an English plantation, and realise that, in a sense, history is repeating itself. Those immigrants were rapidly absorbed. This new generation have made a life as a separate community; but gradually, through work, music, pubs and school, they are being integrated. Crucially, their children see themselves as Irish, and within a generation or two their English antecedents will have melted away. Heritage tourists will be taken up to the mountain to see the strange old houses. 'This is where English hippies used to live,' the guide will be able to say. 'It's all Irish here now.'

Select Bibliography

FURTHER IRISH TRAVEL NARRATIVES

As suggested above, there is a great number of travel narratives relating to Ireland, many out of print, many more in manuscript form. Below is a supplementary list of published works, roughly the same number as chosen for this text, and covering the same period. This list is neither prescriptive nor exhaustive, merely a way of alerting scholars of Irish travel to the wealth of available material.

Barrow, John, *A Tour round Ireland in the Autumn of 1835* (London: Murray, 1836)

Binns, Jonathan, *The Miseries and Beauties of Ireland* (London: Longman, 1837)

Brewer, James, *The Beauties of Ireland* (London: Sherwood, 1825)

Butler, Elizabeth, *From Sketch-book and Diary* (London: Black, 1909)

Carlyle, Thomas, *Reminiscences of my Irish Journey in 1849* (London: Sampson, 1882)

Carr, John, *The Stranger in Ireland; or a tour in the Southern and Western parts of that Country in the year 1805* (London: Phillips, 1806)

Carter, Nathaniel, *Letters from Europe* (New York: Caravill, 1829)

Cowie, Donald, *Ireland, the Land and the People* (London: Barnes, 1976)

Cromwell, Thomas, *Excursions through Ireland* (London: Longman, 1820)

Curtis, William, *One Irish Summer* (New York: Duffield, 1909)

Dallas, Rev. Alexander, *A Mission Tour-book in Ireland* (London: ICM, 1860)

De Tocqueville, Alexis, *Journeys in Ireland* (Dublin: Wolfhound, 1990)

Edwards, Lionel *My Irish Sketch-Book* (London: Collins, 1938)

Frédérix, P., *Irlande, Extrême-Occident* (Paris: Gallimard, 1931)

Gamble, John, *A View of Society and manners in the North of Ireland in 1812* (London: Cardock, 1813)

Gardner, Raymond, *Land of Time Enough* (London: Hodder, 1977)

Greene, John Baker, *Notes on Ireland made from Personal Observation* (London: Sampson, 1886)

Griscom, John, *A Year in Europe comprising a Journal of Observations* (New York: Collins, 1823)

Hamilton, Cecily, *Modern Ireland as seen by an Englishwoman* (London: Dent, 1936)

Hardy, Evelyn, *Summer in another World* (London: Gollancz, 1950)

Harrison, John, *The Scot in Ulster* (Edinburgh: Blackwood, 1888)

Harrison, Marie, *Dawn in Ireland* (London: Melrose, 1917)

Hartley, Dorothy, *Irish Holiday* (London: Drummond, 1938)

Hayward, Richard, *Border Foray* (London: Baker, 1957)

Head, Francis Bond, *A Fortnight in Ireland* (London: Murray, 1852)

Hilditch, Neville, *In Praise of Ireland* (London: Muller, 1951)

Hoare, Sir Richard Colt, *Journal of a Tour in Ireland, A.D. 1806* (London: Miller, 1807)

Hogg, Garry, *Turf beneath my Feet* (London: Museum, 1950)

Howard, John, *The Island of Saints, or Ireland in 1855* (London: Seeleys, 1855)

Hutton, Mark, *The Cruise of the Humming Bird* (London: Tinsley, 1864)

Jaouen, Herve, *Journal d'Irlande* (Quimper, Calligrammes, 1985)

Johnson, James, *A Tour in Ireland, with Meditations and Reflections* (London: Highley, 1844)

Joynes, James Leigh, *The Adventures of a Tourist in Ireland* (London: Kegan Paul, 1882)

Lancaster, Joseph, *A Brief report of a Tour in Ireland in the Winter of 1811-12* (Tooting: Pickton, 1812)

Lazenby, Elizabeth, *Ireland – A Catspaw* (London: Boswell, 1928)

Lyons, Anthony, *Observations on my First Visit to Ireland* (Malton: Norton, 1904)

Mackay, John, *Porcelain, the Soul of Ireland* (London: Benn, 1927)

Martin, Hugh, *Ireland in Insurrection: an Englishman's record of Fact* (London: O'Connor, 1921)

Mathieson, G., *Journal of a Tour in Ireland, during the months of October and November 1835* (London: Bentley, 1836)

Millman, Laurence, *Our like will not be there again: Notes from the West of Ireland* (Boston: Little, 1977)

Morton, H.V., *In Search of Ireland* (London: Methuen, 1930)

Neillands, Robin, *Walking through Ireland* (London: Little, 1993)

Pendleton, Henrietta, *Gleanings from the Islands and Coast of Ireland* (Dublin: White, 1856)

Pook, Leonard, *A Holiday in the North of Ireland* (London: Harrap, 1915)

Poucher, W.A., *Journey into Ireland* (London: Country Life 1953)

Rashad, Ibrahim, *An Egyptian in Ireland* (Dublin: Privately published, 1921)

Raymond, Josephine, *The Remembered Face of Ireland* (Chicago, Willcox, 1946)

Reid, Thomas, *Travels in Ireland in the year 1822* (London: Longman, 1823)

Renshaw, Charles, *Impressions of the North-West of Ireland* (Manchester: Falkner, 1895)

Retler, Wolfgang, *Ireland Explored* (London: Thames, 1966)

Richardson, Ralph, *Ireland in 1880* (London: Stanford, 1881)

Roussel, Napoléon, *Trois mois en Irlande* (Paris: Grassart, 1853)

Somerville, Alexander, *Letters from Ireland during the Famine of 1847* (Dublin: IAP, 1994)

Speakman, Harold, *Here's Ireland* (New York: Dodd, 1927)

Staples, John Alexander, *A Tour in Ireland in 1813 & 1814* (Dublin: Gough, 1817)

Sutherland, Halliday, *Irish Journey* (London: Bles, 1956)

Templar, A., *Six weeks in Ireland* (London: Faithfull, 1862)

Tillotson, John, *Ireland and its Scenery* (London: Allman, 1863)

Waugh, Edwin, *Irish Sketches and Miscellany* (Manchester: Heywood, 1882)

Weld, Charles, *Vacations in Ireland* (London: Longman, 1857)

Welsh, John, *Ireland Afoot* (Boston ; Badger, 1931)

Wheeler, Mortimer, *Ireland today: a Political Pilgrimage* (London: Hodder, 1911)

Whelpton, Barbara, *Unknown Ireland* (London: Johnson, 1964)

Wilson, Mary, *Sketches of North and West Ireland* (London: Stockwell, 1913)

Wood, John, *With rucksack round Ireland* (London: Elek, 1950)

Wright, Rev. G. N,. *Tours in Ireland* (London: Baldwin, 1823)

IRISH TRAVEL CRITICISM

The number of scholars actually writing about 'Irish' travel literature is still relatively modest. Below are a number of works – including criticism and anthologies – that reflect something of the developing interest in the area. Although critical works lag significantly behind anthologies and readers, and several of the latter include an eclectic range – incorporating historical and imaginative literature – they nevertheless encompass some fascinating material. I have not included in this list recently republished and edited versions of travel accounts, several of which I have already cited.

Cronin, M., *Across the Lines: Travel, Language, Translation* (Cork: Cork UP, 2000)

Deane, S. (ed.), *The Field Day Anthology of Irish Writing* (Derry: Field Day, 1991)

Hadfield, A. & McVeagh, J. (eds), *Strangers to that Land: British Perceptions of Ireland from the Reformation to the Famine* (Gerrards Cross: Smythe, 1994)

Harrington, J. (ed.) *The English Traveller in Ireland* (Dublin: Wolfhound, 1991)

Litton Falkiner, C., *Illustrations of Irish History and Topography, mainly of the Seventeenth Century* (London: 1904)

Maxwell, C., *The Stranger in Ireland, from the reign of Elizabeth to the Great Famine* (London: Cape, 1954)

McVeagh, J. (ed.), *Irish Travel Writing: a Bibliography* (Dublin: Wolfhound, 1996)

O'Connor, B. & Cronin, M. (eds), *Tourism in Ireland: a Critical Analysis* (Cork: Cork UP, 1993)

O'Dalaigh, B. (ed.), *The Strangers Gaze: Travels in County Clare, 1534–1950* (Ennis, Clasp, 1998)

Ryle, M., *Journeys in Ireland: Literary Travellers, Rural Landscapes, Cultural Relations* (Aldershot: Ashgate, 1999)

THE IRISH HISTORICAL AND POLITICAL CONTEXT

This list includes secondary texts that specifically contextualise the period covered by the anthology. Literary criticism, social and political history, historical surveys: the Irish modern period is extremely well catered for, even if occasionally caught up in the political maelstroms of their day.

Bardon, J., *A History of Ulster* (Belfast: Blackstaff, 1992)

Brady, C. (ed.), *Interpreting Irish History: the Debate on Historical Revisionism* (Dublin: IAP, 1994)

Brown, T., *Ireland: a Social and Cultural History, 1922–79* (London: Fontana, 1981)

Buckland, P., *A History of Northern Ireland* (Dublin: Gill & Macmillan, 1981)

Carty, A., *Was Ireland Conquered? International Law and the Irish Question* (London: Pluto, 1996)

Daly, M., *A Social and Economic History of Ireland since 1800* (Dublin: Educational Co., 1981)

Deane, S., *Strange Country: Modernity and Nationhood in Irish Writing since 1790* (Oxford, Clarendon, 1997)

Eagleton, T., *Heathcliff and the Great Hunger* (London: Verso, 1995)

Fanning, R., *Independent Ireland* (Dublin: Helicon, 1983)

Farrell, M., *Northern Ireland: the Orange State* (London: Pluto, 1976)

Foley, T. & Ryder, S. (eds), *Ideology and Ireland in the Nineteenth Century* (Dublin: Four Courts, 1998)

Foster, R., *Modern Ireland, 1600–1972* (London: Penguin, 1988)

Geary, L,. *The Plan of Campaign, 1886–1891* (Cork: Cork UP, 1986)

Harkness, D., *Ireland in the Twentieth Century: Divided Island* (London: Macmillan, 1996)

Hooper, G. & Litvack, L. (eds), *Ireland in the Nineteenth Century: Regional Identity* (Dublin: Four Courts, 2000)

Hoppen, T,. *Ireland since 1800: Conflict and Conformity* (London: Longman, 1989)

Howe, S., *Ireland and Empire: Colonial Legacies in Irish History and Culture* (Oxford: Oxford UP, 2000)

Jackson, A., *Ireland, 1798–1998* (Oxford: Blackwell, 1999)

Kelleher, M., *The Feminization of Famine: Expressions of the Inexpressible?* (Cork: Cork UP, 1997)

Kelleher, M. & Murphy, J. (eds), *Gender Perspectives in 19th Century Ireland: Public and Private Spheres* (Dublin: IAP, 1997)

Keogh, D., *Twentieth-Century Ireland: Nation and State* (Dublin: Gill & Macmillan, 1994)

Kiberd, D., *Inventing Ireland: the Literature of the Modern Nation* (London: Cape, 1995)

Kinealy, C., *This Great Calamity: the Irish Famine, 1845–52* (Dublin: Gill & Macmillan, 1994)

Laffan, M., *The Partition of Ireland, 1911–1925* (Dundalk, Dublin Historical Ass., 1983)

Lee, J., *Ireland, 1912–1985* (Cambridge: Cambridge UP, 1989)

Leerssen, J,. *Mere Irish and Fior-Ghael: Studies in the Idea of Irish Nationality* (Cork: Cork UP, 1996)

Lyons, F.S.L., *Ireland since the Famine* (London: Weidenfeld, 1971)

MacDonagh, O., *Ireland: The Union and its Aftermath* (London: Allen, 1977)

MacDonagh, O., *States of Mind: a Study of Anglo-Irish Conflict, 1780–1980* (London: Allen, 1983)

Miller, D. (ed.), *Rethinking Northern Ireland* (Harlow, Longman, 1998)

Morash, C. & Hayes, R. (eds), *Fearful Realities: New Perspectives on the Famine* (Dublin: IAP, 1996)

Ní Dhonnchadha, M. & Dorgan, T. (eds), *Revising the Rising* (Derry: Field Day, 1991)

O'Brien, C.C., *States of Ireland* (London: Hutchinson, 1972)

O'Farrell, P., *England and Ireland since 1800* (Oxford: Oxford UP, 1975)

O'Grada, C., *A New Economic History of Ireland, 1780–1939* (Oxford: Oxford UP, 1994)

Phoenix, E., *Northern Nationalism: Nationalist Politics, Partition and the Catholic Minority in Northern Ireland, 1890–1940* (Belfast: Ulster Historical Foundation, 1994)

Vaughan, W.E., *Landlords and Tenants in Mid-Victorian Ireland* (Oxford: Clarendon, 1994)

Whyte, J.H., *Interpreting Northern Ireland* (Oxford: Clarendon, 1990)

Woodham-Smith, C., *The Great Hunger: Ireland, 1845–49* (London: Hamilton, 1962)

TRAVEL CRITICISM AND ANTHOLOGIES

Rather than give the impression of an isolated work, I include here other anthologies of travel (women travellers, travellers to the Orient, Black Atlantic travellers), many of which have only recently appeared, and all of which concern nineteenth and/or twentieth century travel. The need for anthologies of this sort should be obvious enough: out of print, in manuscript form, sometimes simply side-lined by other, more canonical, concerns, these works address the genuine need to provide readers with difficult-to-access material. Of course, despite this the majority of work undertaken in the last ten or fifteen years has been of a critical nature. Below are also listed a number of works that connect travel to contemporary issues and theories (autobiography, postcolonialism, empire, gender, leisure tourism and cultural anthropology, for example), although several also reflect more empirical interests. Though not related to Irish issues as such, these texts provide a useful template against which to situate Irish travel.

Behdad, A., *Belated Travellers: Orientalism in the Age of Colonial Dissolution* (Durham: Duke UP, 1994)

Birkett, D. & Wheeler, S. (eds), *Amazonians: the Penguin Book of Women's New Travel Writing* (London: Penguin, 1998)

Blanch, L., *The Wilder Shores of Love* (London: Phoenix, 1954)

Blunt, A., *Travel, Gender and Imperialism* (London: Guilford, 1994)

Bohls, E., *Women Travel Writers and the Language of Aesthetics 1716–1818* (Cambridge: Cambridge UP, 1995)

Brendon, P., *Thomas Cook: 150 years of Popular Tourism* (London: Secker, 1991)

Buzard, J., *The Beaten Track: European Tourism, Literature, and the ways to Culture, 1800–1918* (Oxford: Oxford UP, 1993)

Carrington, D., *The Traveller's Eye* (London: Pilot, 1947)

Clark, S. (ed.), *Travel Writing and Empire: Postcolonial Theory in Transit* (London: Zed, 1999)

Clifford, J., *Routes: Travel and Translation in the late Twentieth Century* (London: Harvard, 1997)

Cocker, M., *Loneliness and Time: British Travel Writing in the Twentieth Century* (London: Secker, 1992)

Croll, E., *Wise Daughters from Foreign Lands: European Women Writers in China* (London: Harper, 1989)

D'Oyley, E. (ed.), *Great Travel Stories of all Nations* (London: Harrap, 1932)

Dodd, P. (ed.), *The Art of Travel: Essays on Travel Writing* (London: Cass, 1982)

Duncan, J. & Gregory, D. (eds), *Writes of Passage I: Reading Travel Writing* (London: Routledge, 1999)

Duncan, J. & Gregory, D. (eds) *Writes of Passage II: Travel Writing, Place and Ambiguity* (London: Routledge, 1999)

Elsner, J. & Rubies, J.-P. (eds), *Voyages and Visions: Towards a Cultural History of Travel* (London: Reaktion, 1999)

Foster, S., *Across New Worlds: Nineteenth-Century Women Travellers and their Writings* (Hemel Hemstead, Wheatsheaf, 1990)

Frawley, M., *A Wider Range: Travel Writing by Women in Victorian England* (London: Associated U Presses, 1994)

Fussell, P., *Abroad: British Literary Travelling between the Wars* (New York: Oxford, 1980)

Ghose, I., *Women Travellers in Colonial India: the Power of the Female Gaze* (Delhi: Oxford UP, 1998)

Gilroy, A. (ed.), *Romantic Geographies: Discourse of Travel, 1775–1844* (Manchester: Manchester UP, 2000)

Glage, L. (ed.), *Beings in Transit: Travelling, Migration, Dislocation* (Amsterdam: Rodopi, 2000)

Grewal, I., *Home and Harem: Nation, Gender, Empire, and the Cultures of Travel* (Durham: Duke UP, 1996)

Hodge, A. (ed.), *Varieties of Travel* (Edinburgh: Oliver, 1967)

Holland, P. & Huggan, G., *Tourists with Typewriters: Critical Reflections on Contemporary Travel Writing* (Ann Arbor: Michigan UP, 1998)

Hulme, P., *Remnants of Conquest: the Island Caribs and their Visitors, 1877–1998* (Oxford: Clarendon, 2000)

Hulme, P. & Whitehead, N. (eds), *Wild Majesty: an Anthology of Encounters with Caribs from Columbus to the Present Day* (Oxford: Clarendon, 1992)

Jarvis, R., *Romantic Writing and Pedestrian Travel* (London: Longman, 1997)

Kaplan, C., *Questions of Travel: Postmodern Discourses of Displacement* (Durham, Duke UP, 1996)

Kaur, R. & Hutnyk, J. (eds), *Travel Worlds: Journeys in Contemporary Cultural Politics* (London: Zed, 1999)

Keay, J. (ed.), *Exploration* (London: Robinson, 1993)

Korte, B., *English Travel Writing: from Pilgrimages to Postcolonial Explorations* (London: Longman, 2000)

Kroller, E.-M., *Canadian Travellers in Europe, 1851–1900* (Vancouver: British Columbia UP, 1987)

Leed, E., *The Mind of the Traveler: from Gilgamesh to Global Tourism* (New York: Basic, 1991)

Lockwood, A., *Passionate Pilgrims: the American Traveler in Great Britain, 1800–1914* (New York: Cornwall, 1981)

MacCannell, D., *The Tourist: a New Theory of the Leisure Class* (New York: Schocken, 1976)

MacCannell, D., *Empty Meeting Grounds: the Tourist Papers* (London: Routledge, 1992)

Michael, M.A. (ed.), *Traveller's Quest: Original Contributions towards a Philosophy of Travel* (London: Hodge, 1950)

Mills, S., *Discourses of Difference: Analysis of Women's Travel Writing and Colonialism* (London: Routledge, 1991)

Mulvey, C., *Anglo-American Landscapes: a Study of Nineteenth-Century Anglo-American Travel Literature* (Cambridge: Cambridge UP, 1983)

Newby, E. (ed.), *A Book of Traveller's Tales* (London: Picador, 1985)

Ousby, I., *The Englishman's England: Taste, Travel and the Rise of Tourism* (Cambridge: Cambridge UP, 1990)

Pettinger, A. (ed.), *Always Elsewhere: Travels of the Black Atlantic* (London: Cassells, 1998)

Porter, D., *Haunted Journeys: Desire and Transgression in European Travel Writing* (New Jersey: Princeton, 1991)

Pratt, M.-L., *Imperial Eyes: Travel Writing and Transculturation* (London: Routledge, 1992)

Rennie, N. *Far-Fetched Facts: the Literature of Travel and the Idea of the South Seas* (Oxford: Oxford UP, 1995)

Robertson, G. et al. (eds), *Traveller's Tales: Narratives of Home and Displacement* (London: Routledge, 1994)

Robinson, J., *Wayward Women: a Guide to Women Travellers* (Oxford: Oxford UP, 1990)

Rojek, C., *Ways of Escape: Modern Transformations in Leisure and Travel* (London: Macmillan, 1993)

Rojek, C. & Urry, J. (ed.), *Touring Cultures: Transformations of Travel and Theory* (London: Routledge, 1997)

Schiffer, R., *Oriental Panorama: British Travellers in 19th Century Turkey* (Amsterdam: Rodopi, 1999)

Smith, V. (ed.), *Hosts and Guests: the Anthropology of Tourism* (Oxford: Oxford UP, 1989)

Spurr, D., *The Rhetoric of Empire: Colonial Discourse in Journalism, Travel Writing and Imperial Administration* (Durham: Duke, 1994)

Thomas, N., *Colonialism's Culture: Anthropology, Travel and Government* (Cambridge: Polity, 1994)

Turner, L. & Ash, J. (eds), *The Golden Hordes: International Tourism and the Pleasure Periphery* (London: Constable, 1975)

Urry, J., *The Tourist Gaze: Leisure and Travel in Contemporary Societies* (London: Sage, 1990)

Van Strien, K. (ed.), *Touring the Low Countries: Accounts of British Travellers, 1660–1720* (Amsterdam: Amsterdam UP, 1998)

Youngs, T., *Travellers in Africa: British Travelogues, 1850–1900* (Manchester: Manchester UP, 1994)

Contents